CONSUMERISM

CONSUMERISM

As a Way of Life

Steven Miles

SAGE Publications
London • Thousand Oaks • New Delhi

First published 1998

SAGE Publications Ltd
6 Bonhill Street
London EC2A 4PU

SAGE Publications Inc.
2455 Teller Road
Thousand Oaks, California 91320

SAGE Publications India Pvt Ltd
32, M-Block Market
Greater Kailash – I
New Delhi 110 048

British Library Cataloguing in Publication data

A catalogue record for this book is available from the British Library

ISBN 0 7619 5214 4
ISBN 0 7619 5215 2 (pbk)

Library of Congress catalog card number 98–060536

Typeset by Mayhew Typesetting, Rhayader, Powys
Printed in Great Britain by Biddles Ltd, Guildford, Surrey

I dedicate this book to Tom Lamb and Violet Miles

CONTENTS

ACKNOWLEDGEMENTS

Several people offered their invaluable support and advice while I was writing this book. I would therefore like to thank the following: Jim Brown, Viv Burr, Stephanie Church, Penny Clark, Dallas Cliff, Glenn Duckworth, Harvie Ferguson, Andy Furlong, Eric Harrison, Kevin Meethan and last, but certainly not least, Ian Roper. I would also like to thank Chris Rojek, Robert Rojek and everybody at Sage who helped bring this project to life.

1

CONSUMERISM THEN AND NOW

The Church of England is to adopt a corporate logo in an attempt to rid the Church of its muddled image and provide a 'common visual identity' for its 13,000 parishes . . . The Rev. Eric Shegog said . . . 'The Church is one of thousands of bodies competing for attention in the media market place and we have got to do it efficiently.' He said the Church sought a symbol that had 'gravitas with a contemporary feel'.

(Combe, 1996: 1)

Consumerism appears to have become part and parcel of the very fabric of modern life. Areas of social life that were previously free of the demands of the marketplace, including religion, have had to adapt to a world where the needs and desires of the consumer are apparently paramount. How we consume, why we consume and the parameters laid down for us within which we consume have become increasingly significant influences on how we construct our everyday lives. Whether you live in Plymouth, England, Paris, Texas, or Moscow, Russia, the benefits of consumerism, though to varying degrees, are apparently available off the shelf. And the parallel with religion is not an accidental one. Consumerism is ubiquitous and ephemeral. It is arguably *the* religion of the late twentieth century. It apparently pervades our everyday lives and structures our everyday experience and yet it is perpetually altering its form and reasserting its influence in new guises.

Everyday life in the developed world appears, at least at a common-sense level, to be dominated by our relationship with consumer goods. The question this book intends to ask is: how far are we in control of this relationship? Wherever we go, whether in the High Street, the museum, the airport, the sports stadium, the doctor's surgery or our very own living room, consumerism is touted as the answer to all our problems, an escape from the mundane realities of everyday life. Our city centres are more remarkable as sites of consumption than they are as cultural centres; our homes might be described as temples to the religion of consumerism; our lives apparently amount to little more than a constant juxtaposition of diverse consumer styles and tastes. From this point of view, it could well be argued that we are indeed what we consume. But can this really be said to be the case? Do the superficial appeals and attractions of consumer lifestyles have a profound impact upon who we are as individuals or do they simply amount to images and representations which we disregard at our will? Can we assert personal choice through the things we consume or is such choice merely prescribed for us?

I shall begin this chapter by briefly considering *why consumption* is an important focus for social scientific enquiry. I will then go on to take the important step of identifying how best to distinguish between the two terms, *'consumerism'* and *'consumption'*. Having done so, I will ask *how did the consumer society come about?* I will then briefly consider the relationship between *consumerism and politics*, at which point I will summarize the main points to be taken from this chapter by identifying the significance of consumerism in the context of *social, economic and cultural change*. I will conclude Chapter 1 by outlining the *structure of the book* as a whole.

Why consumption?

In recent years, a sociology of consumption has developed which has begun to acknowledge the fact that our lives are not solely determined by our relationship to the means of production or to where we work. Previously, the productivist vision of modernity had seen the relations and experiences characteristic of work as fundamental to the shaping of social life. Sociologists have traditionally seen people's relationship to production as being the fundamental determinant of their life experience. In this context, the impact of consumption was largely ignored. Indeed, it is possible to identify

> a series of trends which have led to an overwhelming concentration on the area of production as the key generative arena for the emergence of the dominant social relations in contemporary societies, and a comparative neglect of consumption, together with a concomitant failure to observe the actual changes which have taken place over the last century in the balance of influence between these two forms of interactions with goods. (Miller, 1987: 3)

Commentators have traditionally focused on developments in the production process and how it is that production imparts influence on social structures. In this context, consumption has for too long been perceived to be little more than a by-product of production. This over-emphasis on production has, in fact, been counterproductive in so far as important aspects of social life have for too long been neglected by sociologists. Several commentators have noted that the productivist vision of modernity is an oversimplification and that consumer goods have an active and significant role to play in the experience of social life (see Lee, 1993; Gabriel and Lang, 1995). Consumer goods and services *potentially* play an important role in who we are and how we construct our social lives, in terms of how we use such goods and services and how we relate to other people *through* such goods and services. But what is consumerism? Is its influence on our everyday lives merely superficial or does it really amount to a fundamental focus for the construction of contemporary social lives? Before I go on to consider these issues, it must be noted that no clear-cut definition of consumerism is readily available. All too often commentators fail to distinguish between definitions of 'consumption' and 'consumerism'. It is therefore important that I begin by distinguishing between these two terms.

'Consumption' or 'consumerism'?

Any attempt to define the relationship between 'consumption' and 'consumerism' is fraught with difficulty. Consumerism is not coterminous with consumption. The *Concise Oxford Dictionary* defines *consumption* as the 'purchase and use of goods'. Similarly, Campbell (1995: 102) defines consumption as 'the selection, purchase, use, maintenance, repair and disposal of any product or service'. Useful as this definition is, Campbell himself acknowledges that it is far from completely satisfactory since at its heart lies an economic conception of the role of consumption. What is of more interest here, as Lee (1993) notes, is the way in which, during the 1980s, the object of consumption, the commodity, came to take on some form of magical quality, to such an extent that consumption took on a dual role as both an economic and a *cultural* touchstone. The problem here is that discussions of consumption, and particularly those which can loosely be described as contributing to a 'sociology of consumption', have been slow to deal with the complex nature of the interrelationships that exist between the economic and the cultural. This is a problem that this book will seek to redress.

One author who has gone some way towards coming to terms with the complexities inherent in an understanding of the social significance of consumption is McCracken (1990), who describes consumption as a thoroughly cultural phenomenon and who argues in turn that

> in Western developed societies culture is profoundly connected to and dependent upon consumption. Without consumer goods, modern, developed societies would lose key instruments for the reproduction, representation, and manipulation of their culture . . . The meaning of consumer goods and the meaning creation accomplished by consumer processes are important parts of the scaffolding of our present realities. Without consumer goods, certain acts of self-definition and collective definition in this culture would be impossible. (McCracken, 1990: xi)

McCracken argues that any study of consumption should take into account the ways in which consumer goods and services are created, bought and used. The significance of this definition is that it extends the traditional view of consumption as an act of purchase in order to address the sorts of influences and experiences that are undertaken by both the product and the consumer before and after such a purchase.

If we are therefore to accept the contention that consumption is more than a mere economic phenomenon, then its cultural dimensions cannot be addressed in isolation. Indeed, what is most interesting about consumption is that, 'as a set of social, cultural and economic practices, together with the associated ideology of consumerism, [it] has served to legitimate capitalism in the eyes of millions of ordinary people' (Bocock, 1993: 2). It is in this sense that the notion of *consumerism* can be said to be of more sociological interest than consumption *per se*. The study of consumerism is a broader and more reflexive enterprise than a concern for the relatively straightforward process of simply purchasing and consuming a particular good or service. I will suggest that a study of consumerism should actually attempt to come to terms with the complexities that lie *behind* the act of consumption. In effect, while consumption is an act, consumerism is a way of life. From this point of view, consumerism is the cultural expression and manifestation of the apparently ubiquitous act of consumption. What is it about social life in the developed world in the late twentieth century that provides a set of circumstances where the adoption of consumerism as a way of life becomes a feasible alternative? What is it that attracts consumers to this way of life and what does the fact that people choose such a way of life say about the state of the world in general?

It is worth noting that the word 'consumerism' is often used to refer to a life 'excessively preoccupied with consumption' (Gabriel and Lang, 1995: 3). In this sense the word 'consumerism' takes on negative overtones. I prefer to describe the social impact of consumption as ubiquitous rather than excessive. Consumer goods and services appear to surround us, but need not necessarily be a negative influence on our lives. As such, I suggest that consumerism should not and cannot be morally condemned, but must rather be considered in a systematic fashion as an arena within which social lives are currently constructed. Having said that, this is essentially a critical text. My intention is to highlight some of the more important sociological debates that surround consumerism as a way of life, providing a basis upon which readers can decide upon their validity as I do so. The arguments which I present amount to considered judgements which I hope will provoke the reader into reflecting upon his or her own assessment of the social and ideological impact of consumerism.

To reiterate, what is crucial to the study of consumerism as far as my definition is concerned is how the ubiquitous nature of consumption is reconstructed and interpreted on a day-to-day basis; how it is that structural expressions of consumption come to affect our everyday lives and how we negotiate our life experience within those structures that consumerism provides. Consumerism *is* an important topic for social scientists precisely *because* it appears, at a common-sense level, to be somewhat inconsequential. Because we accept the routine of the consuming experience as legitimate, powerful ideological elements of that experience go largely unnoticed. What I will go on to suggest is that consumerism should be considered as an issue that has a fundamental influence upon the everyday experience of social life in advanced capitalist societies. Not only does consumerism structure our everyday lives, but it does so by offering us the illusion of consumer freedom when, at least to a certain extent, such freedoms are inevitably constructed and constrained.

In this sense, I call for a broader definition of consumerism than has generally been offered in the literature. Definitions of consumerism, notably in the United States, have tended to describe consumerism in the context of the development of a movement to protect consumer interests. I suggest here that the word 'consumerism' is of more use in a sociological sense when it is differentiated from its derivative, namely consumption, as a means of addressing the *psycho-social* impact of the consuming experience. The definition of 'consumerism' that I adopt throughout this book highlights the interactive nature of the consuming experience and how this experience owes much to the interaction between the personal appeal and the ideological power of consumerism. Consumerism can be defined as a psycho-social expression of the intersection between the structural and the individual within the realm of consumption. The consuming experience is psycho-social in the sense that it represents a bridge that links the individual and society.

What impact *does* consumerism actually have on our everyday experience? Though consumerism arguably amounts to what is a fundamental influence upon the ways in which we conduct our personal and social lives, there appears to be little consensus about precisely what constitutes 'the consuming experience'. This book will attempt to come to terms with the nature of that experience and, in particular, with what I describe as 'the consuming paradox': the fact that in terms of our individual experience consumerism appears to have a fascinating, arguably fulfilling, personal appeal and yet simultaneously plays some form of an ideological role in actually *controlling* the character of everyday life. In effect, consumerism is, at one and the same time, psycho-socially constraining *and* enabling and this is what makes it such a fascinating topic for social scientific investigation. The key point here is that consumerism is not purely of sociological interest, but its significance crosses disciplinary boundaries. Consumerism is quite possibly the key concern of contemporary social science inasmuch as it transcends everyday life and does so in such a way that consumers take it for granted. Indeed, consumerism is arguably *the* realm within which the tensions of late twentieth-century social life in the developed world are most graphically played out.

How did the consumer society come about?

In order to make further sense of some of the above debates we need to consider how it was that a consumer society began to take root. McKendrick et al. (1982) identify a consumer revolution in England as early as the eighteenth century, when, for the first time, it is possible to identify a society within which material possessions became prized less and less for their durability and more and more for their fashionability. Yet Braudel (1974) goes one step further than McKendrick et al. (1982) in arguing that exchange relations had developed in a sophisticated manner even before industrialization, notably in the guise of the seventeenth-century French market – fairs and carnivals being focal points of consumption.

One of the most interesting accounts of the rise of a consumer society is Benson's (1994) chronicle of events in Britain between 1880 and 1980. Benson considers the material changes which served to increase consumers' capacity for consumption during this period. Though there is little agreement as to when the 'consumer revolution' occurred (McKendrick et al. 1982), apparently anywhere between the sixteenth century and the 1980s, Benson (1994) sees this as a long-term development and in particular focuses on the increased demand produced by a rapidly expanding population between the early nineteenth and late twentieth centuries. These changes in demand were accompanied by changes in supply in an increasingly expanding marketplace which came to direct its goods to the attention of those consumers whose purchasing power was increasing most rapidly (Benson, 1994).

Such developments can be closely related to the emergence of what many commentators, and not least members of the Frankfurt School, refer to as a 'mass society', the concentration of the population in urban centres exposing urban dwellers to an increasing plethora of consumer goods (see Horkheimer and Adorno, 1973). The rise of a consumer society clearly came into its own with the onset of industrialization. As production for subsistence came to be replaced by wage labour, people inevitably became consumers as well as producers. As such, from a long-term historical point of view, there emerged evidence of a radically different way of life in terms of social structures, social values and attitudes. Gradually, then, a new type of society developed: a society built upon the thirst for novelty – novelty that the economic system became more than willing to perpetuate.

A crucial development in the emergence of the consumer society was the growth of working-class purchasing power. The years after the Second World War saw the emergence of a mass market based at least to some extent on the principles of Fordism. Fordism refers to the ideas and principles of the American industrialist Henry Ford, who is generally accredited as the pioneer of the modern mass-production system, notably in the guise of the car assembly line. Fordism was based on principles of size, uniformity and predictability and on the notion that to keep demand high wages needed to be kept up, while government investment provided an essential means of ensuring full employment and prosperity. As far as the individual consumer is concerned, what was crucial about Fordist practice was that he or she was provided with the surplus necessary for him or her to be able to purchase consumer goods. Indeed, Henry Ford proffered the notion that workers should be encouraged to be consumers of the very products they produced.

In this environment, while mass production ensured, on the one hand, that standardized, easily produced goods could be introduced to the market at minimum cost, on the other, the surpluses made available to the workers offset a periodic danger, one that capitalism had up to now always been forced to face: the effect of a slump or depression. A wide variety of large-scale industrial sectors, including clothes, furniture and processed food, were subsequently transformed (see Murray, 1989). Gradually, luxurious consumer goods became everyday items. The Fordist economy was dependent upon the fact that workers had a surplus of disposable income which they could invest in the increasing diversity of goods that were being made available to them. This was a crucial development. Consumption came to play an increasingly important role in people's everyday lives. People were not only offered what they needed but also what they desired, while simultaneously 'wants' actively became 'needs'. For instance, whereas previously a very basic functional pair of spectacles may have been sufficient for the partially sighted consumer, in a consumer culture functional items became designer items in the sense that a pair of spectacles became another means by which the individual could express his or her self-identity. Consumer capitalism was able to exploit a situation where the *symbolic* value of consumer goods was endowed with an increased social significance. It is in this sense that the ideological impact of consumerism became increasingly subtle in nature.

Some commentators saw these developments as inherently liberating for the working classes in that the active nature of consumption meant that the 'masses' became incorporated in a society from which they were once excluded (see Bell, 1976). On the other hand, it could equally be argued that consumers were robbing themselves of individuality inasmuch as they were willing to buy standardized undifferentiated 'mass' products (Murray, 1989). Either way, it could be argued that the impact of consumerism in modern societies amounted to a qualitatively new experience of society. In this context, Cross (1993) considers various sets of figures that reflect the emergence of a consumer society. He identifies an unprecedented degree of access to durable goods in the latter half of the twentieth century. Focusing in particular on the American example, Cross notes that disposable household income in the USA rose from $15,110 in 1940 to $26,313 in 1970 and $28,607 in 1979, while between 1935 and 1970 home ownership nearly tripled for white, wage-earning families and doubled for black families. The impact of consumerism was equally impressive in Britain, although tempered slightly, in the first instance, by the need to recover from the Second World War. Generally speaking, however, consumerism appeared to be emerging as a way of life on an unprecedented global scale.

As far as sociology is concerned, consumption did not emerge as a serious subject of concern until the second half of the twentieth century, and most dramatically during the 1980s and 1990s. Despite the general tendency to see consumption as ahistorical, as Gabriel and Lang (1995) note, commentators have increasingly come to acknowledge that the social significance of consumption began to emerge far earlier. While I accept the suggestion on the part of many of the authors cited above that consumption has always been part of the experience of modern life, I will argue, during the course of this book, that this experience has increased during the course of more recent history, notably towards the end of the twentieth century. It is during this period that consumerism emerged on the day-to-day level as what might be described as a 'way of life'. I therefore suggest that consumerism did not become a way of life for the *majority* of the population of the developed world until the aftermath of the Second World War. Those works that have charted the long-term historical significance of consumption are convincing inasmuch as they illustrate the infiltration of consumer lifestyles into bourgeois realms (see McKendrick et al., 1982; Williams, 1982). This much can be accepted. But my argument is that it was not until much later that consumption became a way of life for the majority of the population and, in particular, the working classes. Although the long-term implications of a consumer revolution were being felt gradually by an increasing percentage of the population of the Western world, the experiential impact of such a revolution was in fact variable. It was not until the 1950s that the accessibility of consumer goods began to transcend social classes and that the status-conferring qualities discussed decades earlier by Thorstein Veblen (who I will consider in more detail in Chapter 2) came to have a more general social relevance. More specifically, I agree with Whiteley (1993), who sees the introduction of the credit card in 1950 as a particularly symbolic event. Interestingly, in the USA, as Whiteley notes, short-term consumer credit rose from $8.4 billion in 1945 to almost $45 billion in 1958. Of equal interest is the fact that the production of cars in the USA rocketed from two million in 1945 to 40 million in 1950, 51 million in 1955 and 62 million in 1960.

With developments in the economy, post-war workers came to have access to resources that meant that they could consider purchasing new objects such as television sets and cars, as well as providing for their families' more basic needs (Bocock, 1993). Accompanied, indeed encouraged, by the rise of advertising, a whole new world of consumerism was on offer to the working majority, most especially to groups of young people who were able to exploit this new situation as long as the resources were available to them. What was emerging was not merely a consumer society, but a consumer *culture*. What had emerged by 1980 was a consumer culture in which, as Lunt and Livingstone (1992: 24) note, 'involvement with material culture is such that mass consumption infiltrates everyday life not only at the levels of economic processes, social activities and household structures, but also at the level of meaningful psychological experience – affecting the construction of identities, the formation of relationships, the framing of events.' What we can identify during this period is a process whereby the consumer society (a society predicated on a market economy which had been in existence for centuries) was superseded by the consumerist society (an advanced state of consumer society in which private affluence on a mass scale emerged as the dominant force in the marketplace) (Whiteley, 1993).

Bocock (1993) therefore suggests that it was after the 1950s that consumption sectors became ever more specific and focused. As capitalism developed alongside improved technology and management practices, usually discussed in the context of post-Fordism and flexible specialization (the emergence of a multi-skilled flexible workforce who work on small-batch production runs which are readily adaptable to the whims of the consumer), there was an argument for saying that fixed status groups and social classes were being undermined as consumer lifestyles became the order of the day (see Piore and Sabel, 1984; Featherstone, 1991). Post-Fordist consumption was apparently more volatile and diversified, as market segmentation emerged to serve the interests of the consumer (see Lash and Urry, 1994; Lury, 1996). In this new world, consumption no longer appeared to be determined by the producer. On the contrary, the producer was increasingly subject to the demands and tastes of the consumer. What was emerging was a shift from homogeneity to heterogeneity, from principles of size, uniformity and predictability to those of scope, diversity and flexibility.

In this context, the work of Martyn Lee (1993), who talks about the rebirth of consumer culture, is of particular interest. Suggesting that consumption represents the point at which economic practice and cultural practice combine, Lee charts the rise and fall of a mass consumption society in the post-war years, followed by the re-awakening of the consumer society in which we live today. In particular, he identifies the role played in this process by the emergence of a new diversified commodity form. Most markedly, it was during the 1980s that the aesthetics, design and style of consumption became increasingly diverse, as the marketplace became ever more sophisticated with regard to what it knew and what it wanted to know about its consumers (Lee, 1993).

Lee therefore suggests that if there have been any significant changes to the regime of accumulation and its mode of regulation then such changes are revealed not so much in the production side of the equation, but more in terms of the changing composition and design of the symbolic commodity form in the late twentieth century. It is in this sense that consumption came to play a fundamentally formative social role in modern societies, and that we can begin to talk about consumerism as a way of life.

The politics of consumerism

The trends that have been identified by authors such as Lee (1993) have been amplified in the past 15 years by political ideologies and rhetoric (both of which are often neglected by contemporary theorists) that have served to transform the cultural as well as the political landscape (Hall and Jacques, 1989). The relationship between consumption and identity and its emergence as a topic of sociological debate is related to the way in which the individualistic ethos of the New Right has come to pervade consumers' experiences of everyday life. It would not be an exaggeration to suggest that consumerism was proposed by the British and American governments of the 1980s as a prime focus of people's lives and, in Britain in particular, that this proposal was gratefully consumed by sections of the population keen to take advantage of the opportunity to purchase their own council houses and to take their annual holidays abroad.

Consumption has clearly been hijacked by politicians of various creeds, parties and ideologies. The freedoms provided for consumers by the marketplace have always been a key arena within which political battles have been fought, most notably in the United States, because such freedoms appear to be intuitively positive in nature. In effect, as Keat et al. (1994) note, consumer freedom has come to be equated with political freedom, as a part of a long-term historical process. This process culminated in the Labour party being elected to power in Britain in 1997 on the basis of a manifesto which incorporated consumerist policies traditionally associated with the Conservative party. Consumerism has come to be seen as essentially democratic and has been marketed to the population as such, despite the inevitable question marks over access to resources and the extent to which consumption can provide all players with a level playing field. As Ewen (1976) notes in his book *Captains of Consciousness*, democracy does not merely flow out of people's desires, but actively reflects their ability to participate in a value structure. Consumerism offers an apparently democratic value structure which parties from both ends of the political spectrum have sought to exploit for their own political gain. Thus, while superficially appearing to withdraw state intervention, what has happened appears to be that government influence over consumers' everyday life is arguably intensified at the core through the transmission of a new mode of ideology, namely consumerism. The problem here is that politicians have found it very hard to sustain a high-quality public sector which incorporates adequate welfare provision, in a system in which consumerism is intended to provide all the answers. As such, a theme that I will return to throughout this book centres on the *potentially* divisive nature of consumerist ideologies.

In Britain, the ideology of consumerism proffers the 'rights' of the individual consumer and, as such, political citizenship is defined through charters (for example, The Patient's Charter, The Citizen's Charter) rather than in terms of active domestic participation. It is in this sense that the citizen as a consumer is essentially passive. I will discuss the ideological implications of consumerism in more detail in Chapter 9. In summary, however, I agree with Bocock (1993) who argues that, while consumption may appear to be rooted in the satisfaction of natural and actual needs, in a sense it has emerged historically as an increasingly 'unnatural' social force: shopping for cars or roller blades is not actually natural in any sense at all and is, indeed, potentially dangerous in so far as it actively accentuates social divisions.

Consumerism as social, economic and cultural change

At a common-sense level, what and how people consume appears to be significant in the maintenance of people's everyday lives, and yet the role consumerism plays as an ideological beast remains uncertain. If we accept that the study of consumerism is potentially more beneficial than the study of consumption *per se*, then the following economic, social and cultural factors enter the equation:

1 *Social change* Modern society appears to be characterized by exchange rather than subsistence as it was in the past. All sorts of aspects of social life, such as gender relationships, class relationships and social relationships in general, appear therefore to be impinged upon by aspects of consumerism, which is potentially as divisive as it is liberating.
2 *Economic change* More specifically, spending power has grown in recent decades as people have enjoyed access to increasing levels of disposable income. This has had significant political implications which governments have been keen to exploit as they have come to recognize the social benefits and appeal that consumerism appears to command.
3 *Globalization* The above changes have also been accompanied by a move towards globalization, a process whereby the common economic currency of consumerism plays a key role most evidently

through the influence of multinational companies such as Coca-Cola and Nike. In this context, there is considerable debate whether consumerism encourages global standardization or diversity and thus whether consumerism as a way of life is in itself desirable.

The above trends combine to ensure that consumerism is not only significant at a social and economic level but also in the context of cultural change. Yet, despite the above trends, little research has been conducted into the everyday manifestations of consumerism as a way of life. Discussions have tended to be speculative in nature. It might indeed be argued that sociology has had little tangible success in coming to terms with the changing role of consumption. Though the long-term historical changes have been discussed and analysed in considerable depth (Benson, 1994; Lansley, 1994), particularly in Britain in relation to the emergence of the New Right and the implications of its policies in lionizing the attributes of consumerism, little has been achieved in analysing the effect of such social change at the micro-level (see Hall, 1988). The societal impact of consumption cannot be fully realized without equal consideration of its micro-social expression. As such, this book will consider the broader macro-issues through their micro-expression. It will therefore use in-depth discussions of particular realms of social life in which consumerism appears to be especially influential as a means of drawing out of this material some conception of the ideological nature of consumerism as a way of life.

Structure of the book

In order to illustrate the impact of consumerism upon social life, I will use a series of case studies which will in turn serve to highlight the sociological significance of consumerism. In Chapter 2, I will present an overview of some of the key theoretical approaches to questions of consumption and consumerism. Extending this debate in Chapter 3, I will consider a more specific and often neglected argument which focuses on the extent to which the consumer society is in fact a designer society. How far does a consumer society allow for the self-expression of its citizens? How far, indeed, are the parameters of consumption laid down in a carefully constructed designer society where what is most important is the designer and his or her profit margin first and the consumer second? In Chapter 4, I will present my first case study in the form of a discussion of the nature of sites of consumption. This is an important section because it addresses the geographical contexts within which people consume. What is it about city life, for example, that makes it a magnet for consumerism? Are contemporary cities anything more than mere centres of consumption? Chapter 5 then considers technology as an especially influential and arguably socially divisive focus for the everyday expression of consumerism. What can tech-nology tell us about the so-called democratic nature of consumerism as a way of life? Chapter 6 discusses the role of fashion in a consumer culture. Fashion is often assumed to be the most expressive, creative and, indeed, graphic arena within which the benefits of consumerism are cosseted. Is this really the case? Similarly, Chapter 7 goes on to consider how far the production of popular music has been undermined by commercial values and whether consumers of popular music are consuming creative expressions of musical talent or a pre-packaged product which guarantees commercial success. Are such commercial values actually in the interests of the consumer? Chapter 8 addresses an area of life that has arguably become infiltrated more by values associated with consumerism in recent years than any other, namely sport. Is the sporting spectacle anything more than a money-making exercise and what role does the spectator play in the commercialization of sport?

Chapters 5 to 8 are intended to illustrate the significance of con-sumerism in the conduct of everyday life. Within these chapters I will therefore discuss literature that was not necessarily originally intended to contribute to the sociology of consumption, but which, none the less, provides a means of extending the debate on the role of consumerism as a way of life. The five areas of life I have chosen are intended to illustrate the diverse influence that consumerism plays in the con-struction of social life. Other areas of social life, such as education, health care or transport, could equally have been used. I do not intend to present a comprehensive discussion of the ways in which con-sumerism imparts influence upon our everyday lives. Rather, I will present a series of case studies that serve as pertinent illustrations of the significance of consumerism as a way of life. In Chapter 9 I will discuss what I identify as the two major theoretical issues that arise out of the case studies I present: the relationship between consumerism and inequality and the ideological implications of consumerism.

This book aims to discuss the sociological significance of consumerism in the context of areas of life in which students and academics alike have direct experience. It represents a conscious effort to steer discussions of consumerism away from abstract conceptions of the commodity form in order to assess the sociological actualities of the experience of consumerism. The emphasis here, then, is on consumerism as lived experience. By presenting a critical analysis of the active, everyday ways in which consumerism imparts influence on our lives, the intention is to perceive consumerism as an active and negotiated realm of life. This will be achieved partly through an in-depth discussion of what I see as key questions or debates affecting each of the realms of life I discuss. This book represents an attempt to address the extent to which sociologists can reasonably argue that we do indeed live in a world where con-sumerism is a way of life. If this can be said to be the case, the ultimate question must then centre on whether or not consumerism can provide us, as consumers, with what we actually want.

Recommended reading

John Benson (1994) *The Rise of Consumer Society in Britain, 1880–1980*. London: Longman. A thorough introduction to the historical emergence of the consumer society in Britain.

Robert Bocock (1993) *Consumption*. London: Routledge. A succinct discussion of the significance of consumption in contemporary society which includes a useful section on the emergence of modern consumption.

Yiannis Gabriel and Tim Lang (1995) *The Unmanageable Consumer*. London: Sage. An exhaustive account of the various dimensions of consumption.

Martyn Lee (1993) *Consumer Culture Reborn: The Cultural Politics of Consumption*. London: Routledge. An account of the relationship between economic and cultural dimensions of consumption. Particularly useful as an introduction to theoretical conceptions of the commodity.

Grant McCracken (1990) *Culture and Consumption*. Bloomington, IN: Indiana University Press. Provides a detailed treatment of theoretical aspects of the symbolic character of consumer goods.

2

CONSUMERISM IN CONTEXT

Although the intention of this book is to avoid an overly theoretical conception of consumption, and as such to perceive consumerism as a situated activity rather than as an abstract social phenomenon, it is necessary to provide some theoretical foundations from which the broader issues I identified in Chapter 1 can be developed. From this basis it might be possible to begin to construct what might be described tentatively as a 'sociology of consumerism'. In this chapter I will therefore consider relevant approaches to the following questions. *What role does consumption play in classical social theory? Which key figures are associated with the more recent emergence of a sociology of consumption? What is the relationship between consumption and postmodernism?* And, finally, *what other approaches have furthered an understanding of the everyday significance of consumption?* I will conclude by highlighting the complexities involved in coming to terms with the social scientific significance of consumption.

Consumption in classical social theory

While historically the sociology of consumption has incorporated what I describe as 'macro-structural' issues, in recent times it has been more concerned with 'macro-cultural' issues. In other words, the significance of consumption has traditionally been developed from a structural point of view in terms of the experience of whole classes or even societies. More recently, sociologists have moved away from perceiving consumption as little more than a by-product of production as part of a move towards understanding cultural aspects of consumption for their own sake. It is in this context that I want to consider the particular contributions of four especially influential 'classical' theorists, each of whom has made a marked contribution to the long-term development of a sociology of consumption. The brief discussions that follow are not intended to be comprehensive theoretical accounts, but should rather provide theoretical tasters which are meant to encourage readers to pursue their own avenues of thought.

Karl Marx

Although it could be argued that the tendency has been to exaggerate
the extent to which sociology has neglected consumption as a focus for
debate in its own right, it would be fair to suggest, as I argued in
Chapter 1, that sociology has traditionally emphasized the role of
production in the development of capitalism at the expense of cultural
aspects of consumption (see Fine and Leopold, 1993). The work of Karl
Marx (*Capital*, 1867) was formative in this respect. Marx's conception of
the commodity does, however, retain its role as a springboard for many
theorists of consumption. Before I briefly consider the role of consumption in Marx's work, I should point out that his contribution is
underpinned by an analysis of what constitutes human needs and how
those needs are met, notably through the application of the production
process (see Lee, 1993). As Lee (1993) points out, Marx therefore sees the
object of labour, that is the material artefact or product, as having a
crucial role in the construction of people's lives and, in turn, in their
sense of personal well-being. In this respect, Marx's understanding of
the commodity is contextualized purely by the production process. It
was the production of commodities, rather than their consumption
upon which he focused his attention. Marx describes a commodity as a
product that has not been produced for direct personal consumption on
the part of the consumer, but rather for the intention of selling it in the
marketplace. It is in this sense that the commodity becomes significant
for its exchange-value rather than simply its use-value. The key point
here, as Lee (1993) notes in his discussion of Marx, is that the value of a
commodity appears to be natural or objective when, in fact, the actual
value of a good bears no relation to its use-value. Rather, this value is
dependent upon the concrete social relations of capitalist production
which actively camouflages the exploitative social and labour relations
that underlie the process as a whole.

What is so fascinating about consumption for the sociologist is that
the processes Marx identifies, and in particular the formative role of the
commodity, are apparently far more salient now than they were when
he conducted his original work during the mid to late nineteenth
century. Whereas Marx saw the worker's relationship to the means of
production and thus to the commodity as a key influence on that
person's life, the actual reception and consumption of that commodity
has become proportionally more influential. Marx discusses the process
of 'commodification' whereby all aspects of social life become subject to
the laws of the marketplace. As well as goods and services, people and
relationships are reduced to a monetary value in an increasingly
alienating capitalist world. Perhaps in the late twentieth century this
consumer society has reached its zenith. It might well be argued that
Marx's vision of the demise of capitalism was misplaced. Indeed, what
undermines Marx's limited conception of the commodity, above all, is

the fact that capitalism went on, undeterred, to develop ever more subtle means of commodification and regeneration until the latter half of the twentieth century, at which point consumer capitalism emerged apparently all powerful. In this sense, there might be evidence to suggest that Marx underestimated not only the versatility of capitalism, but also the everyday impact of the commodity and of consumption, to the extent that consumerism actually became a way of life.

Despite or perhaps because of these reservations, Marx left the sociologist with an invaluable, albeit historically specific, legacy in terms of an analysis of the role of consumption in the development of capitalism. Marx's understanding of the alienation of the worker through the extraction of a surplus-value represents a key to understanding the ways in which workers are 'forced' to become consumers by buying the products they or their fellow workers have made. By earning wages or salaries, and by being obliged to become embroiled in consumer culture (though far more so than Marx could have possibly envisaged), the wheels of capitalism effectively came to be oiled by the workers themselves. Marx was therefore the first theorist to touch upon the inherent contradictions of the 'consuming paradox'. In this context, the sociologist of consumption owes a debt to Marx for addressing questions that would later provide a significant, though incomplete, basis for a sociology of consumption in its own right.

Max Weber

Other theorists offer valuable contributions not only to an understanding of the impact of consumption upon the societies in which they lived, but also as a means of furthering an understanding of the contemporary role of consumerism. In some respects the work of Weber (1920) serves this function. Of particular interest is Weber's discussion of the role of Calvinism in encouraging hard-working, pious attitudes which, in turn, encouraged workers *not* to consume the surplus they had at their disposal. From this point of view, capitalism emerged precisely because of a work ethic that encouraged re-investment rather than consumption. This work ethic could, however, be said to provide a strong material basis from which a consumer ethic could emerge in its own right. Weber saw capitalism as being characterized by 'the pursuit of profit by means of continuing rational capitalistic enterprise: that is . . . the constant renewal of profit, or "profitability"' (Weber, 1978: 333). What is interesting here, as Lee (1993) notes, is that the prioritization of the need to accumulate capital came to have significant social as well as economic consequences. Although Weber's work is centred on the argument that the Industrial Revolution constituted a massive worldwide upheaval in the ways in which manufactured goods were produced, the implications of this process as far as consumption is concerned were not necessarily followed through to the full by Weber (see Campbell, 1987). In effect, as a product of his time much like Marx, Weber did not, and understandably so, realize the long-term significance of the revolution in consumption and its relationship to that of production (Campbell, 1987: 8). Although Weber identified the under-lying social conditions which would make this revolution possible, this was not the key focus of his analysis. Having said that, the more recent work of Colin Campbell (1987) provides an interesting slant on some of the insights provided by Weber through an extension of Weberian conceptions of the social significance of consumption.

Campbell (1987) points out that, though Weber saw consumption as unproblematic, his discussion of the essentially irrational nature of the 'spirit of capitalism' and the thirst for more and more money, which was accompanied by an actual avoidance of the spontaneous enjoyment of life, provided a forerunner of contemporary desires for pleasurable and gratifying forms of consumption. Thus, Campbell describes the emergence of the Romantic ethic in the late eighteenth and early nine-teenth centuries which, though fostering puritanical values of reinvest-ment and piety, included a propensity towards an emotionalist way of life in which people gradually became more aware of their own pleas-ures. Though Campbell tends to exaggerate the role of the Romantic movement in encouraging the emergence of modern forms of hedonism, he does provide an intriguing historical account of the emergence of contemporary forms of consumption, as well as an illuminating critique of Weber. As Bocock (1993) notes, Campbell (1987) identifies a shift towards an increasingly symbolic role for consumption in a world where consumption is equated with desirous day-dreaming. Campbell (1987: 89–90) therefore argues that

> the spirit of modern consumerism is anything but materialistic. The idea that contemporary consumers have an insatiable desire to acquire objects rep-resents a serious misunderstanding of the mechanism which impels people to want goods. Their basic motivation is the desire to experience in reality the pleasurable dramas which they have already enjoyed in imagination, and each 'new' product is seen as offering a possibility of realizing this ambition.

Campbell's work represents an illuminating attempt to extend Weberian conceptions of consumption and as such serves to highlight how the *symbolic* value of consumption came to play a primary role in the ways in which people consume in the late twentieth century.

Thorstein Veblen

One of the most significant classical contributions to a sociological understanding of consumption, bearing in mind the centrality given to the question of consumption in his analysis, is that of Thorstein Veblen, who saw consumer goods as markers of social prestige and status. In his analysis of the American *nouveaux riches* of the late nineteenth century, Veblen (1899) described a 'new leisure class' intent on mimicking the lifestyles of the upper classes in Europe. Veblen (1899) argued that higher social groupings continually updated their consumption habits in order to stay one step ahead of the *nouveaux riches*. As such, consumption was significant largely for its status-conferring qualities, in that what was emerging was a hierarchically organized social structure based upon the prestigious consumption patterns of the rich and in particular of the gentleman of leisure who,

> In order to avoid stultification . . . must . . . cultivate his tastes, for it now becomes incumbent upon him to discriminate with some nicety between the noble and the ignoble in consumable goods . . . Closely related to the requirement that the gentleman must consume freely and of the right kind of goods, there is the requirement that he must know how to consume them in a seemly manner. (Veblen, 1994 edn: 47; orig. published 1899)

Veblen therefore identifies an elaborate system of rank and grades, the markers of consumption expressing a person's place in the social hierarchies of the leisure classes. Arguably, the processes of emulation which were signposted in Veblen's work have emerged as a growing influence upon the everyday construction of social life, though they are arguably less class specific than he envisaged at the time. In contemporary consumer society, the degrees of demarcation and the role that consumption plays in the ways in which people associate with each other have become highly sophisticated. In addition, they appear to have simultaneously become taken for granted as the 'natural' way of things – as a way of life.

Veblen's work remained in the sociological wilderness until it regained popularity with the realization, notably during the 1980s, that consumption was worth considering for its own sake. After all, only recently have serious efforts been made to redress the balance in an attempt to understand consumption *per se*. Veblen is most memorable, perhaps, for being the first sociologist to recognize the social significance of consumption in its own right.

Georg Simmel

Georg Simmel is another theorist who recognized the increasing significance of consumption to the construction of modern social life. Indeed, writing at the turn of the century, Simmel (1907) sees money and, more specifically, exchange as being central to the experience of modernity. This is interesting in the sense that it raises the possibility that consumption is more than of mere incidental interest and might actually have some instrumental role in structuring people's overall experience of modernity. Identifying the metropolis as the seat of the mature money economy, Simmel argues that the anonymity of relations in the

metropolis is determined by the need for anonymous market relationships. The emergence of the city, argues Simmel, has significant implications for the conduct of social life, and he identifies consumption as
having an increasingly significant role to play in this process. As the
metropolis developed, it began to satisfy the social *and* psychological
needs of its inhabitants; hence the role of consumption. Almost a
century later, the impact of consumer culture within late capitalism, not
least in the form of city life, is so profound that this argument has
become imbued with more significance than even Simmel could have
envisaged.

Interestingly, Simmel (1957) also discusses in some detail the role of
fashion as a social form of class demarcation, juxtaposing the feeling of
individuality with the security of commonality with others (see Chapter
6). In an increasingly commercial society, where the pace of life becomes
more and more intense, Simmel argues that fashion provides the only
apparent means of recovering oneself, of stabilizing the assault upon the
senses which is characteristic of modern life. In fact, from this perspective the whole history of society is seen to be a compromise between
adherence and absorption in a social group and the need for indi-
viduation and distinction from the members of such groups. As such,
consumption provides the consumer with a sort of buffer zone between
him or herself and the everyday tensions characteristic of modernity. In
many respects, Simmel foresaw the formative role that consumerism
plays in the construction of everyday life in the late twentieth century.

An emerging sociology of consumption

Despite the contributions of authors such as Veblen and Simmel, an
actual sociology of consumption did not begin to emerge in its own
right (and it continues to do so) until the 1980s when sociologists began
to take more notice of the legacies provided by some of the classical
theorists discussed above. In this section, I will consider some of the
more valuable of these recent contributions to debates over consumption and consumerism.

Peter Saunders

As far as the emergence of the move towards an academic consideration of consumption in its own right is concerned, the work of Peter
Saunders (1981), who calls for the prioritization of a consumption-
oriented paradigm, provides sociologists of consumption with a particularly important benchmark. Saunders argues that class (or the
relationship to the means of production) is no longer a fundamental
determinant of contemporary life experience. What is more important in

this respect are differences in *access* to consumption. As such, from his free-market liberal perspective, Saunders focuses on the impact of privatized consumption, arguing that the fundamental division in contemporary societies is between those who have the available resources to play an active role in the free market and those whose lives are dependent upon the welfare state. As far as Saunders is concerned, then, owner-occupation is particularly significant in so far as we no longer derive our satisfaction from work in contemporary society but more so from consuming goods and services. In this respect, the ownership of housing provides 'An expression of personal identity and a source of ontological security' (Saunders, 1984: 203).

Saunders's contribution has been criticized on several counts. He somewhat overenthusiastically endorses the opportunities provided by the marketplace, while simultaneously portraying the state as incompetent. He also presents a narrow conception of consumption which is limited by his representation of privatized and collective consumption (see Warde, 1990a). Despite these reservations, Saunders (1981) should be commended for highlighting the significance of consumption in the sociological 'enterprise' by provoking considerable sociological debate around the question of consumption.

Pierre Bourdieu

Pierre Bourdieu, one of the most prominent sociologists of the late twentieth century, is also one of the most important commentators on questions of consumption in the contemporary world. Bourdieu, whose work has something in common with that of Veblen inasmuch as he addresses questions of social comparison through consumption, has had a formative role in highlighting the social significance of consumption. Seeing consumption as a means of establishing, as opposed to merely expressing, variations between social groups, Bourdieu (1984) argues that human beings are motivated by the need to reproduce a collective pattern of preferences based on class demarcation. What Bourdieu describes as 'cultural capital' is crucial in this respect, in that different classes are educationally qualified to take advantage of different aspects of symbolic capital. The dominant classes therefore demonstrate their superiority through access to high culture and high consumption. The implication here, then, is that consumption amounts to a set of cultural resources that underpins consumers' everyday lives.

Of course, access to these resources depends upon access to economic resources. But the important issue here is that the social and cultural *norm* is for the individual to aspire to them. In this context, Bocock's (1993) discussion of Bourdieu is a useful one in that he highlights the fact that consumption is not to be analysed as the satisfaction of a biologically rooted set of needs. Rather, consumption, as Bourdieu (1984) points out, actively involves signs, symbols, ideas and values which are used as a means of marking off one social group from another. What is especially impressive about Bourdieu's approach is that it was based upon findings which emanated from situated empirical research that looked at patterns of consumption in France in the 1960s and 1970s. Equally significantly, Bourdieu did not see consumers' consumption habits as being the mere product of social structures, but rather as an *interaction* between the individual and society. In this context, Bourdieu developed the concept of 'habitus', the everyday knowledge or cultural capital that reflects the routine experience of appropriate behaviour in particular cultures and subcultures. 'Habitus' plays a pivotal role in the construction of lifestyles which

> are thus the systematic products of habitus, which, perceived in their mutual relations through the schemes of the habitus, become sign systems that are socially qualified (as 'distinguished', 'vulgar' etc.). The dialectic of conditions and habitus is the basis of an alchemy which transforms the distribution of capital, the balance-sheet of a power relation, into a system of perceived differences, distinctive properties, that is, a distribution of symbolic capital, legitimate capital, whose objective truth is misrecognized. (Bourdieu, 1984: 172)

The habitus, which can therefore be defined as a group-distinctive framework of social cognition and interpretation, is reproduced *between* generations and thereby generates the schemes by which cultural objects are classified and differentiated (see Waters, 1994). Bourdieu argues that class differences are inscribed in individuals as distinctions in taste. In effect, an individual's social experience is structured by what the social group sees as being the legitimate way to do so according to the correct classifications of taste. Whether class remains a fundamental influence on the day-to-day construction of consumer lifestyles is debatable: it could be argued that consumption is currently so ubiquitous as to fragment the very stabilities that were formerly associated with class formations. The significance of Bourdieu's attempt to address the situated actualities of consumer experience cannot, however, be underestimated.

Consumption as a negotiated realm

Equally significant in this regard are a variety of other approaches to questions of consumption, gradually emerging during the 1980s and early 1990s, which began to see consumption as a negotiated realm in which consumers, and often young people, could express their resistance to dominant orders (for example, de Certeau, 1984; Fiske, 1989; P. Willis, 1990). Paul Willis's (1990) work is particularly significant in discussing how young people use the symbolic resources provided by the cultural industries as a means of creatively fashioning youth experience, identity and expression. Though Willis could be criticized for exaggerating the freedoms that young people have in the context of consumption (Miles, 1995), his work represents one of the first attempts actually to address the experiential nature of consumption:

> People bring living identities to commerce and the consumption of cultural commodities as well as being formed there. They bring experiences, feelings, social position and social memberships to their encounter with commerce. Hence they bring a necessary creative symbolic pressure, not only to make sense of cultural commodities, but partly through them also to make sense of contradiction and structure as they experience them in school, college, production, neighbourhood, and as members of certain genders, races, classes and ages. (P. Willis, 1990: 21)

Such debates have been further extended in the important works of authors such as Miller (1987), Otnes (1988) and McCracken (1990), all of whom have helped to move consumption up the sociological agenda. In this respect, it is certainly fair to say that since Saunders's (1981) call for a consumption-oriented paradigm, sociological approaches to consumption have actually moved more towards addressing the *symbolic* role of consumption. A special edition of the journal *Sociology* was subsequently influential in extending the recognition that consumption is an important sociological topic in its own right (see Warde, 1990b; Campbell, 1995). As such, consumption rapidly became associated with broader discussions concerning postmodernity which firmly established consumption as a primary focus for theoretical debate.

Consumption and postmodernism

The increasingly formative role of consumption in social life has gradually come to be acknowledged by social theorists, and as such the sociology of consumption has increasingly been diverted down what might be described as a 'postmodern' route. Though there is considerable debate and discussion as to precisely what 'postmodernism' is all about and what actually constitutes postmodernity, consumption is generally perceived to have an important role in the emergence of a postmodern culture. Generally speaking, postmodern conceptions of consumption are associated with a recognition that consumption is more significant for its sign-value or symbolic qualities than for its use-value. The tendency among these approaches has therefore been to focus on the symbolic processes characteristic of consumption rather than on the situated social experience and ideological function of consumerism as a way of life. This trend is particularly well discussed by the following authors: Lyon (1994) and Featherstone (1991), who provide useful overviews, as well as Baudrillard (1988) and Jameson (1984), both of whom consider consumption to play a key role in their conceptions of postmodernity.

David Lyon

Lyon (1994) directly addresses the relationship between postmodernism and consumption and goes as far as to argue that in the contemporary creation of the new consumer lies 'a crucial clue for understanding postmodernity and postmodernism' (Lyon, 1994: 55). From this point of view consumption is seen to be the 'linchpin' of a new cultural code in a world where the 'metanarratives' of modernity have collapsed and, as such, can no longer offer answers about the nature of a world in which progress is no longer possible. In this world, consumption is so ubiquitous that even meaning itself is seen to evaporate (Lyon 1994: 56). Reality, in effect, is seen to implode in a postmodern world in the sense that distinctions between high- and lowbrow culture become obscured as history, for instance, becomes heritage and the museum a 'hands-on' multi-media consumer experience (Lyon, 1994). 'Once established, such a culture of consumption is quite indiscriminating and everything becomes a consumer item, including meaning, truth and knowledge' (Sampson, 1994: 37).

The divisions between high and low culture become increasingly blurred in a postmodern culture where choice appears to reign supreme, but where hesitation, anxiety and doubt seem to be the price to pay for such freedom. As such, Lyon argues that consumption provides a means of oiling the wheels of symbolic distinctiveness to the extent that 'If postmodernity means anything, it means the consumer society' (Lyon, 1994: 66-8).

Mike Featherstone

Doing more to establish this fact than perhaps any other contribution to the debate is Mike Featherstone's (1991) work, *Consumer Culture and Postmodernism*, which represents one of the most important efforts directly to contextualize the question of consumption within debates concerning postmodernism. Featherstone notes that the identity-conferring nature of consumption is not something that is merely restricted to the young and the rich, but potentially affects the lives of everybody inasmuch as the postmodern world encourages us to believe that anything is possible. We can be whoever we want, as long as we are prepared to consume. Featherstone therefore discusses the aestheticization of everyday life: the process whereby standards of 'good style', 'good taste' and 'good design' have come to invade every aspect of our everyday life (see Featherstone, 1991: 68-72).

As far as the relationship between consumption and postmodernism is concerned, Featherstone looks at the transformation of reality into images and the fragmentation of time, but, more particularly, at the way in which art and aesthetic experiences become what he describes as 'the master paradigms for knowledge, experience and sense of life-meaning' (1991: 124). In this context, Featherstone argues that artistic cultural markets are growing and, as a result, so are audiences with 'post-modern sensibilities' (Featherstone, 1991: 125). Featherstone's own social position may well lead him, however, to exaggerate the role of 'cultural intermediaries' whose role it is to promote an artistic lifestyle by breaking down the exclusivity of intellectual knowledge and thus the boundaries between high and popular culture. Indeed, in this respect, many contributors to the debate over postmodernism appear to be dependent upon their own very specific experiences of a middle-class social world which is bound to reproduce some of the patterns of consumption they describe, but which is ultimately more likely to be the exception as opposed to the rule. What is of more general interest is the suggestion, not that middle-class artistic values are becoming more important to a large percentage of the population, which they undoubt-edly are even if to a limited extent, but that the production of such culture is increasingly subject to a process of commodification.

Consumerism as a way of life incorporates social processes which are far beyond the direct control of specific social groups. Indeed, there could be some basis to the argument that, far from symbolic specialists becoming increasingly prevalent in a postmodern world, consumption provides *everybody* with a sense of control. The essence of consumerism therefore lies in the feeling that as consumers we are all gaining some semblance of authority over the everyday construction of our lives *through* consumption. The extent to which this control is genuine is a matter for further debate. All that need be said at this stage is that Featherstone is correct when he points out that any definitive under-standing of the role played by consumption in the emergence of a so-called postmodern world must be based on careful sociological analyses of real-world phenomena.

Jean Baudrillard

One of the most well-known and extreme approaches to the influence of a mass-mediated consumer culture is that of Jean Baudrillard, the 'high priest' of postmodernism. Baudrillard (1988: 29) describes the role of consumerism in contemporary society as constituting 'a fundamental mutation in the ecology of the human species'. In this sense, 'Consumer society is . . . the society for the apprenticeship of consumption, for the social indoctrination of consumption. In other words, this is a new and specific mode of socialization related to the rise of new productive forces and the monopolistic restructuring of a high output economic system' (Baudrillard, 1988: 49).

Baudrillard (1988) points out that the idea that human beings have certain 'needs' which have to be satisfied through consumption is a myth inasmuch as human beings are never actually satisfied and thus such 'needs' are never actually fulfilled. In this sense, Baudrillard argues that the consumer good takes on the value of a sign. Discussing the example of the washing machine, Baudrillard argues that consumer objects are no longer actually tied to a function or a defined need, but rather respond to what he describes as a 'logic of desire' (1988: 44). Consumer objects exist in a 'world of general hysteria' where goods become interchangeable (1988: 45). They all signify the potential to fulfil human desire, but can never actually do so. What therefore emerges is a constant fluidity of differential desires and meanings.

On this basis, Baudrillard manages to develop an interesting conception of how it is that consumption actually has nothing to do with pleasure, in that pleasure becomes constrained and institutionalized as a duty on the part of the individual citizen or consumer. In this sense, as Chaney (1996) points out, the essence of Baudrillard's argument is that the signifiers of economic value (i.e. currency) have become entirely divorced from any necessary relationship with the signifieds of real value. In other words, money becomes rootless in a social system characterized by simulation and hyper-reality. What is therefore created is an 'aesthetic' hallucination of reality (Baudrillard, 1993). Consumption becomes important in so far as it provides a means of expressing dream-like representations. The mass media have, as far as Baudrillard is concerned, a fundamental role in extending such representations. Consumption therefore serves as the most influential arena within which this world of superficiality is perpetuated.

Frederic Jameson

Allied to the failure directly to address the experiential nature of the consuming experience, postmodern approaches to consumption have also failed to consider the role that consumption plays as an interface between individual experience and broader social forces and, more specifically, as an arena within which individuals experience the cultural implications of capitalism. In this respect, commentators have prioritized consumption over and above consumerism as I defined it in Chapter 1. Postmodern conceptions of consumption are, in effect, limited by their dependence upon an abstract theoretical discourse that contributes little to an understanding of the actualities of everyday life and even less to an understanding of the role consumerism plays in generating people's experiences of what actively constitutes modernity or postmodernity. The actual experiential impact of consumerism tends to be lost amidst fanciful discussions of consumption as fragmentation (as in Baudrillard, 1988) which themselves tend to misrepresent the ideological nature of consumerism as a way of life.

One author who has gone some way towards addressing this question is Frederic Jameson (1984) in his seminal essay, 'Postmodernism, or the cultural logic of late capitalism'. Arguing that late capitalism amounts to what is in fact a *purer* form of capitalism than has previously been experienced, Jameson proposes that 'every position on postmodernism in culture – whether apologia or stigmatization – is also at one and the same time, and necessarily, an implicitly or explicitly political stance on the nature of multinational capitalism today' (Jameson, 1984: 55). This is a key point, and one that is all too often forgotten by the majority of postmodernists who tend to exist on abstract theoretical foundations while paying scant regard for political realities. In contrast, Jameson presents what he describes as a 'periodizing hypothesis' (1984: 55), a key element of which he sees as being the fact that

> aesthetic production today has become integrated into commodity production generally: the frantic economic urgency of producing fresh waves of ever more novel-seeming goods from clothing to airplanes, at ever great rates of turnover, now assigns an increasing essential structural function and position to aesthetic innovation and experimentation. (Jameson, 1984: 56)

Jameson therefore argues that there is a fundamental relationship between the positioning of postmodernism in the economic system and its impact upon the sphere of culture in contemporary consumer society. The key to his analysis therefore lies in the argument that it is misleading to suggest that contemporary society is about nothing more than cultural difference, randomness and fragmentation, and that such characteristics amount to some form of a new systemic cultural norm. From his Marxist point of view, Jameson therefore argues that the production of culture has been subsumed into commodity production in general and in this sense postmodernism is seen to equate with late/multinational/consumer capitalism (see Featherstone, 1991: 52–9). The relationship between so-called postmodern forms of consumption and the structures of consumer capitalism will continue to be a key concern throughout this book.

Having considered some of the major contributors to postmodern debates about the impact of consumption, the overall point should be made that, whether or not you agree with the substance of the postmodern perspective, such approaches have had an important role in ensuring that commentators have come to acknowledge the formative social role that consumption plays in the make-up of contemporary societies. Indeed, this development is largely a result, as Fine and Leopold (1993) point out, of theoretical concern with the 'post' rather than the past. In particular, broad debates over postmodernity (and to a lesser extent post-Fordism) have highlighted the potential diversities available to consumers, the consequence being that consumption has emerged as an increasingly autonomous focus for debate. Postmodern analyses of the contemporary life experience focus by their very nature on the qualities and experience of mass-mediated consumer culture. Work such as that of Jameson (1984) and Urry (1990), whose reasoned, contextualized analyses of postmodern debates are more effective than most, can be commended for helping to establish consumption as a sociological priority. At the very least, they have served to raise the question whether or not consumer conduct has moved 'into the position of, simultaneously, the cognitive and moral focus of life, the integrative bond of the society, and the focus of systematic management' (Bauman, 1992: 49). A key question here, then, centres on how far choice, especially consumer choice, becomes the foundation of a new concept of freedom in contemporary society to the extent that the freedom of the individual is actively and primarily constituted in his or her role as a consumer.

Despite the acknowledgement that debates over postmodernity have developed our understanding of consumption in so far as 'Product image, style and design take over from modern metanarratives of conferring meaning' (Lyon, 1994: 61), the irony is that the actual construction of that meaning has not been addressed directly. In effect, the sociology of consumption has suffered through a postmodern emphasis on 'macro-cultural' issues. Though postmodernists have prioritized the cultural, they have only done so, by and large, from an overarching conception of what constitutes culture, without consideration of the actual everyday experiences in which culture is actively constructed. In this sense,

> Postmodernist criticism should not be confined to textual analysis alone, or the critique of forms of representation alone, but should be an inquiry into the ways forms of representation structure everyday life. To forget everyday life and the users of culture is to neglect the formative aspects of culture itself. (Gottdiener, 1995: 31)

The value of a sociology of consumerism lies in addressing the relationship between the structures of everyday life and the ways in which the culture of consumption impinge upon the conduct of that life, both experientially and ideologically.

Cross-disciplinary approaches to consumption

So far I have focused on approaches to consumption broadly associated with aspects of social theory. I will now broaden the discussion a little further. The general tone of this chapter has tended to suggest that current conceptions of consumption are insufficient, particularly in terms of what they can say about consumerism as a way of life. In this respect a broader, cross-disciplinary conception of consumerism may well be of use.

Mary Douglas and Baron Isherwood

The first approach I want to consider briefly in this context is that of Douglas and Isherwood (1996) whose anthropological approach to the economic nature of consumption is highly influential. Douglas and Isherwood are important in so far as they recognize that consumption is cultural as well as economic and that the use of consumer goods is always framed by a cultural component. Douglas and Isherwood argue that consumption should be perceived in this context as a mode of communication:

> The theory of consumption has to be a theory of culture and a theory of social life. To cut culture free from organization is to float off into a sea of relativism. If the organization works well enough, it can endow objects with value, being fit for consumption means an object being fit to circulate as a marker for particular sets of social roles. (Douglas and Isherwood, 1996: xxii–xxiii)

Douglas and Isherwood therefore refer to consumer goods as an information system and as such famously argue that 'Consumption is the very arena in which culture is fought over and licked into shape' (1996: 37). In effect, consumption acts as a non-verbal medium for human creativity. In this context, the two authors point out that, contrary to some of the over-romanticized visions of the past, social interaction actually improves with affluence. Consumption provides degrees of freedom to the rich which are simply not available to the poor. More importantly, what is crucial about the act of consumption is the meaning that is actually invested in it. When a person purchases a particular bar of chocolate he or she is not simply buying sustenance, but a range of symbolic meanings expressing membership of a social world. In this sense, consumer goods actively articulate existing social divisions and structures. But what is especially interesting about Douglas and Isherwood's work, as Lee (1993) notes, is that it provides an antidote to the structure-down model presented by authors such as Baudrillard. From this point of view, consumers are not seen to be the mere products of structural forces such as advertising and the media. Consumers are always subject to certain pre-established patterns of consumption and social convention, but symbolic goods are purposefully managed by consumers within the cultural rules and codes laid down for and by them.

Helga Dittmar

A further approach to consumption that has sought to come to terms with the meanings invested by consumers in consumer goods is that of the social psychologist, Helga Dittmar. Dittmar (1992) discusses the role of subjective social reality; that is, the process by which the objective

world (which the individual experiences outside him or herself alongside his or her symbolic social reality and which, in turn, incorporates
forms of symbolic expression such as language, non-verbal behaviour
and material objects) is internalized in the form of an individual's
awareness and understanding. From this point of view, individuals are
seen to integrate both objective and symbolic aspects of material objects
in constructing their own representations and thereby regard such
objects as symbols of identity which in turn are negotiated in the
context of social interaction. In this context, Dittmar (1992) calls for a
diversified approach to the link between identity and possessions. From
her social constructionist perspective, Dittmar concludes that possessions transcend their instrumental and utilitarian functions, encom-
passing symbolic meanings within social groups or societies, so that
material objects are used as a means of communicating who someone is
(or would like to be) both to others and oneself. In this sense, Dittmar
argues that possessions act as material symbols of identity, counteracting the sense of fragmentation which I discussed above in the context
of postmodernism and simultaneously providing some sense of
historical continuity.

What Dittmar (1992) refers to as the 'materialism–idealism paradox'
is particularly important here. This relates to the commonly accepted
idea that every individual has a unique personality independent of
material circumstances, alongside the paradoxical notion that material
possessions are central regulators, not only of large-scale social processes, but also of interpersonal relations and impressions. In a so-called
postmodern world, an individual may lose his or her subjectivity
amidst a plethora of lifestyle choices and yet the society in which he or
she lives puts considerable emphasis on the uniqueness of each and
every person.

Peter Lunt and Sonia Livingstone

Similar issues are addressed by Lunt and Livingstone (1992) who
present an equally illuminating analysis of the relationship between
mass consumption and the construction of identity. Their work is
unusual, and admirably so, in so far as it depends very much upon
empirical data with which they attempt to chart the above relationship.
As such, the emphasis here is on consumption as *everyday* experience.
Lunt and Livingstone therefore call upon triangulated research methods
in an attempt to elicit people's experiences of money and possessions
and how this might impart influence on the construction of their
identities. From this basis a vision of a sophisticated consumer, whose
involvement in material culture provides a means of actively locating
him or herself in a changing social order, is drawn. Lunt and
Livingstone (1992) point out that the consuming experience is one of
contradictions where people seem to believe that the contemporary

world is characterized by an exciting proliferation of consumer goods, while simultaneously harbouring a sense of loss for the way life used to be, as well as a need for some semblance of continuity in their lives. Lunt and Livingstone ask how far it is possible for consumers to establish an identity within the freedoms that consumption provides. They argue that the transitory nature of social life, notably in the context of consumption, makes the construction of identity a particularly problematic enterprise.

Yiannis Gabriel and Tim Lang

The final approach to consumption I want to mention is that of Gabriel and Lang (1995) who discuss the characteristic diversities of life as a consumer. The two authors manage to highlight very effectively the paradoxes that characterize the consuming experience:

> The consumer has become a god-like figure, before whom markets and politicians alike bow. Everywhere it seems, the consumer is triumphant . . . And yet the consumer is also seen as a weak and malleable creature, easily manipulated, dependent, passive and foolish. Immersed in illusions, addicted to joyless pursuits of ever-increasing living standards, the consumer, far from being a god, is a pawn, in games played in invisible boardrooms. (Gabriel and Lang, 1995: 1)

Gabriel and Lang (1995) use the term 'the unmanageable consumer' to highlight the complex, fragmented and volatile nature of the consuming experience. The two authors go on to argue that in the future such an experience will become increasingly spasmodic, contradictory and insecure. In this sense, they argue, it is just not possible to answer the simple question, 'what is the consumer?' Consumption and consumerism have become hotly contested terrains – terrains which have been invaded by a diversity of disciplines all of which have tried to impose their conceptions of what it is to consume.

The point here is that consumerism is, indeed, a highly paradoxical and contradictory phenomenon. In order to go some way towards understanding why this is so, I will now conclude this chapter by briefly discussing a key issue which lies at the heart of this debate as a whole, namely the relationship between consumerism, structure, agency and ideology. This issue provides the context within which the remainder of this book should be considered.

Conclusion

The structure and agency debate has emerged as a key concern of the social sciences in recent years (see Layder, 1994; Waters, 1994). Discussing, in particular, the influence of the 'macro–micro' issue on contemporary sociological thought, Layder (1994) points out that the structure and agency dualism, and the debate that surrounds it, highlight the fact that people are 'agents' in the social world; that they are actively able to do things which affect the everyday social relationships in which they are embedded. Society then, is inseparable from its human components because the very existence of that society depends upon human activities and, as such, what society is at any given time depends upon those activities. On the other hand, individuals are not immutable as social agents because existence as social beings is also affected by the experience of the society people live in and by their efforts to transform that society (Archer, 1995). The suggestion here is that, at least *potentially*, consumption is a significant cultural resource in this process.

As I suggested in Chapter 1, recent decades have seen the emergence of a historical sea-change whereby people have increasingly come to identify a sense of power and freedom located in aspects of life outside of work. In this sense, Hall (1988) argues that the ideological impact of a consumer culture can be traced back, at least in the short term, to the consumer boom of the 1950s from which time the immediate lives of many working-class families were transformed. The new opportunities that consumption appeared to offer helped to mould new habits, patterns and models of everyday life, significantly altering people's aspirations and expectations as to how they felt they should lead their everyday lives. What was emerging was a mode of life that was very much less constrained, thereby implanting itself in the minds of ordinary people as an essentially expansive and liberating social system, both personally and in terms of the development of society as a whole (Hall, 1988).

The paradox of consumerism is that it offers a vision of personal freedom through economic means – the opportunity for individuals to take advantage of their own means for extravagant display – and yet maintains a dominant order that potentially constrains personal liberty. Developing this point, Bauman notes how consumer conduct steadily moves into the simultaneous position of the cognitive and moral focus of life, amounting to what is, in effect, the integrative bond of society: 'Consumer freedom has moved in – first perhaps as a squatter, but more and more as a legitimate resident. It now takes over the crucial role of the link which fastens together the lifeworlds of the individual agents and the purposeful rationality of the system' (1988: 807).

Arguing that there might at least be some truth in this proposition, the question I will be considering throughout this book is concerned with the actual consequences of consumption as a significant force in the construction of contemporary forms of social life. In effect, what I am suggesting here is that an agenda for a sociology of consumerism should be focused upon the everyday expressions of consumerism and how those expressions reflect the relationship between structure and agency. I will argue that this is an important development, largely because the sociology of consumption has become preoccupied with what amount to unbalanced, overgeneralized and uncontextualized discussions of the consumption question and more recently the culture of consumption. In effect, commentators in the field have failed to contextualize the situated everyday manifestations of consumerism as a way of life.

The problem seems to lie in an apparent temptation on the part of sociologists of consumption to adopt a structural conception of the impact of consumption or, at the other end of the spectrum, a liberal economic choice approach that tends to see consumption as a free expression of people's wants or as an explosion of creative individualism. In effect, as Miller (1995) suggests, this amounts to a division between those who see consumption as *bad* and those who see it as *good*; thus, between theorists such as Horkheimer and Adorno (1973), who feel that in a mass society consumers are compelled to buy and use its products despite seeing through them, and those at the other end of the spectrum who see consumption as freedom-inducing and liberating. As such, Swingewood (1977) disputes Horkheimer and Adorno's (1973) claim that capitalist culture has degenerated into 'barbaric meaninglessness'; preferring to argue that the capitalist economy has actually achieved unprecedented pinnacles of cultural richness 'on a scale unparalleled in human history' (Swingewood, 1977: ix). From this point of view, the market is seen to offer infinite freedoms, one unleashed freedom leading on to another (see Kingdom, 1992). Consumption is therefore celebrated as a source of perpetual creativity and empowerment. This is an approach synonymous with the political right, both in Britain and the USA during the 1980s and into the 1990s. Perhaps one of the most distinctive thinkers on this issue was Milton Friedman, who saw choice as an end in its own right: 'When you vote daily in the supermarket, you get precisely what you voted for, and so does everyone else. The ballot box produces conformity without unanimity; the marketplace, unanimity without conformity' (Friedman and Friedman, 1980: 65–6).

As I suggested above, there is no straightforward answer to the dilemma as to which of these two extreme approaches is 'correct'. Consumerism is far more complicated and far less clear cut than either of these positions allows. But given the fact that sociologists are increasingly coming to accept that consumption has some sort of significant influence on the maintenance of our life experience in the late twentieth-century developed world, it is a great shame that very limited progress seems to have been made in pinpointing exactly how consumption serves to constrain, or indeed enable, our everyday lives. Gabriel and Lang (1995) argue, as I have elsewhere (Miles, 1995, 1996), that such problems are characteristic of a failure to marry varieties of conceptual and disciplinary approaches to questions of consumption.

There are no straightforward means of analysing the pros and cons of a consumer lifestyle. The consuming experience is in itself essentially abstract in the sense that it is simply not possible to map the exact relationship between consumption as a fulfilling individual experience and consumerism as an ideological phenomenon. All we can do is our utmost in attempting to understand the actual experience of consumerism in situated settings, for it is in these settings that we are most likely to come to terms with the meanings consumers endow in their experience of consumerism as a way of life. Only then can the paradoxes characterizing consumerism in the late twentieth-century developed world be fully understood. This book cannot in itself achieve such a goal, but it can attempt to discuss critically at least some aspects of everyday life in which consumerism appears to play a key role.

In this chapter I have presented brief, thumb-nail sketches of some of the major approaches to questions of consumption. In bringing this chapter to a close I want to suggest that the key to an understanding of the sociological significance of consumerism lies in a concerted effort to bridge the gap between economic, cultural and psychological aspects of consumerism. Such an ambition is only attainable if consumer capitalism is considered in context as *lived* experience. After extending this debate in Chapter 3 through a discussion of the role of design in consumer culture, in the following five chapters I intend to address the social impact of consumerism in five thematic spheres of social life: space and place; technology; fashion; popular music; and sport. From this basis, I hope to analyse the sociological implications of consumerism as a means by which social life is constructed, considering the key role played by ideological dimensions of consumerism as I do so.

Recommended reading

Robert Bocock (1993) *Consumption*. London: Routledge. A useful summary of historical and theoretical aspects of consumption.

Pierre Bourdieu (1984) *Distinction: A Social Critique of the Judgement of Taste*. London: Routledge & Kegan Paul. One of the key contributions to the emerging debates concerning the sociological significance of consumption.

Colin Campbell (1987) *The Romantic Ethic and the Spirit of Modern Consumerism*. Oxford: Blackwell. This usefully marries an analysis of the role of consumption in the emergence of the Romantic movement with Weberian theory.

Helga Dittmar (1992) *The Social Psychology of Material Possessions: To Have is to Be*. Hemel Hempstead: Harvester Wheatsheaf. An insightful analysis of the social psychological impact of consumer goods.

Mary Douglas and Baron Isherwood (1979) *The World of Goods: Towards an Anthropology of Consumption*. London: Allen Lane. The classic anthropological assessment of consumption.

Mike Featherstone (1991) *Consumer Culture and Postmodernism*. London: Sage. An important contribution that helped to prioritize the key role played by consumerism in a so-called postmodern world.

Yiannis Gabriel and Tim Lang (1995) *The Unmanageable Consumer*. London: Sage. A comprehensive compendium which does well to illustrate the diversities characteristic of consumer experience.

Frederic Jameson (1984) 'Postmodernism, or the cultural logic of late capitalism', *New Left Review*, 146: 53–93. A key essay that calls for a consideration of postmodernism in its socio-economic context.

Martyn Lee (1993) *Consumer Culture Reborn: The Cultural Politics of Consumption*. London: Routledge. A particularly useful economistic analysis of what constitutes a commodity.

Peter Lunt and Sonia Livingstone (1992) *Mass Consumption and Personal Identity*. Buckingham: Open University Press. Valuable for its attempt to consider the consumption/identity relationship through empirical lenses.

David Lyon (1994) *Postmodernity*. Buckingham: Open University Press. Includes a particularly useful chapter on the relationship between consumption and postmodernity.

Karl Marx (1990) *Capital: A Critique of Political Economy*, Vol. 1. 2nd edn, trans. Ben Fowkes. Harmondsworth: Penguin. A classical work (originally published 1867) which identifies the sociological and ideological significance of the commodity.

Peter Saunders (1981) *Social Theory and the Urban Question*. London: Hutchinson. This brought consumption well and truly into the sociological arena in the context of urban sociology.

Georg Simmel (1957) 'Fashion', in *American Journal of Sociology*, 62: 541–8. A useful insight into how consumption and, in particular, fashion mediates social life (originally published 1904).

Thorstein Veblen (1994) *The Theory of the Leisure Class*. London: Constable. One of the first authors to highlight the way in which consumption is used as a social marker (originally published 1899).

3

DESIGN FOR LIFE OR CONSUMPTION DESIGNED?

The key theoretical issue arising out of Chapters 1 and 2 centres on whether a consumer culture encourages individual freedom and expression or whether it actually serves painstakingly to construct the parameters within which people consume. In effect, do we as consumers design our own lifestyles or are those lifestyles designed for us? As a means of bringing this question into more direct focus, I will concentrate in this chapter on the role of *design* in contemporary society. I have chosen to focus specifically on the question of design because in many ways design appears to be symbolic of the impact of consumerism on contemporary society and, as such, highlights debates concerning the substance or superficiality of consumerism as a way of life.

Although on the surface the nature of design may appear to be relatively inconsequential, it might well be said to play a formative role in the history of capitalism and, in turn, in the social expression of capitalist practices. In this context, the unfortunate tendency to limit design to a purely artistic activity has 'made it seem trivial and relegated it to the status of a mere cultural appendix' (Forty, 1986: 6). The suggestion here is that design does indeed play a key role in maintaining consumerism as a way of life and that, by considering the impact of design in some detail, it may begin to be possible to come to terms with the complexities inherent in any sociological analysis of the day-to-day nature of consumer culture.

Design, like consumption, is ubiquitous. Everywhere we turn as consumers, the impact of design is evident: from the design of a grandiose set at a party political conference or convention to the design of 'corporate' university logos. Is this a case of style over substance? Has our society got so carried away with consumerism as a way of life that the actual substance that constitutes that life – an effective political agenda for improving our everyday lives, perhaps, or a university curriculum that provides us with a stimulating and thought-provoking education – has become immaterial? Does the immediacy of good design override the substance of modern or postmodern life? Can we, indeed, accept Sparke's (1986: xix) judgement that 'design is characterized by a dual alliance with both mass production and mass consumption and that these phenomena have determined nearly all its manifestations'.

One line of thought is that the obsession with style and design was a 1980s phenomenon and that, in the caring, sharing nineties, labels, lifestyle accessories and design-led products and services have become a thing of the past (see Inglehart, 1990). In effect, we have come to live in a post-materialist age where the superficiality of design for design's sake and, indeed, consumption for consumption's sake has been exposed for the counterproductive social trend it always was.

In the above context, I will begin this chapter by considering *how design emerged historically*. I will then discuss two specific areas of design: the *Sony Walkman* and *Levi jeans*. I will then ask *whether there is any such thing as 'green design'*. Debates concerning the greening of design should be able to tell us something about the role of consumerism in contemporary society. I will then move on to consider whether or not *design is merely an expression of postmodernism*. Finally, I will come to an overall conclusion about the role of design in the everyday construction of a consumer society, using this as a springboard from which I can introduce the series of case studies that I present throughout the remainder of the book.

The emergence of design

The historical emergence of design is discussed particularly effectively by Sparke (1986) and Whiteley (1993), both of whom note that, while early developments in industrial production were more concerned with utility than design, during the twentieth century design gradually came to play a more fundamental role in the desirability and saleability of a product. In particular, as Sparke (1986) suggests, the economic demands of industrial capitalism depended upon the constant consumption of goods and it is in this context that design came into its own, providing the variation that was so essential to the development of a capitalist economy. In this context, far from being static over the past century, the meaning of 'design' has shifted along with the evolution of consumer culture as a whole.

Sparke (1986) suggests that it was during the latter years of the nineteenth century when the use of electricity became more widespread in Britain, thereby underlining increased mechanization, that the variety of areas of consumption available to the consumer became extended. Such developments occurred alongside the social changes that necessitated them: 'For these new consumers appearance and life-style were becoming increasingly important and this pointed the way to products becoming a means of offering them style and social status which, in turn, called for increased product elaboration' (Sparke, 1986: 12). The second half of the nineteenth century was therefore a boom period in the history of consumption, and design became a legitimate means of sustaining and expanding markets. Whereas in the early days consumers in general were uneducated about questions of style and taste, and production was able to concentrate on speed and on saving costs, the meanings invested in consumption gradually changed until, by the turn of the twentieth century, status symbolism began to have a more influential role in the construction of middle- and working-class lifestyles.

As noted in Chapter 1, industrialists such as Henry Ford promoted a standardized aesthetic whereby mass taste could be educated to accept mass-produced products such as the Ford Model T (see Sparke, 1986: 10). In this context, Whiteley (1993) argues that the late 1920s, most notably in the USA, represented a turning point in the emergence of design. It was at this time that the industrial strategy of aiming for gradual and constant improvement towards technical perfection gave way to a more thoroughgoing and arguably cynical policy aimed at continual stylistic change in order to stimulate sales and profits. In this respect, the American car industry of the 1920s and 1930s played a key role, as manufacturers saw the economic benefits of giving their products 'eye appeal' or 'added value' (see Whiteley, 1993; 13). Whiteley describes this as a process of 'consumer engineering'. By streamlining the cars they produced, manufacturers were matching consumers to products, rather than products to consumers. As such, the car industry was the first to realize the profits that could be made in promoting short-term, three-year product cycles within which major style changes could be introduced, thereby perpetuating a mentality on the part of consumers that they should be looking to buy a new car triennially (Whiteley, 1993).

The point here is that, as far as the evolution of consumer capitalism is concerned, style was simply not enough on its own. It had to go hand in hand with profit, hence the need for compulsory obsolescence. Compulsory obsolescence is the foundation-stone of the modern design industry and involves the intentional design of products for short-term use. In other words, designers ensure a constant demand for new products by intentionally designing products with limited life-spans. This temporality is most noticeably enforced through the design of intensively designed fashion goods which almost inevitably lose their appeal to consumers within two or three years. The intriguing part of this equation is that the power in this relationship, at least from one point of view, is still with the consumer in the sense that if he or she no longer desires a product he or she will not buy it. Through compulsory obsolescence, however, the designer makes the act of purchase more of a probability than a possibility. In this environment, Whiteley quotes Harley J. Earl (1959: 79) who argued that 'our job is to hasten obsolescence. In 1934 the average car ownership span was five years; now it is two years. When it is one year, we will have a perfect score.' Design, then, was emerging as an industry intent on stimulating demand, regardless of the need on the part of the consumer, and yet it maintained a semblance of democracy in the sense that, if one consumer traded in his or her car for the latest model, the old model could be passed on down the chain to those consumers with less disposable income.

By the 1950s, the USA was well ahead of Europe in embracing a design-led consumer culture. This state of affairs was reiterated by a process of Americanization or 'Coca-colanization', whereby American products and consumer-based lifestyles were held up as the aspirational ideal, notably through the images portrayed by Hollywood (Sparke, 1986). Britain was undergoing considerable social change at this time – social change that was exacerbated by the sudden abundance of consumer goods that the USA had experienced about 30 years earlier. A thriving economy and the fact that consumers had more disposable income encouraged the development of an increasingly eclectic marketplace. The 1960s, symbolized by the emergence of the Habitat lifestyles stores in Britain, saw a proliferation of this 'mass culture' on both sides of the Atlantic, notably as a result of the expansion of the mass media (see Whiteley, 1993: 18). As such, Sparke (1986) argues that design was well and truly appropriated as one of consumer society's major communicative forces. In effect, then, design was a business strategy in what amounted to a self-conscious attempt to give consumer goods added value.

It was in this sort of socio-economic climate that consumerism became a way of life. Consumer goods became fashionable and design had a fundamental role to play in this process. I am not arguing here that design alone had a formative role in structuring the nature of everyday life, but that design both reflected and reinforced the climate of the times. This fits in with Featherstone's (1991) description of the aestheticization of everyday life which I discussed in Chapter 2. Design had an important role in ensuring that such social change was possible. The value of a consumer and design-oriented life was rapidly being disseminated throughout society (see Barthel, 1989). In this context, Barthel quotes Forty (1986: 6) who argues that 'Far from being a neutral, inoffensive artistic activity, design, by its very nature, has much more enduring effects than the ephemeral products of the media because it can cast ideas about who we are and how we should behave into permanent and tangible forms.' In this respect, design has an especially important role in the visualization of class positions and status. Style, and hence the meanings people invested in design, became a social value in its own right. In effect, style itself became a commodity, a new way of selling old products. Consumers came to buy products not necessarily for what they did but for what they said about them as consumers. The role of design is therefore not to meet human needs but to create and stimulate those needs in increasingly diverse ways. In order to illustrate this point I want very briefly to consider the design of two particular types of consumer goods: the Sony Walkman, as discussed by du Gay et al. (1997), and Levi jeans, as represented in the work of Fiske (1989).

The Sony Walkman

Paul du Gay et al. (1997) present an illuminating analysis of all aspects of the Sony Walkman's production and consumption. They argue that the Walkman is closely allied to the culture of late modernity through the nature of its design. The Walkman is designed to be worn as a lightweight appendage to the human body through which an individual can express aspects of his or her self-image. Describing it as an 'extension of the skin', du Gay et al. go on to argue that the Sony Walkman is also designed for mobility, as a required piece of equipment for the modern 'self-sufficient urban voyager' (du Gay et al., 1997: 23). Such mobility is also apparently symbolic of the social mobility of modern life in general and the way in which individual choice and flexibility has become increasingly apparent in the everyday experience of modern societies.

In this context, Sony presents itself as a design-led corporation and particular efforts are made to encourage consumers to identify with its products. This is reflected in the way in which the Sony Walkman has constantly reinvented itself since its first incarnation in 1979. Paul du Gay et al. (1997: 66; original emphasis) point out that the Walkman had far broader appeal than the company originally thought:

> Gradually, as Walkman sales increased worldwide it was not simply representations of the Walkman that began to change but the *very 'look' and 'feel' of the product itself*. In other words, Sony shifted from registering the increasing diversity of consumer use through changes in its advertising and marketing materials alone to inscribing those changes onto the 'body' of the Walkman itself, through changes in its *design*. Instead of a single Walkman model sold worldwide, Sony began to customize the product, targeting different sorts of Walkman at different consumer markets or niches. Or to put it another way, Sony began to *lifestyle* the Walkman.

In other words, Sony came to realize the benefits to be gained from tailoring and designing the Walkman according to the lifestyle specifications of a specific market segment. In fact, the Walkman is currently available in over seven hundred versions worldwide (du Gay et al., 1997). More specifically, du Gay et al. go on to discuss the 'My First Sony' range, a primary intention of which was to build brand loyalty among young consumers. The marketing of this range was focused on middle-class parents. In this context, du Gay et al. argue that the actual design of the 'My First Sony' range played a crucial role. Interestingly, they go as far as to maintain, and this is a key point, that such design operates on the cusp of production and consumption. Thus, this particular type of Walkman had to be made durable enough to suit the needs of young children while allowing them to establish their own identities or looks through the product. As well as producing an effective product, Sony also observed the behaviour of parents and children at first hand in order to finalize decisions about product construction, packaging and visual presentation. In effect, 'through the deployment of their particular "symbolic" expertise, designers made a series of products achieve a *new register of meaning*' (du Gay et al., 1997: 69; original emphasis). The issue at stake here, then, centres on how far such meaning is created by the consumer and how far it is the construction of the producer who, in effect, appears actively to go about convincing the consumer that he or she constructs such meaning him or herself.

Jeans and the 'designer fallacy'

In order to develop this point, I want briefly to consider jeans as another example of a designed and often design*er*, item, particularly with reference to the work of Fiske (1989). During an informal exercise undertaken with students, Fiske asked what meanings people had for their jeans and many people argued that their jeans gave them the 'freedom to be myself' (Fiske, 1989: 2). Fiske points out that the paradox here is that the desire to be oneself encourages consumers to purchase and wear the same product as everybody else. In this context, popular culture appears to be inherently contradictory in the sense that it expresses aspects of domination (for example, of consumerism) and resistance (for example, by using the wares of consumerism such as jeans in a resistant fashion, i.e. ripped jeans). Fiske (1989) argues that jeans are semiotically rich and therefore provide a rich source of potential meanings. The point here is that it is not necessarily the actual design of the jeans themselves, but the *perception* of that design that is important. Manufacturers can therefore be said to exploit the feeling on the part of consumers that their particular design of jeans serves their own needs when in fact one pair of jeans is very much like any other. Marketers appear to target specific social groups in order to create niches in the market, thereby maximizing their profits. By creating a society dependent upon the exploitation of undifferentiated design –

design which is lauded as individualistic when it is patently not – consumer capitalism is able to reproduce itself.

Fiske considers a particular advertisement for Levi 501s which portrays three young people in a run-down city street who are sharing the hard-living lives they have been born into. His argument is that the advertisement simultaneously expresses an underlying current of living through this hard life *and* succeeding as an individual, despite all the odds. In other words, this advertisement reinforces the ideologies of meritocratic capitalism; the idea that whatever your station in life, the opportunities provided by capitalism, and in particular by consumer capitalism, mean that anything is possible (Fiske, 1989; 5–6). What is crucial here, then, is that the design of the jeans, as well as the advertising that sells the jeans, become a vehicle for the maximization of profit and the perpetuation of the consumerist ideal.

> Jeans are no longer, if they ever were, a generic denim garment. Like all commodities, they are given brand names that compete among each other for specific segments of the market. Manufacturers try to identify social differences and then to construct equivalent differences in the product so that social differentiation and product differentiation become mapped onto each other. (Fiske, 1989: 6)

In other words, consumer capitalism actively creates the illusion that there are differentiations in design between products. The differences in design between alternative types of jeans, between makes of jeans and types of jeans made by a single manufacturer, are often quite minor in nature and are arguably more the product of advertising and marketing than design itself.

In this sense, the cultural value of designer clothing is vastly exaggerated by consumers who read meanings off such goods according to their interpretation of the dominant mode of cultural capital. In this context, I conducted some research into the relationship between youth consumption and the construction of identity (Miles, 1995, 1996). The results gleaned from a 'Consumer Meanings Questionnaire', completed by approximately three hundred young people, illustrated the significance that designer labels played in young people's lives. Several of my respondents identified Versace suits as a consumer good which gave them particular pleasure. The question whether or not young people could actually afford to buy a design-intensive suit costing hundreds of pounds and whether their parents would indeed sanction such a purchase is an interesting one. The possibility that these particular answers were fabricated cannot be dismissed. But what is important here is the fact that a culture has emerged where designer labels can command a significant degree of cultural capital which young people themselves are keen to tap into in order to establish their identities in communal settings, regardless of their ability to purchase.

What is also interesting here, and something I discuss further in Chapter 6 in the context of fashion, is that, as Sparke (1986) argues, designer labels offer the consumer nothing more than run-of-the-mill brands with fancy names. Consumerism is safeguarded by what I describe as a 'designer fallacy'. Consumers are encouraged to become members of a consumer society by purchasing goods primarily through the attraction of superficial differentiations in design. Levi 501s are essentially the same as any other pair of jeans that are made available on the marketplace. Consumers convince themselves that 501s are better designed and of a higher quality than their competitors when what in fact separates them from the competitors is merely the added-value appeal of Levi's as a lifestyle product. What this means as far as design is concerned is that:

> Every product, to be successful, must incorporate the ideas that make it marketable, and the particular task of design is to bring about the conjunction between such ideas and the available means of production. The result of this process is that manufactured goods embody innumerable myths about the world, myths which in time come to seem as real as the products in which they are embedded. (Forty, 1986: 9)

The intention of design and aspects of the production process associated with design, such as advertising, is therefore to alter the way in which consumers see commodities. It is in this respect that design has increasingly come to be perceived negatively in so far as it is often accused of being responsible for the vast excesses of consumerism, notably during the 1980s. In this sense, design 'has come to imply spurious value, cynical manipulation, the justification of inflated price through a false impression of status and exclusivity' (Conran, 1996: 17). Conran goes on to defend design, arguing that questions of marketing and styling often get confused with design which is, in fact, a more fundamental process. Design, argues Conran, brings with it choice and with choice comes freedom. From this point of view, design is a democratic process, a process that far from pulling the wool over the eyes of a gullible public actually allows consumers to vote with their wallets. Thus, it can be argued that:

> Design can offer something beyond the chink of coins in the till or the rising curve of a sales graph. As well as promoting turnover, good design can be a progressive force, creating a momentum of confidence and a 'feel good' factor which bolsters a society's – or a company's – image of itself. (Conran, 1996: 21)

This point raises an interesting question: can the power of design be actively harnessed to promote the emergence of a new type of society? By considering this question in the context of debates over 'green design' I hope to construct a critical basis for addressing the role that consumerism plays as a way of life in contemporary consumer societies.

Is there such a thing as 'green design'?

The debate as to whether design can be harnessed for the benefit of the planet as a whole provides an interesting angle on the relationship between consumerism and design. In this respect, the work of two authors, Papanek (1995) and Whiteley (1993), are of particular interest. Papanek argues that design needs to become more environmentally and socially progressive and that consumers' attitudes and lifestyles need to be radically altered if the ravages of consumerism are to be contained. He therefore points out that the continued progression of the world's population, and thus of production, consumption and waste, camouflages the fact that one-quarter of humanity experiences the benefits of consumerism at the expense of the remaining three-quarters. As such, 'unless we learn to cut back dramatically and at once, and demonstrate *by example* that the industrialized world can find frugal ways out of the consumer dilemma, all will be lost' (Papanek, 1995: 185).

In this context, Papanek argues that design needs to take on a more humane face as part of a concerted commitment to a deep spiritual concern for the planet, the environment and its people. As such, in the late twentieth century, designers find themselves working in increasingly paradoxical situations. While the intention of design has traditionally been to stimulate demand through obsolescence and fashion, nowadays designers are finding themselves under more pressure to design things that will last and yet can also be recycled and reused. What Papanek wants to emerge, then, is a new aesthetic where consumers are more knowledgeable about the things they consume and where they can use that knowledge in order to make repairs when necessary, while also reducing waste.

Similarly, Whiteley (1993) argues that the role of design in contemporary society is essential in reproducing a socio-economic system that assumes limitless growth and a continual state of desire. In this sense, Whiteley argues that it is disingenuous to talk about 'consumer-led' design inasmuch as it is marketing and not consumers that are the driving force behind design and, in this respect, 'The choice that consumer-led design offers may be attractive, but it is often phoney' (Whiteley, 1993; 37). Whiteley goes on to argue that the word 'green' has often been used by designers as little more than a marketing ploy and that, though the needs of the 'green consumer' appeared to have an increasingly high profile during the 1980s, this blip represents little more than the temporary exploitation of yet another consumer *niche*. In any real sense, the 'green consumer' is a consumer first and green second. The Body Shop, which produces environmentally and ethically green cosmetics, is a good example of a company that purports to be green. However, the Body Shop must inevitably operate as part of the cosmetics industry as a whole and thus must, at least to a certain extent, prioritize financial profits before ecological concerns. A cynic might argue that even companies with credentials as green as the Body Shop have done nothing more than discover and exploit previously under-explored opportunities in the marketplace (see Whiteley, 1993: 59).

Whiteley's argument is that the world of consumerism we live in encourages the consumption of unnecessary products which waste human and material resources 'as well as contributing to a materialistic and competitive ethic that increases personal anxiety and stress' (1993: 60). It is in this sense that the notion of 'progress' plays a paramount role in the maintenance of a consumer society. A vast plethora of overdesigned products are offered to the consumer who is persuaded that he or she needs to buy into new technology in order not to be left behind in a world of passive consumption where proactive respect for the environment is a long-lost goal (see Chapter 5). Indeed,

> the problem is that we can all be seduced by [design] modifications that make a task slightly simpler and easier, but which thereby perpetuate the system of consumerism. There is no single or definite answer to the question 'Do I need this product or service?' because people – Greens included – have differing values, expectations and visions of material and non-material standards. It is, however, a question which needs to be continually asked. (Whiteley, 1993: 62)

The diversity of human beings and their opinions about the world are arguably exploited in the sense that consumerism is presented to them as the *only* legitimate way of life. Any movement against that way of life is merely subsumed within the capitalist system as yet another market niche.

In this context, Whiteley argues that, although the designer must assume more responsibility for what he or she designs, this is not always possible when designers have to contend with directive clients. Though the emergence of a green aesthetic has been held back some-what by the propagation of green values by all corners of the market-place, Whiteley argues that there is no reason that the lip-service which is generally paid to green issues in the realm of consumption should not itself be transformed into a way of life or at least an aesthetic, partly through the influence of design and designers. In this respect, he sees packaging as an aspect of design that demands urgent action. Ulti-mately, argues Whiteley, marketing-led design is shallow and irrespon-sible. The problem is that socially useful design is not amenable to the imperatives of capitalism in that, as Whiteley notes, it is often the manufacturer and not the consumer (despite any illusions to the con-trary) that has the real power in the marketplace. Meanwhile, the pivotal role of designers as a focus for social change is undermined by the fact that they are equally vulnerable to commercial reward as the rest of us. Designers operate in a world where the creation of wealth is a prime motivation. As such, Whiteley (1993: 159) suggests that design provides a snapshot of a society's priorities and values: 'If we are to distance ourselves from our condition in order to understand society's values, we need critically to examine the relationship between design and society. We have to remind ourselves that a cultural condition is not natural, but socially, politically and economically constructed.' Here Whiteley seems to be describing consumerism as a way of life. His image of consumer society is one where human needs are constantly created and where human desires are constantly stimulated. Thus, the market which is regenerated by the design profession provides a constant stream of new or at least apparently new goods, thereby perpetuating consumerism as a way of life. From this point of view, it could well be argued that there is nothing more to consumerism than the rapid consumption of surface imagery which is in fact perpetuated by symbolic differentiations in design.

Design as an expression of postmodernism

The above argument is closely related to the issues I raised in Chapter 2 relating to debates about postmodernism. Postmodernists such as Baudrillard (1988) discuss the emergence of an increasingly eclectic society in which we consume surfaces and not substance. Thus, it might be argued that the consumer is subject to such a vast array of imagery – imagery that is perpetuated by the design industry – that reality itself becomes unsettled so that eventually meaning itself evaporates. In this context, Baudrillard's (1988) analysis of hyper-reality is worth considering in more depth. Baudrillard argues that for too long cultural dimensions of social relations have been neglected and that the roots of repression, which were in fact misread by Marx, actually lie in the oppressive nature of the play of commodities as signs (see Lee, 1993). In effect, then, the goods purchased by consumers are characterized by their 'hyper-reality', that is, the realm of signs incorporated in those goods which are entirely unrelated to actual needs. What is more important in a consumer culture is the symbolic value of a consumer good. It is therefore in the interests of consumer capitalism to promote the symbolic value of goods and hence the primary role of design. In this Baudrillardian world of superficialities and surfaces the individual is left to exist without any sense of the social to fall back on. Social classes and social groups become irrelevant in a world where spectacular combinations of imagery become more important than reality itself. As Lee (1993) notes, Baudrillard sees the logic of sign-value as the great final triumph of capitalism in its attempt to impose a cultural order compatible with the demands of large-scale commodity production.

Objects are *categories of objects* which quite tyrannically induce *categories of persons*. They undertake the policing of social meanings, and the significations they engender are controlled. Their proliferation, simultaneously arbitrary and coherent, is the best vehicle for a social order, equally arbitrary and coherent, to materialize itself effectively under the sign of affluence. (Baudrillard, 1988: 16–17; emphasis added)

This is an interesting argument and, though Baudrillard can undoubtedly be criticized for underestimating the creative abilities of consumers, what he does do is highlight how design might fit in to an ideological model of consumerism. There is an argument for suggesting that since the early 1980s, and possibly before, it is not the actual nature of material goods but the signs evident in such goods that have served to accentuate our experience of consumerism as a way of life.

In order truly to understand the significance of design in a consumer society, it really needs to be considered in a broader economic and ideological context. The key point arising out of the above discussion is that design appears to play a fundamental role in the active *construction* of consumerism as a way of life. In this respect, a particularly useful approach is that of Lash and Urry (1994) who argue that the aesthetic qualities of consumer goods have come to be prioritized in the production process, thereby giving the design component an increasingly important role in determining the value of goods. But what is equally significant in this regard is the fact that the actual labour process, the human investment in the production of goods, has simultaneously come to play an increasingly minor role in adding value to a good. Thus, multi-national companies spend millions of pounds or dollars on research and development (R&D) in order to ensure that their consumer aesthetics are perfected and that design gives consumers what they want or at least what designers thinks they *should* want. It should not necessarily be assumed, however, that this is an entirely negative process. Lash and Urry (1994) argue that the individual consumer can become an agent of aestheticization in so far as he or she is consulted by manufacturers through the process of branding, for instance. Lash and Urry therefore suggest that far from being the controlled dupe of structural forces there is at least some potential for the individual to be reflexive in the context of the aestheticization of everyday life. Ultimately, we may live in a world saturated by the commercial and design-led manipulation of images which are intended to tap and create desires, but it should not be assumed that individuals cannot be aware and critical of the surroundings in which this occurs.

Lash and Urry (1994) go on to argue that the culture industries, such as advertising, film, publishing, music and television, have traditionally been innovative and design-intensive and that what is happening today is not that cultural production is becoming more like commodity production in the manufacturing industry, but rather that ordinary manufacturing industry is becoming more and more like the production of culture. In effect, the culture industries have provided a template from which an increasingly design-led industrial base has emerged. Production has in this sense become more cultural in nature.

Lash and Urry therefore identify a de-differentiation of culture and economy whereby cultural industry firms are becoming more like business *services*. Nowadays all aspects of capitalism appear to be emphasizing sign-value (Lash and Urry, 1994). The computing industry is an ideal example of this process in that it is currently not merely concerned with producing the best version of the latest technology, but also of reacting to innovations in design, as well as to the symbolic meanings applied by consumers themselves. In this respect, it is worth considering the massive hype that surrounded the release of Microsoft's operating system, Windows 95. What appeared to be important about this launch was the *image* of Windows 95, rather than the technological innovations which it incorporated. The PC operating system's symbol-led launch appeared to tap into an image of cutting-edge technology but without any real effort to explain the nature of that technology; instead, it preferred to exploit an abstract image of the mysterious world of computing which would allow consumers access to any aspect of the world of imagery they pleased (see Chapter 5). In this context, what Lash and Urry describe is very much an ideological process.

> [In] modern societies cultural domination has been effected through the already emptied out abstract ideologies of liberalism, equality, progress, science and so on. Domination in post-modern capitalism is effected through a symbolic violence that has been even further emptied out, even further de-territorialized, whose minimal foundations have been swept aside. (Lash and Urry, 1994: 15–16)

In particular, while modern ideologies are transmitted through abstract ideas to do with equality of opportunity and socialism, in the postmodern world the media come to play a fundamental ideological role. The media have control of a world apparently devoid of meaning and are more concerned with maximizing viewers, readers and profits than in reproducing the interests of the dominant class. The media, in effect, marginalize the social through prioritizing spectacle and thus undermine the significance of social problems in general, the problem being that postmodernism appears to provide no alternative outlet for the masses (Lash and Urry, 1994: 16–17). Their only outlet seems to be the realm of consumerism which continues to be perpetuated by the superficial differentiations which are imposed through design. How-ever, I would add to Lash and Urry's comments by pointing out that the maximization of profit is more often than not actually in the interests of the dominant power groups.

Conclusion

This book is essentially concerned with the ideological construction of consumerism as a way of life. While the success of design is, in itself, fundamental to the success of products, it is also crucial to the reproduction of consumerism as a way of life.

The critical point to be made about design is that it transcends the economic and the cultural. Colin Campbell (1987: 37) argues that modern society is, in effect, characterized by what he describes as an 'apparently endless pursuit of wants'. From this point of view, the contemporary consumer can never actually be satisfied in that as soon as one want is satisfied consumer capitalism simply creates another. The point I am making here is that design plays a fundamental role in this process. The consumer is constantly seeking novel rather than familiar products regardless of their use-value. There is, indeed, always a feeling on the part of consumers that a novel good will provide them with an experience they have never had before. Design activates this process.

There is, however, a further point to be made about design. Though Lash and Urry (1994) talk about the potentially liberating role of design, there could be a strong argument for suggesting that the values inherent in well-designed goods are actually socially *divisive* and that design is actually symbolic of the socially divisive nature of consumption in general. The promotion of desire and consumerism as a way of life divides societies between the 'haves' and the 'have-nots', so much so that the 'have-nots' are compelled to adopt consumerism as a way of life through the black hole that is consumer credit (see Ritzer, 1995). Consumerism therefore creates desires that individuals cannot fulfil without having to deal with some often dire economic consequences. Meanwhile, for those people who are unable to partake in the world of opportunity that consumerism offers there is always the unsavoury prospect of a constant state of longing and low self-esteem as a direct result of this immediate lack of resources. Such individuals are never able to live up to the expectations that the consuming world perpetuates through the media.

This point about the socially divisive nature of consumerism is an interesting one in so far as it highlights the double-edged nature of consumerism. Design is not always liberating, creative or artistic. It is often oppressive, conforming and dictatorial. Dorfles (1979: 11) asks how far the products of design are actually imposed upon the public, 'which accepts them because it has no alternative to "enduring" them'. He goes on to suggest that contemporary society is essentially constituted in an artificial environment surrounded by artificial objects and artificial 'nature'. What is called for in this context are new systems of design that provide the consumer with 'polyvalent' objects or systems that can actually be modified by the consumer at his or her will.

Design should in effect become more of a negotiation between the designer and the consumer. The problem currently, as far as Dorfles (1979: 12) is concerned, is that:

> Just as uncontrolled economic expansion can lead to a loss of equilibrium in our ecological system, so an incessant supply of graphic, cinematic, televisual and musical images, unanswered by an equivalent response on the part of the consumer, may lead to a sterilisation of the imaginative quality of the individual . . . Even the most prestigious object of 'good design' may become unsatisfactory if it does not permit the user to develop his [sic] own imagination.

In effect, Dorfles argues that through design many consumer objects have lost their meaning inasmuch as they are essentially anonymous and inauthentic. What design needs to do, then, is to instrumentalize choice, to oppose the influence of advertising and activate some sense of autonomous consumption in the minds of consumers. In this sense, 'there is a pressing need to restore to the consumer the possibility of exercising his [sic] own choice and of enhancing his own preferential capacity, in rebellion against the framework of pre-established conformism' (Dorfles, 1979: 13).

Dorfles's concerns about the nature of a design-led society may be extreme, but there does seem to be evidence to suggest that design has an important role to play in maintaining a society of consumerist conformity. Whether design is powerful and free enough of the ideologies of consumerism to re-invent itself in the ways in which Dorfles suggests is another question. In the final analysis, it would be fair to see that Dorfles's ambitions are currently even further from being fulfilled than when he published them nearly 20 years ago. The beauty of design could therefore be said to emanate from the fact that it convinces the consumer that he or she can have control over what he or she consumes when he or she simply cannot. In this respect, at least, life in a so-called postmodern world is inevitably hollow.

I want to end this chapter by suggesting that the role of design in consumer capitalism appears to be to accentuate the idea that the temporal experience of consumerism *is* a legitimate way of life. Design is a progressive force only inasmuch as it ensures the perpetuation of consumerist lifestyles. But, ultimately, the most significant myth peddled within the consumer society seems to be that presented by authors such as Whiteley (1993) and Papanek (1995) regarding the salvational impact that design may have upon our society in the future. This appears to be a forlorn hope. The progress offered by design is a false one. Consumer goods may be superficially improved through the efforts of designers but, far from promoting the progress of an ecologically aware and ethical humanity, design is likely to continue to promote consumerism as a way of life, as consumers continue to be seduced by the constant turnover of consumer goods. Design is indeed socially, politically and economically constructed and it is constructed in such a fashion that the cultural condition that is perpetuated is *perceived* to be a natural one. In the remainder of this book I will consider a cross-section of aspects of contemporary life in which consumerism appears to have established a significant hold. On this basis, I can consider the pros and cons of a world in which consumerism is apparently a way of life. To this end, I will begin in Chapter 4 by considering the sites within which consumerism is manifested.

Recommended reading

Jean Baudrillard (1988) 'Consumer society', in Mark Poster (ed.), *Selected Writings*. Cambridge: Polity Press. One of the most significant and original attempts to contextualize consumption within the postmodern debate.

Paul du Gay, Stuart Hall, Linda Jones, Hugh Mackay and Keith Negus (1997) *Doing Cultural Studies: The Story of the Sony Walkman*. London: Sage. A stimulating and detailed discussion of the Sony Walkman and its relationship to the cultural construction of everyday life.

John Fiske (1989) *Understanding Popular Culture*. London: Unwin Hyman. Two particularly useful chapters on 'Commodities and culture' and 'The jeaning of America'.

Scott Lash and John Urry (1994) *Economies of Signs and Space*. London: Sage. Argues that today's economies are increasingly economies of signs in which design plays an important role.

Victor Papanek (1995) *The Green Imperative: Ecology and Ethics in Design and Architecture*. London: Thames and Hudson. An analysis of how design might be harnessed in order to lead the way towards a greener planet.

Nigel Whiteley (1993) *Design for Society*. London: Reaktion Books. Discusses the role of design within consumer society and looks at how design might develop in order to become more humane and less consumerist in nature.

4

CONSUMING SPACE, CONSUMING PLACE

Having already outlined some of the main theoretical and contextual debates concerning the potential social impact of consumerism, in this chapter I want to begin to map this impact further by considering in some detail the role that sites of consumption play in the *construction* of consumerism as a way of life. To this end, I will begin by outlining how consumption affects our lived environment, considering in turn the sociological implications of the experiential nature of sites of consumption. I intend to do so, first of all, by briefly asking, what are *the spatial dimensions of consumerism*? I will then move on to discuss *the impact of retail development on the lived environment*, before looking, more specifically, at *the role of the shopping mall in a culture of consumerism*. I will then consider *the significance of Disney as a site of consumption*. This should help to develop some conception of 'postmodern' expressions of both tourism and consumption.

As noted in Chapter 1, consumerism appears to be becoming increasingly global in its influence. However, it would also be true to say that the geographical impact of consumption is primarily an urban one. As such, one particular issue that will arise throughout this chapter centres upon the role that consumption plays in the construction of urban life in everyday contexts. Consumerism may often have an invisible part to play in a city's life through the influence of money markets, stocks, shares and so on (for example, the City of London). This chapter, however, will be more concerned with how consumerism appears to affect the actual physical character of the cities people inhabit. The city of Glasgow, Scotland, for instance, is currently promoted with the by-line 'Glasgow's Miles Better'. But is it? Equally, is it appropriate to describe another city, Plymouth, in which I live, as being synonymous with 'the Spirit of Discovery'? Do these slogans amount to anything more than a determined effort to further the consumer ethic in the context of tourism? Is there, indeed, anything more to our physical environments than the outward expression of ideologies of consumerism? Are, in fact, the only smiles in Glasgow on the faces of those retailers who are riding high and low upon the ups and downs of the retail market; the only spirit in Plymouth a consumption-based entrepreneurial one? How far have our city centres become no more than mere sites of consumption? In order to address this question, I want to begin by discussing some of the spatial dimensions of consumerism.

The spatial dimensions of consumerism

There should be no doubt that consumerism, notably in the post-war years, has come to have a significant impact upon the nature of the physical environment throughout the developed world. Authors such as Knox (1991) go as far as to suggest that the whole of the contemporary landscape is being geared towards consumption, as a direct result of the emergence of an increasingly flexible form of production which is itself more and more dependent upon the demands of consumers.

> Mediated by a new, more intense and flexible development industry, the result is a consumer landscape based around the aesthetic values of historic preservation and postmodern architecture, which is gradually overwriting the older urban landscapes and, at the edge of cities, is able to forge its own distinctive landscape forms. (Jackson and Thrift, 1995: 207)

In this respect, it could be argued that the urban landscape of the modern world amounts to a spatial reaction to the new productive forces of the modern age (Lee, 1993). Thus, Harvey (1995) talks about the era of the 'Keynesian city' whose character was shaped around the new forces of consumption and by the need to establish commodity consumption as a 'way of life', as a necessity rather than a luxury. In this context, Chaney (1990) goes as far as to argue that contemporary culture has, in fact, been *de*territorialized. That is, with the development of metropolitan-based mass communication and entertainment networks which disseminate the wares of consumer culture, what has emerged is a cultural homogeneity that overlays the diversity of places and spaces. In this context, Chaney focuses, in particular, on the suburban expression of consumerism and sees the suburban home as a privileged site for the creative display of a consumer lifestyle. In effect, Chaney sees suburbia as a consumption-based locale largely constructed through transport links. As part of a consumer culture the suburbs are seen to emerge as exporters and importers of workers and services to and from the city centre, the car being an especially important piece of symbolic display. From this point of view, consumer culture has focused on the car as an icon of suburban consumer lifestyles and as a result cars and roads provide a framework within which contemporary lifestyles are enacted. Privatized experience becomes the order of the day in a consumer society and in this sense consumer lifestyles have fundamentally altered our everyday experience of city life.

Many geographers prefer to emphasize gentrification when they discuss the urban impact of consumerism (see Jackson and Thrift, 1995). In this context, Beauregard (1986) considers the advent of a new urban lifestyle generated by 'urban pioneers', who risk all to turn run-down parts of the city into sophisticated and attractive centres of urban living to the extent that 'Urban culture is now a commodified form, leagues removed from the sense of "community" which it was once meant to convey' (Beauregard, 1986: 36). In the same vein and from a more sociological viewpoint, Featherstone (1991) discusses the impact of culture industries, such as publishing, broadcasting and tourism, on city life. Featherstone focuses on how the cultural dispositions of those employed in such industries, the new middle class, help to develop new sites of cultural consumption. This group is seen to be particularly sensitive to the question of style and aesthetics and subsequently stamp this preoccupation upon the character of city life. All this is suitably summed up by Jaeger (1986: 86–7), who argues that:

> Today the inner urban 'scene' has become an important stage for promoting fashion and new urban life-style. The elaboration of consumption techniques is increasingly centred in the private residential and cultural domains, rather than in the public or occupational spheres. Thus the redevelopment necessitated by urban conservation involves the reworking and recycling of consumption objects at an accelerating rate.

Sharon Zukin (1988) considers some of these themes in depth as part of her detailed study of the influence of capital investment in the SoHo district of New York during the 1960s and 1970s. As such, she identifies the transformation of the real estate market in SoHo during this period as reflecting the repositioning of cultural producers in contemporary society. Zukin argues that big cities represent important foci for cultural production and innovation. This reflects David Harvey's (1988: xi–xii) contention in the introduction to Zukin's work that:

> Big cities have long been important arenas of cultural reproduction, forcing-houses of cultural innovation, centres of fashion and the creation of 'taste'. In a world in which large cities have lost many of their traditional manufacturing functions but in which the imperialism of shifting tastes and fashions appears ever more important, it may well be that this traditional role of large cities can become part of a vital strategy for urban survival.

Largely an American phenomenon, 'loft living' came of age in the early 1970s, reflecting the emergence of an increasingly design and style-intensive culture as well as a transition from a production-based urban culture to one centred on cultural and artistic production. The decline of small businesses, which previously occupied loft space, and the subsequent expansion to industrial plants by those companies that did survive, saw vacancies emerge which were later largely taken up by artists. Gradually, other middle-class occupiers tapped into the creative potential of what was a distinctive new housing market. Starting, in Zukin's eyes, as a trend, loft living gradually became a movement and finally created a niche market as the recycling of new buildings captured the feeling of the times as part of the development of a so-called 'post-industrial' city where consumption plays a key role in developing a focus for the economic development of cityscapes.

Zukin therefore sees the development of loft living as being very much tied in with processes of gentrification whereby a middle-class population moves into the centre of the city, causing market prices and tax assessments to rise and thereby driving out other residents in the area who cannot afford to stay. In effect, the rise of loft living can be seen to be synonymous with the increasing role of consumption in city life as new gentrified markets are seen to emerge. Middle-class consumption is therefore promoted, arguably at the expense of working-class manufacture. Loft living amounts to what, in effect, is a consumer showcase. Such developments are seen to reflect the commercialization of cultural change and, as such, loft living reflects the cultural underpinnings of consumerism.

Some of the cultural and social changes Zukin describes are discussed by O'Connor and Wynne (1993) in their discussion of Manchester as a postmodern city. They argue that culture has become more and more commodified as a result of which social identities have become increasingly fragmented, notably in the context of the 'bricolage' of consumer goods. In this respect, cities such as Leeds in Yorkshire have attempted to exploit the heritage of their city through various consumer-led tourist initiatives including the opening of the Tetley Brewery Wharf.

The Scottish city of Glasgow might equally be described as a classic illustration of how cities, and in particular local authorities, actively endeavour to alter their overall economic and cultural focus from a production-oriented base to one increasingly dependent upon consumer lifestyles. In 1990 Glasgow became 'The European City of Culture', having hosted an International Garden Festival in 1988, as well as, more recently, the Festival of Design in 1996. Glasgow has also been awarded the title of 'The City of Architecture 1999' and is hoping to attract considerably more investment to the city as a result. All these consumer-led initiatives are intended to promote Glasgow as a centre of tourism and consumption. Meanwhile, deprived parts of the city have been redeveloped in a similar fashion. The Gorbals area of Glasgow, once notorious as a run-down slum area of the city, still has its problems, but is nowadays equally renowned for its 'Citizens' Theatre'. In addition, during the 1980s an archetypal 'Zukinesque' area of Glasgow city centre, the Merchant City, has been developed with its prime focus being the Italian Centre, a new development for the location of businesses as well as designer shops, cafés and restaurants (Booth and Boyle, 1993).

The Glasgow example illustrates how gentrification can alter the focus of a city and arguably transform that city's image apparently for the common good. Retail gentrification tends to encourage a more diverse and specialized retailing environment than is typical of the uniform experience that tends to characterize most city centres. However, there might also be an argument for suggesting that such gentrification is in fact not only rare but divisive. In this context, sites of consumption such as the Italian Centre in Glasgow might be seen to reassert broader social divisions by providing middle-class, designer shopping enclaves that merely serve to highlight what most consumers simply *cannot* afford. As such, loft living might be seen to be an extreme illustration of a process of gentrification which has limited rewards for the majority of the population.

Some commentators might therefore argue that consumerism is inherently divisive; that the advantages of a consumer culture will always be outweighed by the disadvantages because in the end consumerism can never benefit consumers in an equitable fashion. In this respect, consumerism will always have negative implications for the everyday experience of our towns and cities. The key point to make here is that the parts of those towns and cities that are lauded as havens of consumerism are more accessible to some sectors of the population than to others. Perhaps this represents a crucial component of what actually constitutes the spatial dimensions of consumerism. Perhaps we can shed some further light on this debate through a brief discussion of the development and nature of retail provision in contemporary consumer societies.

Retail provision and the lived environment

In their book *Retailing*, O'Brien and Harris (1991) outline the considerable amount of retail development that has occurred in Britain since the 1950s and suggest that on the whole these developments have done little to improve the appeal of urban environments. Developing this point, the following quotation from Gardner and Sheppard (1989: 126) sums up many commentators' feelings about the impact of consumerism upon city life:

> Bleak, windswept, grey concrete wastelands, discarded litter blowing along the gutters, threatening groups of bomber-jacketed youths lounging in shop doorways, down alleys, or rampaging spray-can-in-hand across graffiti splattered walls. Boarded-up shops, an abandoned supermarket trolley, a dog

meandering across an anonymous, brutal urban landscape . . . Instantly recognisable, the images are an immediate visual shorthand for all that's wrong with our cities.

Such images are seen to be a direct result of the investment decisions of retailers and planners, decisions which are actively determining our everyday experience of city life. In Britain, this development has been reinforced as the long-term American trend towards establishing retail centres out of town has, until recently, been extended, creating a situation where the 'haves' drive to the purpose-built out-of-town shopping centres, while the 'have-nots' are forced to live and shop in what Gardner and Sheppard (1989) describe as little more than a war-zone.

The evolution of our cities as centres of consumption mirrors the historical emergence of a consumer ethic. In this respect, developments in the United States have had an influential role, the first shopping centre being built in Baltimore as early as 1907 (Simmons, 1992). Indeed, the early development of shopping centres was more rapid in the United States than in Europe (the first edge-of-town shopping centre was built in the suburbs of Kansas City in 1923), the growth of car ownership and the expansion of the suburbs having an especially important influence on the development of edge-of-town centres, as O'Brien and Harris (1991) note. The fact that the public sector has had virtually no role to play in determining the nature of retail development in the United States has, indeed, helped to ensure the omnipresence of a consumer ethic.

As far as retail development is concerned, since the 1970s Britain can be seen to have mirrored the American example in many respects, not least in the form of a major decentralization of retail facilities which has served to alter the character of Britain's city centres radically. In particular, the development of edge-of-town retailing centres really took off in Britain during the 1970s, reaching a peak in the 1980s, largely through the influence of free-market Conservative ideologies and, more particularly, through the availability of prime sites in Enterprise Zones which offered government inducements for businesses to develop in these areas. What emerged in the 1980s, then, was a new shopping culture symbolized in Britain by massive regional shopping centres such as Sheffield's Meadow Hall, Gateshead's Metro Centre, and Merry Hill in Dudley which echoed their North American counterparts, arguably creating architectural blights on the landscape as they did so.

But the key issue here remains the broader effect of retail develop-ment upon the nature of city life. In this context, Hinde (1994) considers the plight of Dudley town centre which declined rapidly with the opening of the Merry Hill centre. Major chain stores such as Marks & Spencer, C&A, and British Home Stores moved out of Dudley town centre to be replaced by a rag-bag collection of discount stores, charity

shops and struggling family businesses. Hinde (1994) estimates that the
number of empty shops in Dudley rose by 50 per cent between 1987 and
1994. The Merry Hill centre was subsequently dubbed 'Merry Hell' by
locals as a testament to its negative impact on the city centre. Cities
appear to have become so dependent upon a successful retail profile to
survive that when that profile deteriorates there is a distinct danger that
the very heart of the city centre goes with it.

Authors such as Thomas and Bromley (1993) argue that the disadvantages of developing regional shopping centres, hypermarkets and
retail warehouses on the edge of our cities are exaggerated. They point
out that traditional centres are often redeveloped for the common good
in the face of fierce competition. For instance, they quote the example
of Newcastle upon Tyne, where money was invested in the city centre
in the form of the refurbishment of a major shopping centre (Eldon
Square) in face of the competition presented by the Metro Centre, a
development on the outskirts of the city. Newcastle city centre continues to be relatively prosperous. Other positive reactive benefits of
developing retail outlets on the outskirts of a city might include the
improvement of transport links to the centre, the introduction of pedes-
trianization or the implementation of a more coordinated process of
town-centre management. Meanwhile, out-of-centre developments offer
one main advantage to city centres in so far as they actively *reduce*
congestion in city centres (Thomas and Bromley, 1993).

Thomas and Bromley (1993) go on to discuss the international
impact of regional out-of-town shopping centres. They argue that it is
impossible to make direct comparisons between the American
experience and that in Britain. They point out, in particular, that
decentralization in American cities owed more to lower suburban
residential densities, higher levels of car ownership and the ethnically
diverse nature of the inner city which apparently acted as a disincentive
to affluent suburban consumers. One thing for certain is that, in Britain
at least, the trend towards out-of-town shopping centres is on the wane,
reflecting a ground-swell of political opinion that emerged in response
to the perceived environmental effects of such developments, notably
through car pollution and urban blight. Meanwhile, the increased status
of approved local plans in the planning system, as Guy (1994) notes, has
tended to restrict the potential for further out-of-town development.
Indeed, more recently, commentators, including Hinde (1995), have
argued that major retailers are being increasingly attracted back to city
centres in Britain as a result of governmental planning policies which
have sought to encourage this trend. Indeed, Hinde (1995) quotes the
surveyors, Hillier Parker, who estimate that the number of stores in
Britain's high streets actually rose by 5 per cent between 1993 and 1995.
Such developments apparently reflect the emergence of an increasingly
discerning consumer determined to be given the opportunity to
investigate the benefits of specialist shops with high-quality produce

and a personal service. There may well be a trend emerging to this end, but the fact is that Britain, like the USA, has gone far enough down the out-of-town shopping centre route as to leave an indelible effect upon the urban fabric.

Consuming the shopping mall

Having briefly discussed the broad implications of retail development, at this juncture I want to go on to consider, more specifically, the actual nature of the shopping mall and what it says about the impact of consumerism on our experience of everyday life. Clearly, as Friedberg (1993) suggests, the shopping mall is symbolic of the global dissemi-nation of late capitalist economies, but what meanings are engendered in malls by those people who visit them? A good place to start in this respect might be America's largest mall, the Mall of America, in Bloomington, Minneapolis, which covers a surface area of 4.2 million square feet and is quite literally a temple of consumerism which self-consciously extends the shopping experience into the realms of enter-tainment. The Mall of America offers the consumer dozens of bars and restaurants, 14 cinema screens and its very own funfair – a lifestyle experience where consumers can get married, hang out and feel safe doing it.

> The shoppers, moving from lift to walkway to shop to food court, like drones in a climate-controlled, glass-walled ant farm, are oblivious participants in a lifestyle revolution . . . Today, the spectacle that is the Mall of America is part circus, part city and 100 per cent all-American consumer madness. (Corrigan, 1994: 40)

The problem here is that, far from being a mere monument to the freedom of consumer choice and to the market economy, the Mall of America could be seen to be actively constructing an image of what life 'should' be all about, namely consumerism, regardless of the less savoury connotations of a consumerist lifestyle. The mall endows con-sumerism with almost religious-like qualities. It actively camouflages the inequalities that underlie it. Though, in Britain at least, it is past its peak as far as future urban plans are concerned, on a global scale the shopping mall is more socially influential than ever before. Consumer-ism has brought with it a whole new menu of social conduct – social conduct, most crucially, that is controlled by developers and retailers rather than the consumers themselves. The shopping mall appears to provide all the immediate gratifications of consumerism but at the same time shields that consumer from the social prescription that this entails.

Shopping malls are highly controlled environments. The sense of security engendered in the fact that security guards patrol the shopping mall is offset by the fact that those same guards operate as a quasi-police force able to eject people from the urban space they patrol as and when they see fit. In the same breath, closed circuit television (CCTV) cameras provide the consumer with the sense that they can shop in a crime-free environment while invading consumers' personal space and the right to privacy in public places. With the desertion of city centres by retail outlets in Britain during the 1980s, the aim of CCTV was to create more user-friendly cities. The shopping mall therefore came to represent what Bulos (1995) describes as a physical enclosure from which the problems of the outside world could be excluded. The downside of this equation appears to be the emergence of a world reminiscent of George Orwell's *1984*, a controlled environment where nobody is free from the gaze of 'Big Brother'.

The impact of CCTV on our retail spaces was intended to offset the impact of urban crime and to increase public consumption, to create, in effect, an unreal world of 'enclosed consumption mono-economies' in which shopping could be conducted trouble free (Bulos, 1995: 2). Bulos points out that such developments are actively in the interests of commerce, particularly in so far as they help to regenerate city centres. But, aside from the obvious benefits of CCTV, there are a variety of more sinister implications. Most worryingly, by its very nature, CCTV involves a high level of monitoring of everyday activities. This ensures the isolation and monitoring of so-called problem individuals, notably through the use of 'computerized face recognition', in order to spot any new crimes before they have even been committed. Critics of CCTV might well describe this as a monitoring of the law-abiding majority, as opposed to the criminal minority.

The question here, then, centres on how far our rights as individuals, let alone those we have as consumers, are actually protected when we enter sites of consumption. British consumers, for instance, are not legally protected from the encroachment of private surveillance. There is no licensing system in Britain to regulate or monitor the number of private schemes operating and yet the consumer is monitored from the moment he or she collects money from the cash dispenser.

The original attempt to create a safe and environmentally controlled commercial shopping area was Southdale Mall in America which was based on a classical visionary ideal of citizenship, whereby the mall reproduced the spirit of the ancient Roman and Greek marketplace (see Corrigan, 1994). Evidently, the architect of this first mall saw it as the utopian modern-day equivalent to the ancient marketplace serving our civil, cultural and social needs as well as our needs as consumers. But the problem today is that much of this idealism has fallen by the wayside as controlled environments seem to dominate every aspect of the consumer's experience to the extent that surveillance now appears to be concerned with controlling the *social* environment as well as the physical one. Malls and shopping centres may be perceived at a superficial level to be utopian modern environments, but as places which are owned privately, which only open at very particular times and which monitor our every move, they in fact provide a physically tangible justification for the dominant and controlling role of consumerism in contemporary society. In this sense, the shopping mall might be seen not only as a symbol of the virtually global domination of consumer capitalism but also of the personal infringements that such a domination engenders. Shopping malls are in this respect symbolic of the ideological impact of retailing and consumerism upon contemporary society.

It would be going too far to dismiss what shopping can offer the individual out of hand. In this context, there may be something in Lauren Langman's (1992) contention that late twentieth-century shopping malls provide centres of social life or 'pseudo-communities'. From this point of view, shopping malls provide consumers with a sense of community that is perhaps missing in the outside world. This point can be illustrated with brief reference to the Woody Allen film *Scenes from a Mall* in which the two main characters, played by Woody Allen and Bette Middler, experience marital woes during the course of a day out at the mall. The mall is seen to provide a bright, cheerful, musical, community-based environment which appears to soften the blow of their respective affairs, reflecting the idea that, though life is generally unstable, the joys of a consumer culture will always be available to fall back on in times of woe. Not only can people escape from their everyday problems through the physical and mental stimulation of shopping, but by becoming part of consumer culture they begin to feel part of something *real*, when arguably that experience is not real at all. Thus, the architectural historian, Margaret Crawford argues in Susan Marling's (1993) book, *American Affair: The Americanisation of Britain* that:

> Shopping malls, Disneyland, television, are all examples of the new stage of hyper-reality – the falseness that is better than the reality. Reality always has its detrimental aspects like crime, homeless people, dirt. In a situation of hyper-reality like a shopping mall, everything is reduced to a set of agreed upon themes, so people feel more comfortable here than in a real situation. The accurate urban reality is replaced by the falsehood of the shopping mall. (Marling, 1993: 27)

In this sense, as Butler (1991) notes in a discussion of the tourist potential of West Edmonton Mall, many shopping malls are remarkable inasmuch as they have been deliberately planned to create an image of 'elsewhereness'. In effect, West Edmonton Mall 'has falsified place by creating an appropriately entitled but spatially restricted Fantasyland' (Butler, 1991: 291). Such sites of consumption amount to what Friedberg (1993) describes as a 'contemporary phantasmagoria' which blinds consumers from the realities of urban blight. More crucially, as Urry (1990:

149) notes in his book *The Tourist Gaze*, in a shopping mall you become part of a community of consumerism. By frequenting the shopping mall, you are recognized as a legitimate citizen of contemporary society. Meanwhile, shops seem to be adopting ever more sophisticated ways of monitoring shopping habits such as the use of loyalty cards through which, though they reward consumers, retailers can build up a comprehensive and somewhat invasive computer profile of the consumer concerned. At the same time, researchers in Boston are developing 'Can-Scan', an intelligent dustbin which can read the bar codes of discarded containers and which relays such information to the supermarket in order that next week's groceries can be delivered directly to your home (Lloyd, 1995). Furthermore, in both Britain and the USA, Safeway, the supermarket chain, has begun to introduce a system whereby customers can scan their own food as they go around the store, thereby cutting down on the extent of the shopping trip, the check-out queue and thus reducing human contact in this context. These examples appear to suggest, if anything, that shopping will become an increasingly dehumanized and controlled experience.

One approach that might help us come to terms with the apparently controlling nature of aspects of the retail experience is that of George Ritzer (1993) whose discussion of *The McDonaldization of Society* expands upon some of Max Weber's ideas on rationalization. As Brubaker (1984) notes, Weber (1920) identifies three main aspects of rationalization all of which are relevant to this discussion. First is the fact that in modern societies scientific knowledge and calculation have come to replace religious knowledge systems and that, in order for capitalism to advance, reason and scientific knowledge had to be applied. Secondly, as market relations come to dominate modern society, sources of authority become increasingly abstract and impersonal. An individual's life is increasingly subject to the rules of 'the system', while he or she is increasingly evaluated in terms of material success rather than according to aspects of his or her personal achievement. Thirdly, Weber argues that modern societies are increasingly characterized by control. That is, in the modern world individuals are obliged to conform to the instrumental needs of the organized industrial system. In other words, the individual becomes reduced to the function he or she performs in that system.

George Ritzer (1993) has attempted to apply some of the above ideas to an analysis of the global consumer culture which, far from encouraging diversity, actually promotes, as far as Ritzer is concerned, a high degree of standardization through global consumer cultures and communication flows. Ritzer argues that the highly standardized and rationalized experience consumers have when they visit McDonald's is symbolic of the rationalized and dehumanizing nature of modern society in general. In any McDonald's, wherever it might be in the world, both the worker and the customer go about their business seeking the most rational means to their individual end, whether that end be to eat a predictable 'safe' meal as quickly as possible or to dispense with the queue at the 'drive-thru' in an efficient fashion. The point is that this is a highly automated system which is completely rational in the sense that it is entirely efficient, though irrational in the sense that it undermines interactive and creative aspects of what it is to be a human being. This approach might explain why aspects of the consuming experience in sites of consumption appear to be so 'controlling'. It is actually in the interests of the system as a whole for this to be the case. Life would be impossible if each individual entered a fast-food restaurant demanding his or her own idiosyncratic meal, just as it would be if the employees of McDonald's were to spend 10 minutes chatting to each and every customer they encountered. The social system needs predictability and so too do individuals, if only in order to cope with 'information overload' (see Milgram, 1992). However, this does not stop commentators such as Ritzer (1993) lamenting the essentially sterile and anti-creative uniformity of modern life.

In fact, the rationalized nature of contemporary society is exaggerated by Ritzer (1993) who underestimates the ability consumers have to interpret the social structures at their disposal. Despite being aware of the creative limitations of fast-food restaurants, those consumers entering McDonald's do not perceive themselves to be controlled, but gain their own sense of enjoyment and invest their personal meaning in the framework which that structure provides. This is a point I will develop further below, having discussed the example of Disney as a site of consumption.

In concluding this section, I should point out that, regardless of the individual benefits of a rationalized society, there is arguably a distinct lack of creativity expressed in the character of our city centres in general and that this is directly the result of the perception of sites of consumption as being rational. A key issue here, as O'Brien and Harris (1991) note, is the increasing dominance, notably in the British retail scene, of multiple retail companies. Both inside and outside town centres, British urban environments in particular appear to be increasingly characterized by uniformity as major companies seek to establish market dominance. The identities of retail outlets are therefore virtually identical from one shopping centre to the next, such familiarity being intended to garner customer loyalty. In recent years, there has been a particular tendency to attempt to gain an advantage on competitors by regularly revamping the image of a particular store. But this generally only affords a short-term advantage for the company concerned as competitors soon 'jump on the refurbishment bandwagon' in order to protect their market share (O'Brien and Harris, 1991: 110). As a result, what emerges is a retailing system in which competitors perpetually tend to clone one another, with retail developments, in British cities especially, being characterized by a predictable and uniform tenant mix and a distinct lack of any creativity, so much so that 'high streets are becoming almost indistinguishable from one another' (O'Brien and Harris, 1991: 110). It is interesting to note that Deyan Sudjic (1993), in charge of Glasgow's plans for the City of Architecture 1999, blames planning controls for encouraging the growth of multiple retail chains which have arguably resulted in our city centres becoming no more than Identikit shopping centres.

> The central question about shops is whether it is the form of shopping that dictates the nature of a city, or if it is the city's nature that dictates how shopping, its primary communal activity, is carried out. Perhaps the truth is somewhere in between; that the different incarnations of shopping, from the market to the department store, the high street to edge-of-town, are the signals that confirm the direction a city has taken. (Sudjic, 1993: 252)

The central question about sites of consumption focuses upon how far consumers can consume *individually* in such contexts. This is a question that may begin to be resolved in light of a brief discussion of Disney as a site of consumption.

Disney as a site of consumption

As I illustrated in my discussion of Zukin (1988) above, there is evidence to suggest that consumption exerts its influence on urban life beyond the shopping centre, mall or out-of-town supermarket. Tourism undoubtedly has a significant role to play in this process. An important illustration of the physical manifestation of consumerism are therefore the Disney parks, Disneyland and Disney World, a brief examination of which tends to reinforce some of the arguments I raised above. Consumerism appears to provide some form of an escape from the real world, while the real world is in fact characterized to begin with by the everyday expression of consumerism as a way of life. In this sense consumerism provides no form of escape at all.

In discussing Disney World and Disneyland as sites of consumption, I will consider the work of two authors in particular, namely Robert David Sack (1992) and Alan Bryman (1995). Sack (1992) discusses the ways in which Disney World symbolizes the tensions that exist between reality and fantasy in contemporary consumer culture. As such, he acknowledges the fact that the Disney parks sell enormous quantities of commodities and argues that the prime commodity in this respect is the actual experience of commodified landscapes which are billed as the 'happiest places on Earth'. In this context, Sack (1992: 121) quotes Walt Disney himself: 'I don't want the public to see the real world they live in while they're in the park . . . I want them to feel they are in another world.' Crucially, the vast infrastructure that underlies the Disney operation is out of sight of the consumer, creating a 'front stage without a backstage' (Sack, 1992: 165). Meanwhile, as Sack points out, even national cultures become a ubiquitous commodity: the consumer is invited to journey to a variety of foreign lands within the confines of Disney World's national showcases. These showcases might more critically be referred to as shopping expeditions which reinforce the experience of a world of escapism within which consumption is all.

> Disney World promises to release us from our own contexts and place us at the center of other contexts: we can be astronauts journeying to Mars, physicists living in a satellite community near the moon, children drifting along the Mississippi River on Tom Sawyer's barge, or forty-niners in the gold rush. It provides us with an opportunity to find our roots, to return home to Main Street USA, and to create a 'world of our own'. (Sack, 1992: 166)

Through the intricate juxtaposition of commodified fantasies, Disney creates a simulated 'instant' world which has much in common with mega-malls such as the Mall of America (Sack, 1992: 167). In essence, what a Disney park does is construe the good life as being directly equated with our identities as consumers and with what we buy. As such, the New Innovations buildings at Disney World can be viewed as a showcase for the latest products being touted by multi-national companies such as IBM and Sega (Bryman, 1995: 154).

Disney parks are exciting and mystifying places which, as Sack (1992) notes, can also be dismissed as serving to distort the real condition of social meaning and social relations. This is a key point. Consumer culture actively distorts reality for its own ends. Consumer culture works because consumers *want* reality to be distorted. As such, much of the imagery with which the Disney parks deal are targeted at the family, a key locus of consumption.

> Stimulating this image acts as a prompt to remind the visitor of his/her identity as consumer of both the corporation's products and the Disney merchandise itself, though this is not to suggest that visitors are automata who rush to buy character dolls and tee-shirts as soon as they can, but that image is a convenient, self-serving one. (Bryman, 1995: 154)

Disney builds upon such images in order to naturalize the process of consumption. Thus, as authors such as Yoshimoto (1994) and Bryman (1995) point out, shopping will always be a key focus of the Disney experience. Disney provides consumers with narratives that make consumption part of the experience itself in order that the actual act of consumption is not explicitly acknowledged. The themed nature of the consumer experience is a tendency that many shopping malls have duplicated in the apparent realization that the more that the consumer feels he or she is escaping into another world, the more he or she will be prepared to consume (see Bryman, 1995: 159). In this sense, we should perhaps consider the validity of Ritzer and Liska's (1997) contention that Disney theme parks (much like McDonald's) are symbolic of the increasingly efficient, calculable, predictable and arguably controlling nature of social life in general. In this sense, Ritzer and Liska (1997) see Disney as a mall, another carefully designed structure intent on encouraging people not only to visit but also to spend, spend and spend some more.

One further approach that attempts to come to terms with the significance of Disney in the context of consumption is that broadly associated with postmodernism, which I discussed in some detail in Chapter 2. Bryman (1995), in particular, comments on how Disney prioritizes sign-value over use-value; more for a symbolic value than for any practical use it may or may not have. Meanwhile, great emphasis is placed upon the juxtaposition of cultures at Disney with nostalgia for times gone by being a common theme, a theme closely associated, in turn, with postmodernism. Indeed, Bryman (1995: 160) comes to the conclusion that 'Disney parks are sites of postmodernity, since the hailstorm of signs in which we are drenched, and which exist in plentiful supply at the parks, are emblems of the postmodern condition.' Disney parks are characteristically eclectic and are more specifically centres of pastiche inasmuch as Disney thrives in the excitement generated by incompatible architectures (Bryman, 1995). Perhaps most importantly, Disney parks problematize reality in that they thrive on an *illusion* of reality. In this context, Bryman (1995) quotes Willis (1993) who has conducted several observations of the Disney phenomena:

> Many visitors suspend daily perceptions and judgements altogether, and treat the wonderland environment as more real than real. I saw this happen one morning when walking to breakfast at my Disney Resort Hotel. Two small children were stooped over a small snake that had crawled out on to the sun-warmed path. 'Don't worry, it's rubber' remarked their mother. (Willis, 1993: 123)

In effect, then, as Eco (1986) points out, Disney glorifies the fake and the stimulation of desire for the fake (Bryman, 1995: 172). This only works because reality is inevitably a disappointment in that consumerism as a way of life is never as fulfilling as advertisers and retail planners would have consumers believe. Ultimately, as Ritzer and Liska (1997) suggest, the consumption of tourism and of sites of consumption more generally satisfies our desire to consume the inauthentic in an increasingly simulated world.

Conclusion

One issue that might be said to bring together the above debates and concerns is that of globalization. Though it could be argued that globalization has fractured consumption groups and has cut across traditional barriers of non-access to provide a liberating realm of self and, indeed, urban expression (see Buffoni, 1997), there may, in fact, be more evidence to suggest that globalization has resulted in the construction of a standardized and uniform urban landscape, notably in the guise of Americanization. In this context, Harvey (1989: 147) talks about 'time–space compression', the way in which in the capitalist world the time horizons of both the public and the private worlds have shrunk alongside associated advances in communication. The implication here is that products have become internationalized; commodity exchange has become global. You can, for instance, purchase a bottle of Czech beer at your local corner shop more or less wherever you might live in the developed world.

Our relationship to space is therefore seen to be increasingly uncertain. Above and beyond the impact of commodification, our geographical identities are continually being undermined in a so-called postmodern world. In this respect, the impact of consumerism on place and space is far from clear cut. While, on the one hand, consumption has become such a powerful and fundamental influence upon contemporary society that this influence is asserted without any long-term concern for the creative experience of our physical environment or for our cities as diverse social centres, on the other, the globalization of consumer life-styles intensifies the instability of social life, while arguably undermining localized identities. Urban diversity has in many respects been displaced by a retail mono-economy (see Bulos, 1995). The limitations of such centres are compounded by the fact that, despite the enjoyment people get from spending money in a mass consumer culture, such enjoyment is 'frequently frustrated by a retail system that strips the "pleasure" from shopping and reduces it to a mere exchange of goods for money' (Newby, 1993: 208) and where spatial realities are increasingly disrupted.

Our cities have arguably become functional centres of consumption rather than liberating foci for personal or social creativity. In this context, Benjamin's (1973) discussion of the *flâneur* is particularly relevant. The *flâneur* is a playful and transgressive figure, originally associated with nineteenth-century Paris, who strolls through the urban space of large cities dispassionately gazing around the arcades of the urban landscape. With the development of the department store, the *flâneur*'s relationship with the commodity became a more direct one to the extent that he became as actively involved in the expanding realm of capitalism as the shopper him or herself (see Parkhurst Ferguson, 1994). Authors such as Featherstone (1991) discuss the extent to which the *flâneur* can be seen to have an equally influential role to play in late twentieth-century urban life.

> Within . . . postmodern cities people are held to engage in a complex sign play which resonates with the proliferation of signs in the built environment and urban fabric. The contemporary urban *flâneurs*, or strollers, play with and celebrate artificiality, randomness and superficiality of the fantastic mélange of fictions and strange values which are to be found in the fashions and popular cultures of cities. (Featherstone, 1991: 24)

The above approach tends to romanticize what urban expressions of consumption are all about and as a result aids the legitimization of consumerism as a way of life. Indeed, generally speaking, many commentators, including Zukin (1988), portray a rather overidealized image of consumer-driven lifestyles. In this atmosphere policy-makers, in particular, take the risk of being persuaded by the image of a middle-class consuming nirvana, an image which is, in fact, artificially constructed by 'image managers' with vested interests in encouraging investment into the areas concerned (see Beauregard, 1986). Meanwhile, in considering the impact of consumerism in urban settings, disenfranchised 'consumers', who are unable to partake of the excesses of a consumer culture, continue to be neglected. Beggars on the streets of major European cities provide us with a clear indication of the limitations of even the most vibrant of consumer cultures and of the fact that consumerism cannot always provide what it promises.

In the final analysis, exciting and inventive opportunities to consume in urban environments *do* exist. As such, Zukin (1995: 190) is keen to stress the nature of cities as lived centres of consumer experience where 'identities and communities are formed and which owe more to the unmediated theatricality of medieval and early modern markets than to the calculated stage settings of merchant princes of mass consumption'. The sort of expressive cross-cultural vitality that Zukin argues is acted out in colourful and ethically thriving locales of consumption are, however, more the exception than the rule. Developments such as that in Leeds, England, towards the liberation of a 24-hour city *are* exciting as far as the consumer is concerned. But the fact is that all too often consumers live in what are at best 15-hour cities where the most dramatic act of consumption might be found in the form of a busker whose musicianship is drowned out by the hustle and bustle of a culture in which nobody has the time or the inclination to consume the architectural images around them.

Consumption has become so fundamental to the character of our urban environments that cities could in fact be construed to be 'unreal' in the sense that they could be anywhere; they have, in effect, lost a sense of place (see Clarke, 1991). Globalization has had a fundamental role to play in this process. Though on the surface our towns and cities appear to provide a consumerist escape from the harsh realities and resource divisions that characterize consumer society, in reality all they do is reinforce the very problems, stresses, not to say environmental strains, that they purport to resolve. The joys of consumerism are, in this respect, apparently skin deep. Everywhere consumers turn, notably in the context of the urban environment, consumerism is apparently there to offer a way out. Ultimately, far from providing a way out, what consumerism actually does is ensure that there can never be any such thing. It appears that, at least in a spatial sense, consumerism has indeed become a way of life. In Chapter 5, I will consider how far the same can be said about the consumption of technology.

Recommended reading

Alan Bryman (1995) *Disney and his Worlds*. London: Routledge. An insightful discussion of the cultural dimensions of Disney. The section on postmodernism is particularly useful.

Larry O'Brien and Frank Harris (1991) *Retailing: Shopping, Society, Space*. London: Fulton. A useful geographical account of retailing which includes a particularly good section on the development of retail in Britain.

George Ritzer (1993) *The McDonaldization of Society*. Newbury Park, CA: Pine Forge. An interesting angle on the potentially controlling aspects of commodification which draws upon Weber's theories of rationalization.

Robert D. Sack (1992) *Place, Modernity, and the Consumer's World*. London: Johns Hopkins University Press. Looks at the way in which place and space define the world of the consumer.

Sharon Zukin (1988) *Loft Living: Culture and Capital in Urban Change*. London: Radius. A key contribution to debates over the gentrification of cities and the impact of consumer lifestyles in urban centres. The significance of loft living itself is, however, debatable.

5

CONSUMING TECHNOLOGY

The world that Libby inhabits is very different. It's 1996; she's three. If her sister is watching the four-channel television downstairs, she can choose one of her many Disney videos to keep her company on the floor above. Her dad is in the study, writing articles on the word-processor, which he then sends by fax to various places. Her mum is always in contact, using the mobile phone, or she can be bleeped. Dad is waiting for a new computer to be delivered – one with the CD-ROM programmes she's seen advertised, and access to something called the Net. He'd like cable telly. She's heard the rows this has occasioned between her parents, who have sharply opposed views about where all this – this deluge of electronic information – is headed.

(Aaronovitch, 1996: 7)

If we were to believe everything we read in the newspapers and saw on the television, it would not take us long to be convinced that consumer society is, in fact, essentially a technological society, a world of virtual reality where the only limitation is the extent of the human imagination. In this respect, as far as Druckery (1995: 1) is concerned, 'Technology forms the core of the cultural transformations that are generating startling changes in every cultural and political activity.' Authors such as Silverstone and Hirsch (1992) acknowledge that such developments have significant implications for the nature of contemporary forms of consumption and that, in particular, information and communication technologies are becoming a key component of household cultures of consumption. Indeed, the impact of technology on contemporary society, and more specifically on consumers, provides a fascinating barometer of the apparently irresistible temptations of consumerism. During the course of this chapter I will therefore consider how far the consumption of technology is actually closely constructed *for* consumers and how, in turn, this relates to the role of technology as a liberating force in the experience of contemporary consumer culture.

As a means of addressing the above questions, I shall begin this chapter by asking whether there is any such thing as *virtual consumption*.

I will then go on to assess whether or not we might usefully describe *consumer society as a post-industrial information society*. I will then consider two examples of technological consumption, *home computers* and *television*, as a means of extending this debate. Before concluding this chapter, three key questions will be considered: *Is technology really egalitarian? What is the relationship between technological consumption and power?* And *Is technology necessarily progressive?*

Virtual consumption or virtual myth?

Is there any such thing as virtual consumption? Or are consumers merely consuming a myth in accepting the apparently inevitable attributes of a technological future? In his book, *The Third Wave*, Alvin Toffler (1981: 10) argues that:

> The computer can be asked by us to 'think the unthinkable' and the previously unthought. It makes possible a flood of new theories, ideas, ideologies, artistic insights, technical advances, economic and political innovations that were, in the most literal sense, unthinkable and unimaginable before now. In this way it accelerates the historical change and fuels the thrust towards Third Wave social diversity.

Bearing these thoughts in mind, in this chapter I want to consider the sort of role technology really does play in constructing contemporary consumer lifestyles and the extent to which such a construction is potentially socially divisive. One aspect of technological consumption that is constantly lauded as an illustration of the democratic nature of new technology is the Internet. Politicians and media commentators alike constantly refer to a computer-driven utopian future in which the Internet plays a key role in liberating a virtual world within which every individual is equal (see Aaronovitch, 1996). But what is often overlooked in this analysis is the fact that access to computers, and to cutting-edge innovations in technology in general, is largely limited to a privileged academic and business-based minority. In this respect, consumers' experiences of technological consumption are often inevitably negative. Access to technology is inherently divisive in so far as it creates a distinction between those who have the resources to partake in technological consumption and those who do not. The majority of consumers do not have the resources to tap into the technology that is supposedly going to liberate them. The argument I will be considering in this chapter therefore centres on whether the only areas of social life in which technology has a *real* impact are either areas that require expert knowledge, which people do not have, or those that do not require any expertise and which are therefore unfulfilling as a result.

Before addressing these debates in any detail, we need to consider how influential technology can potentially be in relation to social experience in general. Technological determinists argue that changes in technology are the cause of change in society (see MacKenzie and Wajcman, 1985). In this sense, technologists apply the principles of science in order to work out the principal benefits of new scientific discoveries, introducing those benefits into society, often in the form of products. Technological change can be seen, from this point of view, to cause social change in the construction of a new type of society. Such a society is often seen to have been liberated from the restricted practices of capitalist production. In effect, it is argued that technologies have social legacies. But the problem here, touched upon by MacKenzie and Wajcman (1985), is that often society has more effect upon the nature of technology than technology has on the nature of society. What is arguably created is therefore a cyclical process whereby technology constantly reproduces the consumerist ideologies that constituted it in the first place. It could therefore be argued that technology is subject to economic imperatives and subsequently that

> if technological systems are economic enterprises, and if they are involved directly or indirectly in market competition, then technical change is forced on them. If they are to survive at all, much less to prosper, they cannot forever stand still. Technical change is made inevitable, and its nature and direction profoundly conditioned by this. (MacKenzie and Wajcman, 1985: 14)

This point raises some important issues about the role of technology in a consumer society which I will consider in more detail towards the end of this chapter. At this stage, I will develop some of the above points by focusing on debates concerning the existence of a post-industrial society and the implications that this sort of society may or may not have for the consumer.

Is consumer society a post-industrial 'information' society?

By considering the contribution of Daniel Bell (1973) and his work on the nature of post-industrial society, I hope to begin to put the above debates into a sociological context. Bell's work represents one of the most significant attempts to address the sociological impact of technology upon the structure of contemporary life experience. Bell identifies the emergence of a society based on the foundations of an age of information and high technology which are seen to supersede heavy industry. He therefore argues that there has been a radical transformation of social life, largely as a result of various advances in science and technology. These advances include: first, a shift of emphasis away from the production of goods and towards the provision of services; secondly, the prioritization of planned technological innovation, whereby science, technology and economics are increasingly integrated in the context of research; thirdly, the subsequent influential role of a professional and technical class whose influence is such that they become, in effect, the new ruling class of society; and fourthly, a fundamental role for theoretical knowledge at the forefront of innovation and policy, to the extent that theoretical knowledge emerges as the axial principle of a post-industrial society.

> Industrial society is the co-ordination of machines and men for the production of goods. Post-industrial society is organized around knowledge, for the purpose of social control and the directing of innovation and change; and thus in turn gives rise to new social relationships and new structures which have to be managed politically. (Bell, 1973: 20)

What is crucial here is that Bell identifies what is at least partially a technological revolution, but argues that this revolution cannot be understood without reference to its social and political context. Indeed, as far as Bell is concerned, the technological revolution is expressed within a cultural revolution where, most notably, time becomes the most precious and enslaving of commodities.

Though Bell's arguments can be commended for stimulating considerable debate as to the nature of contemporary developed societies, they have been criticized on a number of counts. Most significantly perhaps, Kumar (1978) argues that Bell overestimates the decline of the manufacturing sector and the subsequent rise of the service sector. Meanwhile, research and development (R&D), which Bell sees as being a crucial influence on the emergence of a new society, is arguably something that has always been associated with industrial societies (Kumar, 1978). Bell (1973) also exaggerates the role of theoretical knowledge. In this context, Swingewood (1991) points out that in modern industrial societies the proportion of gross national product (GNP) devoted to pure science is far less than that invested in practical research projects, thereby contradicting a central tenet of Bell's theory. Quoting academic involvement in government defence and foreign-policy projects, Swingewood (1991) also doubts Bell's (1973) contention that a science-based profession, which is led far more by community and environmentally based motivations than by profits, has actually emerged.

In effect, the argument that the power and influence of the knowledge and scientific elite has in recent decades been extended is greatly exaggerated by Bell. His vision of technology is undoubtedly an idealized one, notably in the way in which he neglects the fact that technological innovation has the less honourable distinction of bringing with it significant increases in unemployment (see Gorz, 1982;

Callinicos, 1989). Authors such as Kumar (1978) therefore argue that
Bell is a technological determinist inasmuch as he reads too much social
change in technological advances which are not in fact as revolutionary
as he might think. What is perhaps of more concern is Bell's woefully
misguided prediction that market forces will actually recede in influence in a post-industrial society. The evidence contradicting this point
of view seems to be overwhelming as so much of the material presented
in this book appears to illustrate. In many respects, market forces
apparently maintain a vice-like grip on the nature of contemporary
society, while:

> The fact that fewer people are employed in material production does not in
> any case alter the fact that no one can survive without the industrial goods
> manufactured by these people. Not only do human beings continue to have
> the same mundane needs for food, clothing, shelter, and the like, but rising
> living standards and the associated expansion of mass consumption entail a
> proliferation of material goods, particularly given the tendency . . . for
> services to be replaced with consumer durables. (Callinicos, 1989: 127)

The prominence of consumer goods within the framework of conduct
in contemporary consumer societies is well expressed in Kumar's (1978)
discussion of long-term historical change in the nature of consumption.
Technology has evidently had a key role to play in consumption's
pacification of the consumer. For instance, whereas previously a
consumer may have had the ability and willingness to repair his or her
car, television set or radio, in contemporary society such skills are
becoming increasingly specialized as a result of the sort of 'progress'
that authors such as Bell discuss. In effect, consumers are becoming
deskilled and the result of this process is the wholescale demoralization
of consumers who become increasingly dependent upon skills and
services which need to be paid for in the marketplace (Kumar, 1978).
Unskilled and apathetic consumers save Bell's (1973) precious
commodity, namely time, by accepting the options provided for them
by the marketplace through, for instance, purchasing a dishwasher they
do not know how to fix. In effect, as Kumar (1978) notes, consumer
capitalism is increasingly moving into unexplored terrain. The vehicle
by which consumerism does so is apparently technological innovation.
Contemporary societies are still based on a capitalist model. To argue
that this model has been superseded by the liberating, socializing
impact of technological innovation is quite simply misleading.
      One author who does much to extend this debate is Lyon (1988) in his
book, *The Information Society*, in which he points out that technology
actively erodes social boundaries. Technology, Lyon argues, has a
significant impact on the nature of contemporary society, not least
through the increased likelihood of home working through remote
computer terminals. Meanwhile, work is becoming increasingly flexible

through the development of mobile computer and telephone technology, while the domestic sphere is increasingly being infiltrated by the public marketplace (Lyon, 1988). In effect, the consumption of technology appears to play a key role in the implementation of cultural transformations.

Equally interesting in this respect is the work of Herbert Schiller (1981) who relates the emergence of an information society to the imperatives of consumer capitalism. Schiller argues that the technologies which are allied to the information society are developed with the primary intention of furthering the interests of the corporate marketplace. Information technology bolsters the powers of corporate capitalism by compressing time and space, while furthering the interests of the apparently decentralized yet increasingly powerful nature of global business (see Webster, 1995). In this context, Webster considers those critics who have extended Schiller's analysis of the capitalist dimensions of technology. Thus, reinforcing a point I made in Chapter 4, surveillance can be seen as restricting social dissent, while strengthening the hold of capitalist relations (see Mosco, 1989). More interestingly, Webster (1995: 95) notes that technology can be perceived actively to consolidate consumer capitalism inasmuch as 'Informational developments are central to the spread of consumerism since they provide the means by which people are persuaded by corporate capitalism that it is both a desirable and an inevitable way of life.' I will now consider this contention in more detail with reference to the consumption of two particular forms of technology: the personal computer and television.

Consuming home computers

In considering the impact of the home computer on consumer lifestyles, Murdock et al. (1992) describe the home computer as one of the most conspicuous consumer products of the 1980s. In this context, they argue that home computers provide a site of continual cultural struggle over the meaning of the machine and its appropriate uses, notably with regard to debates between the educational and entertainment value of computer hardware. Murdock et al. address such issues through an interview-based research project carried out in the mid-1980s. They note that, despite promotional exercises on the part of the computer industry, home computing remains a preserve of the middle classes. Looking at the consumption of home computing from an economic point of view, many of Murdock et al.'s interviewees expressed the feeling that the computer they purchased did not live up to the hype associated generally with the computer 'revolution'. The problem here was that those households with higher income could afford computers that fulfilled their needs, while those lower down the social scale could not and as such were often dependent upon obsolete technology.

Material resources clearly play a fundamental role in consumers' experience of computer technology. What is interesting about the market for home computers is how it has diversified from its original guise as a form of 'rational' recreation. This fed, in Britain at least, upon government and media discourses about the 'information age' in light of the potential educational advantages that a computer could provide for people's children. Gradually, the role of the computer as a games console came to play a more fundamental role. Software companies were becoming aware of the massive potential market they had at their disposal. Despite reservations on the part of hardware manufacturers, who were worried about losing the image of the computer as a general-purpose educational machine, the image of the computer began to change in the early to mid-1980s in both the USA and Britain. Whatever, for instance, happened to the mainstays of British computing education, the BBC micro and the Acorn? In fact, the market has become increasingly divided between companies such as IBM and Microsoft, who provide hardware and software for the serious user, and those concentrating on the games console, such as Sega and Nintendo (Murdock et al., 1992: 159). What this piece of research illustrates is that technology appears to aid capitalism in its exploration of ever-new markets, the above diversification between serious and fun uses for the computer being a typical example.

> [T]his industrial segmentation will be mapped onto social divisions, and . . . self-determined computing will remain concentrated in the relatively affluent and well-educated households of the professional and managerial strata, whilst the rest of the population are largely confined to participating in professionally crafted fantasies. They will have interactivity without power. The consequences of this situation for democratic participation, in a society increasingly organized around screen-based systems, deserves more extended discussion than it has so far received. (Murdock et al., 1992: 159)

Taking this point one step further, it could be argued that computers are beginning to take over our lives; that the benefits of computers are blinding us to the more unsavoury aspects of computer consumption. For instance, in writing this book I was able to benefit from innovations in word-processing software which made the task far less onerous than it would have been, say, 20 years ago. However, in enjoying such benefits I may be guilty of forgetting the sorts of social and economic implications of the hardware and software I use. For instance, Microsoft is a company that virtually controls the nature of the world's computer software. Can this be in the interests of the consumer? Is technology conspiring with consumer capitalism in the way in which it rapidly turns over obsolete technologies? Do specific companies have control, not merely over their markets, but also over their consumers, inasmuch as they actively construct the parameters within which those people consume? Is, indeed, Chancellor (1997: 5) correct in his contention that:

> It is obvious why companies such as Apple and Microsoft keep putting new versions of their products on the market and hyping them to the skies. If they didn't, they would soon run out of customers, for their old products are so good that their owners have to be bullied into feeling discontented with them.

In this context, advances in computer technology are constantly touted by the media. For instance, one application for computer technology in the future may well be the implantation of computer chips into parts of people's bodies in order to allow them to talk and interact directly with computer systems: in effect, the development of technology that actively reads the consumer's mind and transmits instructions in computer code (Levy and Rayment, 1995: 15). This would surely set a dangerous precedent. In particular, it may extend the boundaries of 'inauthentic experience' in that the world of surface and media-based images, which I discussed in Chapters 2–4 in the context of postmodernism, becomes increasingly real to the consumer. This therefore encourages more interaction with the computer and less with the real world and its inhabitants. In other words, computers run the risk of making consumption increasingly *passive*.

Television as technology

Morley and Silverstone (1990) take a more interactive view of technology than some of the above authors in discussing television, which they see as becoming embedded within a diverse technical and consumer culture. They argue that, in contrast to those people marketing television who see it as just another machine for the selling of technologies, consumers construct their own meanings in domestic settings through patterns of use and display. In effect, television is articulated through two sets of meanings: first, meanings created by producers and consumers which focus around the selling and buying of objects and their use as a display of style in relation to the membership of a community or subculture; and, secondly, mediated meanings conveyed by the negotiation and transformation of the technologies on offer.

Using conceptions of time and space to develop their argument, Morley and Silverstone (1990) see the development of television as reflecting the historical transition of leisure time into the domestic sphere. In this context, as far as time is concerned, television provides a common cultural resource or routine. However, the implications of technological developments in cable and satellite television, with the associated increase in available channels, is that the 'simultaneity' of social experience is undermined (1990: 44). In other words, the 'imagined community' that television provides for its consumers becomes lost (1990: 43). Technological developments clearly have significant implications for the way in which consumers consume and for the way in which they structure their everyday lives. However, Morley and Silverstone (1990: 48) continue to emphasize that not only do technologies of consumption 'mobilize, extend, reinforce or transform the metaphors of everyday life', but such metaphors are also actively taken up and *translated* by consumers. It is in this sense that technology might be said to be *interactive*. As a vehicle of consumption, technology might well be argued to be far more than a straightforward expression of social division or a vivid expression of the power of the producer. Rather, the consumption of technology can transform social life, depending, of course, upon the context in which such consumption occurs.

Another author who considers the extent to which television viewers can transform the technologies they consume is Ien Ang (1992). Ang presents an interesting analysis of the consumption of television which she describes as a 'consumer delivery enterprise for advertisers' (Ang, 1992: 132). Moving on, Ang looks at the role technology has played in the creation of a burgeoning number of cable and satellite television stations. As such, Ang notes that 30 or more channels can be viewed in over 20 per cent of American homes, with the number of households taking advantage of video technology being well in excess of 50 per cent. According to Ang, this proliferation in channels has made the business of monitoring what consumers watch increasingly problematic for the industry as a whole. Hence, the television industry has started to use a new piece of technology called the 'people meter' which electronically records viewing patterns. However, this particular approach to the apparently chaotic and diverse nature of viewers' habits is far from a complete solution. Viewers are able to adjust their viewing habits according to their own needs regardless of the industry itself which struggles to keep up with the apparent versatility of the remote control. Ang (1992) therefore quotes Bedell Smith (1985), who argues that viewers are increasingly taking control after decades of tyranny on the part of television programmers. It could therefore be argued that television is not as much of a one-dimensional experience as some commentators imply and, in turn, that consumers have begun to commandeer technology actively for their use, thereby usurping the wishes of dominant players in the television industry. Perhaps consumers do have some control over the consumption of technology after all. Ang does not, however, argue that television viewers have complete freedom: after all, they cannot make the programmes themselves. But what she does try to do is

> foreground and dramatize the continuing dialectic between the technologized strategies of the industry and the fleeting and dispersed tactics by which consumers, while confined by the range of offerings provided by the

industry, surreptitiously seize moments to transform these offerings into 'opportunities' of their own – making 'watching television', embedded as it is in the context of everyday life, not only into a multiple and heterogeneous cultural practice, but also, more fundamentally, into a fundamental indefinite and ultimately ambiguous one, which is beyond prediction and measurement. (Ang, 1992: 142)

Despite such protestations, reservations must remain about how liberating television can really be in an environment where the stimulation of consumption appears to be so important. As Webster (1995) notes, television plays a formative role in reinforcing the stay-at-home ethos of consumerism, and current technological innovations such as flat-screen televisions are likely to aggravate this trend. Television is indeed one of the foremost means of transmitting images and by doing so necessarily promotes consumerism as a way of life. Above and beyond advertising, the television programmes themselves actively promote the sorts of benefits and fulfilment that can be enjoyed through conspicuous consumption.

Is technology really egalitarian?

Is the egalitarian nature of technological consumption therefore exaggerated? As consumers, we feel intuitively that technology *should* be liberating. Indeed, as Lyon (1988) suggests, the increased array of technologically inspired commodities appears to provide more choice for everyone through cable television channels devoted to catalogue shopping and computers that double as television monitors, or through the likely introduction of new technology which allows the consumer to customize his or her favourite track onto a single compact disc. However, as Lyon (1988) goes on to argue, one of the problems of this increased cultural commodification is a diffusion of 'garbage information' that has no real educational value to the consumer. In this respect, technological innovation is arguably having a negative impact upon consumers' life experiences. What appears to be happening in this context is that the expansion of electronic culture is leading to less rather than more choice. Technology is not developing and improving for technology's sake but at the behest and for the benefit of the marketplace. For instance, in Chapter 8, I discuss the increasing preponderance of pay-per-view sporting channels which allow the consumer to see the sporting contest of his or her choice. Such developments are pursued not purely to extend consumer choice, but also because they create a market segment that can be exploited commercially. In effect, the technological choices that are made in the marketplace are made according to the criteria of profitability. Consumer choice only comes into the equation as a means of fulfilling those criteria.

What I am suggesting here is not only that a so-called post-industrial or information society may not be as beneficial to consumers as it may appear to be on the surface, but that, as Jean-Pierre Dupuy (1980) also points out, the social transitions that such an approach attempts to describe do not in any case serve to liberate humankind from material constraints. Bell's (1973) suggestion that the move towards a service-based economy, which he describes as 'a game between people, unmediated by things' (Dupuy, 1980: 4) is quite preposterous inasmuch as:

> far from being a stage in the progressive evolution of mankind, postindustrial society . . . is a phase in the history of capitalism coping with its contradictions. Rather than delivering us from material constraints, the informational society intensifies the struggle for survival and strengthens the radical monopoly of economic activity over the social and political dimensions of our life . . . Instead of fostering harmony among people, then, the new technologies are aggravating alienation, producing a highly unstable, potentially explosive system. (Dupuy, 1980: 4–5)

In the same collection of essays, Baudrillard (1980: 137) argues that, in fact, 'We live in a world of proliferating information and shrinking sense.' Baudrillard sees information, and particularly that propagated through the mass media, as effectively neutralizing social relations. The media actually destroy the social through a bombardment of signs which are given life by technological innovations in the media. The 'masses' are infatuated by what the media offer them, not in terms of the media's message, but through the more general and fascinating imagery that the media constantly reproduce and which thereby creates a situation whereby actual meaning is liquidated.

In contextualizing the above approaches to the impact of technology and information upon society, I want to go on to consider the generally more positive perspective of Yoneji Masauda (1990) and his work, *Managing the Information Society*, in which he considers the future prospects and implications of technological consumption. Masauda argues that as the information epoch emerges social consumption will be expanded. That is, whereas in industrial societies personal forms of consumption became dominant in the form of food, housing, cars and so on, the information society, which he feels is currently emerging, will stimulate social consumption in the form of parks, schools, hospitals and suchlike. Masauda (1990) notes that an industrial society is essentially based on the satisfaction of material needs and that a liberal capitalist system is highly efficient in maintaining the relative satisfaction of the populace. In turn, as long as material productivity raises the level of material consumption, saturation point will inevitably be reached. Meanwhile, social disutility, including air pollution, urban congestion and excessive environmental damage, will continue to increase in inverse proportion to increases in material consumption. As this situation deteriorates and as the implications of consumption in an information society rapidly become evident, Masauda argues that consumers will eventually come to place more importance on social utility, thereby imposing constraints on individual consumption and, in turn, enhancing the tendency for increasingly social forms of consumption. The whole process is apparently exacerbated by the fact that the consumption of computer information is a service generally offered by a public utility and such services are extensively used by public systems such as medical care and education.

The net result of all this would be the emergence of a more socially and environmentally aware society where information is used for the social good. The environment becomes a social resource rather than a resource to be exploited for the benefit of individualized forms of consumption. Consumers or citizens therefore join together to construct public facilities such as homes for the elderly, schools and roads. As far as Masauda (1990) is concerned, then, technology has a fundamental role to play in liberating the consumer from the anti-social world that he or she currently inhabits.

The relationship between technological consumption and power

It is therefore possible to argue that, far from having a negative impact upon the everyday experience of a consumer culture, technology has played an essentially liberating role. Regardless of the perspective you take on this debate, Druckery (1995) points out that technology is no longer simply a mode of participation but represents an important 'operative principle' which plays a fundamental role in maintaining the fabric of contemporary society: 'Beneath the facades of ownership through consumption and conceptualization through use, technology subsumes experience. The relationship between technology and knowledge, class, scarcity, and competition can no longer be framed in strict economic terms; they have encompassed the individual' (Druckery, 1995: 3).

However, the point here, as Druckery (1995) notes, is that the powerful role of technology in contemporary society also has its down side in the sense that, whilst on the surface technology appears to provide the individual with a fascinating realm of self-exploration, actually it serves to undermine individuality through the concentration of power; hence, the increasingly disturbing impact of surveillance technology which I mentioned in Chapter 4. Technological consumption serves the individual in many contexts through broadening the range of available entertainments, improving communications and facilitating more efficient work practices, but as a result it also assimilates 'into popular culture in ways that reinforce its authority but mask the tactic of domination' (Druckery, 1995: 5). In other words, as consumers we are seduced by the benefits of technology, but are simultaneously blinded to the power technology represents. The problem here, as Silverstone and Hirsch (1992) point out, is not only that technology plays an increasingly important role in our everyday lives, but that it brings with it the concern that the consumption of technology is not only beyond our personal control, but that it is actually consuming *us*.

In developing the above argument, the relationship between gender and consumption provides a particularly illuminating illustration of the socially controlling potential of technology. Cockburn (1985), for instance, argues that technology is essentially a medium of power and that the ability to use technology effectively brings with it considerable authority. In turn, the fact that technology is so closely bonded with the accumulation of wealth gives those with access to it, namely men, a formidable social and political resource. In this respect, Cockburn (1985) argues that it is interesting to note that women command the slenderest degree of the technological know-how necessary for the maintenance of such wealth. In effect, technology is a medium of power which men use to further their cause at the expense of women. As far as production in particular is concerned, women may often operate technology, but they are rarely involved in jobs where knowledge of the inner workings of the machine is deemed necessary: 'With few exceptions, the designer and developer of new systems, the people who market and sell, install, manage and service machinery, are men. Women may push the buttons but they may not meddle with the works' (Cockburn, 1985: 11–12).

Technology therefore provides a means for those who have access to the reins of power in a society to control those who do not. In the wrong hands, technology can be dangerous: 'It is often proposed that technology today, like Frankenstein's monster, is "out of control". It is not technology that is out of control, but capitalism and men' (Cockburn, 1985: 255). In this respect, technology benefits the male producer more than it does the consumer, regardless of his or her gender. Technology's veneer of egalitarianism props up the capitalist enterprise.

In a similar vein to Cockburn, Judy Wajcman (1991) considers the historical paths that developments in technology *might* have taken. She argues that computers could have followed one of three routes: a gender-neutral technology; an arena specifically appropriated by women, building upon feminine images of cleanliness, precision and nimble typing fingers; or finally, as male machines. Wajcman argues that there can be no doubt that the last option came to pass and that, traditionally, women have been discouraged from consuming computers, notably at school level. Meanwhile, boys actively participate in technology in the home through computer games, for instance, suitably encouraged by advertisements for games largely aimed at a male market. In effect, Wajcman identifies a series of social and cultural

factors which seem to be conspiring to create a situation where technology is perceived as being alien to women when there is no practical,
or certainly biological, reason why this should be the case. As such, 'We
need to go beyond masculinity and femininity to construct technology
according to a completely different set of socially desirable values . . .
Insofar as technology currently reflects a man's world, the struggle to
transform it demands a transformation of gender relations' (Wajcman,
1991: 166). Technology is clearly a powerful medium which, far from
liberating consumers, can, in the wrong hands, be used actively to
accentuate counterproductive power relationships.

Is technology necessarily progressive?

In this respect, it is worth asking how 'progressive' technology really is.
Could, indeed, technology be taken to be symbolic of the essentially
irrational and 'unnatural' nature of consumerism in general? It is fair to
say that, though authors such as Lyotard (1984) have referred to the
eclectic role of technology in postmodernity, technology is more generally associated with the imperatives of modernity in the sense that
human beings used technology as a means of pursuing 'progress'. The
question is: has technological consumption really brought progress
along with it? One author who considers this issue in detail is Ernest
Braun (1995) in his work, *Futile Progress*. Braun considers the extent to
which progress, which he regards as the most characteristic feature of
our time, has brought with it technological innovations that have
stimulated social advance above and beyond individual happiness.
Braun notes that, although continuous technological innovation is an
absolute necessity if a strong industrial base is to be maintained,
technological progress should not necessarily be equated with progress
towards a better life or society. In particular, technological progress
clearly expands the range of human wants that can be satisfied by
technology.

Braun (1995) sees technology, which is deeply rooted in the dominant
industrial system of progress, as being symbolic of progress in modern
society in general. But the problem as far as Braun is concerned is that
the overpowering rate of technological innovation, which appears to be
getting faster and faster, actually makes the quest for contentment
through the acquisition of products of technology increasingly futile. In
effect, technology provides an engine for the constant quest for desire
that is so important to the long-term effectiveness of the capitalist
economy. Technology may provide plenty of benefits, notably in the
form of medical progress, but

> if progress becomes too fast, if all we own is obsolescent or even obsolete, if
> all we see around us is in constant rapid flux, if sales pressures are such as to

make us buy things beyond our purchasing capacity, then technological change turns the dream of progress into a nightmare. (Braun, 1995: 42)

Braun's concerns therefore focus on the fact that computers, among other forms of technology, have not fulfilled their potential as enablers of 'participative democracy' (1995: 42). They have merely fuelled the roller-coaster of consumerism. More specifically, Braun bemoans the fact that the environment is endangered as a result of its inability to defend itself against the speed of such innovation when, in fact:

> What society really needs are technologies and attitudes that help to solve, or alleviate, societal problems. What we do not need are technologies designed merely to stimulate flagging demand by making products of technology subject to fashion and by producing ever new toys and gadgets . . . We need technologies that solve environmental problems, urban problems, health and safety problems; that help to provide meaningful employment; and those that help developing countries to overcome barriers to development. (Braun, 1995: 185)

Braun's point is that technology does not provide the consumer with what he or she wants, but rather with what is economically viable. On a global scale, technology is inherently divisive inasmuch as it helps very few developed countries and ostracizes the poor of both the developed and developing worlds. It is in this sense that technological progress and the consumption of that progress is essentially futile.

The relationship between technology and progress is also taken up by Winner (1995), who argues that technology does not necessarily bring economic benefits with it. Winner also points out that technological innovation may indeed be socially harmful through the impact of unemployment, urban decay, poverty, illiteracy, dysfunctional families and shattered lives, all of which are potential consequences of technological 'progress'. In this context, Winner (1995) identifies what he describes as the three paradoxes of the information age. First is the fact that, far from enhancing human abilities, technological developments not only appear to assume that consumers are incompetent, but they also invent appropriate roles for these consumers which thereby ensure the demise of the 'paradox of intelligence'. Secondly, although past technologies were expected to create leisure time and as such opportunities for personal freedom and the expression of creativity, what has actually resulted is a bombardment of social life by multimedia communication systems. Hence, the infuriating sound of a train passenger talking on his or her mobile phone and the fact that:

> Our society has begun to look like a vast electronic beehive in which information processing in search of economic gain overshadows other personal and social goods. Places and spaces in our lives formerly devoted to

sociability, intimacy, solitude, friendship, love, and family are now being redefined as susceptible to productivity, transforming social norms and boundaries. (Winner, 1995: 194)

Time, as Daniel Bell (1973) argued, has, indeed, become a precious resource and one that is punctuated by 'time-saving' devices that far from liberating the consumer actually subject him or her to constant stress. The need to do things quickly subverts our need to relax, ensuring that any sense of personal freedom and creativity is further from our reach than when we began. This then, is the 'paradox of lifespace'. Finally, while technology has often been lauded as a means of enhancing democracy, on the contrary, Winner (1995: 195) suggests that such a myth applies only to a minuscule proportion of the population who 'hang out in transnational computer networks'. In reality, television is the major technological innovation impinging on the majority of people's lives and thus serves to promote a situation where people command increasingly limited concentration spans, so much so that American politics, for instance, has become nothing more than a politics of video imagery. Technology is not democratic in any real sense; rather, consumers have become increasingly divorced from democratic practice. There therefore exists a 'paradox of electronic democracy'.

Overall, then, Winner maintains that there is an enormous gap between expectations about how technology can improve consumers' lives and everyday realities. This is basically an ideological issue in so far as 'Beyond the prevailing progressivist ideology of technology lies the attempt to illuminate technology as a sphere of choices and conflicts' (1995: 197). Winner argues that there exists a politics of technology which is hidden from everyday perception. Consumers do not consider what technology presupposes about the people who use it. The politics of technology is a silent politics despite technology having an important role to play in the construction of gender, class, control, community, freedom and so on.

Conclusion

The relationship between technology and consumption represents an important focus for the sociologist of consumerism in the sense that developments in technology clearly have significant implications for the consumer. There is no doubt that recent developments in technology have brought with them a considerable variety of consumer goods previously considered to be the preserve of skilled technical experts. In this sense, technology is democratic. But such democracy comes at a price – a price determined by the marketplace. In this respect, Giedion's (1948) discussion of how technology penetrated domestic space in the years before the Second World War is especially pertinent. Giedion argues that domestic technologies, such as refrigerators, food processors and sophisticated cookers, were introduced to the home precisely because they established commodity consumption as the natural means to need satisfaction (see Lee, 1993). Technology came to be exploited as a stimulator of capitalist demand.

The application of technology to the production process has served to increase standards of living throughout the developed world. This much should not be underestimated. Nor should Bell's (1973) point about the increasing significance of service industries be dismissed out of hand. It is just that such services are entirely dependent upon the relationship *between* consumption and production. In this context, some commentators are very wary of the degree of control that technology appears to command in the context of consumers' everyday lives. Indeed, Dunkerley (1996: 127) argues that, as technology develops, it is increasingly characterized by two aspects, namely: its apparent ability to deliver prosperity and leisure to everyone, and its ability to give those focused on profit more powerful tools with which to garner more and more of the world's wealth for their personal benefit. Other commentators are fearful of the continued polarization of a 'haves' and 'have-nots' situation: 'As things are, the advanced industrial, techno-logical planned economic system is like nothing so much as a great joy-wheel at a fair, of vast size, with power at the centre; those skilful enough to stay furthest from the edge are least likely to be hurled off' (Russell, 1983: 220).

With the arrival of the computer revolution, commentators such as George (1977) became increasingly concerned with the invisible power of technological innovation and its potential for destroying human freedom, particularly in the context of information gathering and data processing. This situation has undoubtedly deteriorated, notably with the advances incorporated in recent years by the retail industry, which has increasingly comprehensive knowledge about the profile of con-sumers. Such knowledge exists alongside more prevalent surveillance technology (see Chapter 4). More particularly, as far as the actual retail of technology is concerned, and as I have learnt to my cost, the financial imperatives are such that manufacturers appear to be cutting corners. A recent attempt of mine to purchase a new television set failed on several technical fronts which were explained rather alarmingly by the manager of the shop concerned as a consequence of having to cut technical corners in light of consumer demand for attractive pricing. In one sense, then, the consumer is in control, but the price of that control is technological incompetence.

Both manufacturers and retailers are sacrificing quality for the needs of a market that is driven by mass production and where the consumer-driven markets of the post-Fordist ideal are conspicuous by their absence. What is ultimately most interesting about technology, as the above example illustrates, is that it transcends the realms of production and consumption and the sociological concerns that emanate from these realms. Technology is having an equal, and arguably more significant, impact in the realm of production than it does in the realm of consumption. As Dunkerley (1996) notes, we live in a consumer society where consumers earn their money by being part of a process of production and by working within the system or at least its offshoots. However, as technology advances, it could be argued that there is less and less need for human beings in this system. Up to now, technology has helped to construct an increasingly efficient system where economic growth has served to pull more people into the system, with higher wages, thereby creating more consumers to purchase the goods that are produced. In this context, consumers have enjoyed higher standards of living. However, as Dunkerley (1996: 13) notes, we may well be on the cusp of a revolutionary transition in our relationship with the production process:

> For the first time in history we are looking at the widespread use of technology that will produce what we need whilst at the same time employing steadily fewer people and ultimately no people. In other words, for the first time in history we are no longer creating consumers for that output.

In effect, Dunkerley identifies a move towards a production process that is winding down, inasmuch as the continual move towards automation will have significant implications for the consumption side of the equation. The prosperity of the industrialized world is based on an arrangement where jobs make consumers and consumers make jobs. The role of technology in this process is to cancel out the job losses resulting from redundant technologies, creating new products which thereby bring with them new, relatively well-paid job opportunities (Dunkerley, 1996: 86). As long as society is dependent upon this sort of a spiral, the fear will always remain that the information technologically driven economy will continue to decentralize work to the extent that part-time and contract work will become the norm, reducing spending power and thereby threatening the very basis of the consumer economy (Dunkerley, 1996).

As far as the consumer is concerned, technology clearly commands a powerful, though tenuous, position in terms of its influence upon the everyday construction of a consumer society. It is in this sense that Silverstone and Hirsch (1992) talk about the fear that technology consumes us, as opposed to us consuming technology. At least to an extent, we do appear to live in an increasingly technological world in which we are obliged to become increasingly passive in how we consume. Consumer goods are increasingly available and it is simply not possible to garner all the necessary knowledge to become an entirely proactive consumer. This means that more often than not the consumer is consigned to being an observer of technical aspects of the world of consumption that surround him or her. One of the words bandied around in the context of technology is 'interactivity', notably in the form of interactive video, television, CDs and so on. But the problem here is that technology continues to seduce us with an *illusion* of interactivity and liberation which in actual fact promotes the passivity of the consumer, while stubbornly regurgitating a market-led agenda within which the consumer is little more than an outsider looking in. In other words, the consumer is left infatuated, dangling on the cusp of a technological future. In the final analysis, that future is no more than a construction of consumer capitalism which seduces consumers into buying the technology that is available today on the basis of technology that will not, in fact, be available today, tomorrow, or perhaps at any time in the future. In this context, Dupuy (1980) argues that a so-called post-industrial society is characterized by more and more information, but at a cost of less and less meaning.

Ultimately, the sorts of benefits that authors such as Bell (1973) read into the emergence of a so-called technologically based service economy have not come to fruition. Science and technology have not brought leisure and prosperity to the whole world, as authors such as Dunkerley (1996) note. Technology has put a man on the moon, but it has not provided people with vast amounts of free time. The only free time that does appear to be available tends to be spent within the confines of consumerism which is constantly regenerated by consumers who seek new ways to consume. The abiding impression here is of a technology that promotes consumer choice, but which apparently does so as a means of maintaining consumerism as a dominant mode of life. As consumers, we can only hope that technology does provide some of the surprises that it perpetually offers us. In the final analysis, we can only trust that Noble (1984) is correct when he contends that technology 'leads a double life, one which conforms to the intentions of designers and interests of power and another which contradicts them – proceeding behind the backs of their architects to yield unintended consequences and unanticipated possibilities' (quoted in Morley and Silverstone, 1990: 35).

The role of technology, which has for so long been associated with human progress, has in recent years become subject to radical change in that the market into which technology is released appears to be increasingly more important than the progressive nature of the technology itself. Meanwhile, as Pepperell (1995) notes, the unique status that technology has given human beings in the world in ensuring our superiority and uniqueness is now being challenged by those very same technologies which are now becoming more powerful than the people actually consuming them. Perhaps the problem here is that consumerism as a way of life is more ideologically powerful than its constituent parts. This is a point I will reconsider in Chapter 6 in the context of a discussion of the relationship between consumerism and fashion.

Recommended reading

Daniel Bell (1973) *The Coming of Post-industrial Society*. New York: Basic Books. A classic, though much criticised, account of the relationship between technology, industry and social change.

Ernest Braun (1995) *Futile Progress*. London: Earthscan Publications. Asks how far technology can really be described as liberating in a world which prioritizes what is economically viable as opposed to what best serves the interests of the people who inhabit it.

Cynthia Cockburn (1985) *Machinery of Dominance: Women, Men and Technical Know-How*. London: Pluto. An important contribution to debates about the relationship between technology, gender and power.

Michael Dunkerley (1996) *The Jobless Economy? Computer Technology in the World of Work*. Cambridge: Polity Press. An insightful analysis of the relationship between computer technology, work and economic growth.

Roger Silverstone and Eric Hirsch (1992) *Consuming Technologies: Media and Information in Domestic Spaces*. London: Routledge. A collection of useful essays which consider the consumption of technology in a direct and empirically informed fashion.

Frank Webster (1995) *Theories of the Information Society*. London: Routledge. A useful overview of some of the debates concerning the role of information and technology in social change.

6

CONSUMING FASHION

Fashion is arguably *the* arena within which the wares of consumerism are most visibly expressed and fervently endorsed as constituting a legitimate way of life. In this respect, there could well be grounds for arguing that 'Fashion is a commercial, industrial art, concerned less with beauty than with making money' (McDowell, 1994: 57). On the surface, fashion appears to provide the consumer with a plethora of choice – a palette from which he or she can paint an identity as he or she pleases. Some critics argue, however, that fashion in fact amounts to little more than an artificial temporal arena within which consumer capitalism cynically renews itself. Alternatively, Featherstone (1991) has argued that consumer culture is characterized by the violation of long-held fashion codes and the emergence of a society of difference, while Ewen and Ewen (1982: 249–51) go as far as to suggest that 'Today there is no fashion: there are only fashions . . . No rules, only choices . . . Everyone can be anyone.' Apparently, fashion has broken free from the shackles of modernist constraint. But is fashion really as emancipatory as it appears on the surface and what does it really tell us about consumerism as a way of life?

Though the term 'fashion' can be applied to virtually all aspects of consumer culture, in reflecting the literature in general I will largely focus on fashion in the context of clothing in this chapter. Before doing so, I will begin by considering *what fashion is*, particularly in light of the contributions made to this debate by authors such as Simmel (1957) and McCracken (1990). I will then move on to consider *the history of fashion*, before I look at whether fashion is characterized by *choice or scam*. This then brings me to a discussion of three further issues that should concern us about fashion *the communicative role of fashion; the global impact of fashion;* and whether *fashion shapes or is shaped by social life*. I will then come to a conclusion about the impact of fashion on consumerism as a way of life.

What is fashion?

Fashion is important because as an issue it encapsulates so many of the tensions characteristic of modern life experience and, in particular, highlights the role that consumerism plays in that experience. In this context, it also serves to enrich an understanding of the complex relationships that underlie questions of structure and agency.

Georg Simmel (1957) is one of the single most important contributors to the sociological debate on the question of fashion. Simmel emphasizes the restless changing nature of modernity and, in effect, sees fashion as a means of coping with such restlessness. Arguing that social life is a battleground, Simmel regards fashion as helping to ensure that people adapt to the complexities of modern life. This reflects his contention that 'The whole history of society is reflected in the striking conflicts, the compromises, slowly won and quickly lost, between socialistic adaptation to society and individual departure from its demands' (Simmel, 1957: 294). As the product of class distinction, fashion not only identifies the individual as being a member of a particular class, but also highlights the fact that he or she is *not* a member of an alternative group. In effect, then, Simmel sees fashion as a product of social demands. The individual feels fulfilled through fashion, but this fulfilment is ultimately a social and not an individual one. In this sense, it could often be argued that fashion bears little resemblance to any reasonable aesthetic judgement or individual taste. 'Judging from the ugly and repugnant things that are sometimes in vogue, it would seem that fashion were desirous of exhibiting its power by getting us to adopt the most atrocious things for its own sake' (Simmel, 1957: 297). As far as Simmel is concerned, fashion represents a means of reacting to the tensions of modern life. In this context, money plays a pivotal role in Simmel's analysis, in ensuring the omnipresence of fashion.

> The increase of wealth is bound to hasten the process considerably and render it visible because the objects of fashion, embracing as they do the externals of life, are the most accessible to the mere call of money, and conformity to the higher set is more easily acquired here than in fields which demand an individual test that gold and silver cannot affect. (Simmel, 1957: 299)

At an individual level, fashion offers social obedience alongside individual differentiation, while from a broader perspective it reflects the underlying workings of a mobile society. In this respect, the needs of the individual and society are meshed. The individual can get from fashion what he or she pleases – a sense of individuality alongside a feeling of belonging – while society itself can reap the concurrent economic benefits.

What makes something fashionable? Although Simmel goes some way towards answering this question, we probably need to delve somewhat further in this respect. One author that discusses this issue in detail is Grant McCracken (1990) in his book, *Culture and Consumption*. McCracken argues that fashion is less of a language than a limited set of prefabricated codes (see also Craik, 1994). That is, it provides a means by which individuals can signal aspects of their identity as well as a way of constructing social interaction. Ultimately, however, the individual's interpretation of fashion is constrained by social conventions. Interestingly, McCracken (1990) argues that in this context there are three main ways in which meanings are transferred to goods in order to become fashionable. First, goods become associated with established cultural categories. This transition from the culturally constituted world to the actual good ensures the transition into the fashion system. Secondly, existing cultural meanings are shaped by social elites and opinion leaders such as pop stars, who therefore disseminate cultural innovations and styles through society (see Chapter 7). Those consumers with less influence imitate these appropriations. Finally, the fashion system radically reforms the cultural meanings invested in goods. As such, McCracken points out that modern societies are characterized by constant change and the instability of meaning (and hence the obsolescence of design which I discussed in Chapter 3) (see Craik, 1994). The key point here is that Western societies actively encourage constant innovation as a means of driving society as a whole. Western industrial societies therefore:

> willingly accept, indeed encourage, the radical changes that follow from deliberate human effort and the effect of anonymous social forces. As a result the cultural meaning of a 'hot,' western, industrial complex society is constantly undergoing systematic change. In contradiction to virtually all ethnographic precedent, they live in a world that is not only culturally constituted but also historically constituted. Indeed it does not exaggerate to say that hot societies demand this change and depend on it to drive certain economic, social, and cultural sectors of the Western world. The fashion system serves as one of the conduits for capture and movement of this category of highly innovative meaning. (McCracken, 1990: 80–1)

The above quotation reflects one of the central concerns of this book as a whole: namely, that economically modern industrial societies *need* consumerism in order to tick over in a satisfactorily productive fashion. Modern societies *need* to promote consumerism as a way of life in order to ensure their viability over an extended period of time. Fashion plays a key role in this process inasmuch as it maintains a constant turnover in demand. By outlining some historical elements to this debate, it might be possible to begin to see why this should be so.

The history of fashion

The historical emergence of fashion, which should be considered in unison with my discussion of the rise of a consumer society in Chapter 1, represents a complex story, beginning in the late Middle Ages (Craik, 1994) and arguably finding expression in the court of Philip the Good, Duke of Burgundy, in the fifteenth century (Rubinstein 1995: 146). Fashion has traditionally been used as a means of stimulating the growth of the world's economies, notably by Louis-Napoléon who opened two Great Exhibitions in 1851 and 1855 which were intended to boost the French economy while displaying how technologically advanced that economy had become (Rubinstein, 1995: 148). Historically, fashion has more often than not been the preserve of the richer sectors of society. But, as Simmel (1957) notes, as money came to have a social currency, this began to change. As classes and individuals attempted to keep up with one another, fashion, in a variety of realms of life – whether in home furnishing, music or dress – came to have an important role in turning over the economy of many societies, by the time of the period after the Second World War fashion was playing an important economic role in both Europe and the USA.

Minchinton (1982) identifies four main factors impacting on the spread of fashion in post-Second World War Britain. First, a general rise in incomes saw the emergence of an increasingly affluent society. Secondly, family sizes were becoming smaller during this period and as a result people were able to draw upon larger disposable incomes which they could invest in aspects of consumption. Thirdly, advertising became more and more professional, focusing its efforts, in particular, on the increasingly affluent 16–26 age range. Finally, marketing was also beginning to develop as an industry in its own right, notably with the emergence of increasingly popular mail-order catalogues in which the delights of the fashionable consumption of a wider range of goods could be extended into the home (see Minchinton, 1982). All these trends had their American equivalents. From a historical angle, it is therefore possible to identify a post-war economic boom which saw the pace of fashion quicken as fashionable ready-to-wear mass produced clothing became popular among middle-class and affluent working-class segments of the market and which required, in turn, long runs of highly standardized products (Wark, 1991).

What emerged after the Second World War, notably with the influence of an expanding youth market, was a popular culture which demanded the appropriation of difference and thus the transformation of the realm of fashion into a series of niche markets. In this context, and apparently by the 1980s, individual choice was all. As innovations in so-called post-Fordist production runs took effect, the fashion industry became increasingly responsive to the needs of the consumer (see Chapter 1). At least on the surface, consumer culture appeared, and

indeed appears, to be beginning to deliver the individuality and difference that it had always promised. Such developments, argues Wark
(1991), reflected a general rise in living standards which allowed the
working classes to become involved in the temporal world of fashion
consumption, leading in turn to significant changes in the way in which
the fashion industry was structured. With the increasing influence of
cheap imports from developing countries such as Taiwan and Korea,
and the developing role of international marketing which depended
upon high advertising budgets and the popular though 'exclusive'
appeal of labels, fashion became an increasingly global phenomenon. By
the 1980s, the by-product of all this was that the fashion industry had
apparently become far more receptive to the needs of its customers.

Fashion as choice or scam?

The apparent transition towards an increasingly democratic fashion
industry, where the needs of the consumer are served as part of a move
towards an increasingly flexible and consumer-oriented industry, is
often illustrated through a discussion of fashion as a post-Fordist
industry and, more particularly, of Benetton as a post-Fordist company
(see Murray, 1989). Arguing that the principles of mass production,
standardization and economies of scale have in recent years been
superseded, the suggestion is that companies like Benetton have in turn
become increasingly responsive to consumer demand; that, as a post-
Fordist industry, clothing fashion is consumer rather than producer
oriented. From this point of view, the relationship between the producer
and the consumer has apparently been turned upside down, giving the
consumer increasing influence over what was previously a one-way
production process. New technology therefore plays a key role in the
new regime in that the rapid collection of data allows designers to
introduce changes to the production process, if and when necessary.
Benetton, for instance, is well known for its sophisticated computer
system which feeds its distribution centre with constant up-to-date
information about the popularity of each product line at each of its retail
outlets. The company can therefore serve customers' needs with maximum efficiency. In this context, post-Fordism is seen to transform time
and space by increasing the efficiency and effectiveness of capitalist
practices. From the consumer's point of view, such developments reflect
a declining interest in mass produced goods in favour of more
specialized products with the emphasis on style and quality rather than
uniformity. In effect, post-Fordism is based on the diversities characteristic of economies of scope, as opposed to the quantities associated
with Fordist economies of scale (see Chapter 1).

The benefits of post-Fordist fashion are not, however, as clear cut as
they might at first seem. Nixon (1996), for instance, argues that post-

Fordist practices have in fact been slow to take root in the British economy in general and in fashion in particular. He points out that the clothing industry is often lauded as a home for new flexible forms of production. Quoting Zeitlin (1988), who in turn highlights the significance of multiple retailers and their move towards an emphasis on fashionable variety as opposed to mass production, Nixon goes on to imply that fashion retailers are a more powerful partner in this relationship with fashion manufacturing than the actual consumer. The point here is that although production in the British fashion industry has arguably become more flexible, it has also concentrated power in the hands of large retailers such as Marks & Spencer and Next. As a result, this has led to an increasing European influence on clothing manufacture in Britain in the middle and higher end of the clothing market, as smaller British manufacturers have struggled to compete.

Meanwhile, Craik (1994) goes as far as to suggest that, in an effort to achieve the authentic look of hand finishing, historically the fashion industry has actively shunned technological developments. Nixon (1996) accepts that a culture of flexible specialization began to emerge in the fashion industry during the 1980s, notably through the influence of new technology such as computer aided design. But the likelihood is that such developments were occurring on the periphery and the industry as a whole has in many respects fallen short of introducing Fordist, let alone post-Fordist, techniques. Perhaps the consumer *is* beginning to have a more influential say in the production process, but such a say is undoubtedly diluted, not only by outdated systems of production, but also by the increased power of influential retailers. As I argued in Chapter 4, these have an increasing and arguably monopolistic hold over the city as a site of consumption.

In effect, the fashion industry is not as flexible as it might seem on the surface. It would be naïve to contest the idea that changes have taken place in the economy – of course they have. Common sense tells us that there are more products on the market. But there could equally be an argument for suggesting that such choice is largely illusory. There may well be hundreds of different versions of the classic pair of jeans available, as I argued in Chapter 3, but essentially each of those jeans offers the consumer the same thing. The choice that is available is not only unnecessary, but barely constitutes a choice in the first place because it so often amounts to little more than a very slight variation on a mass produced theme (see Chapter 3). In effect, consumer choice in the realm of fashion is inherently artificial.

In this context, authors such as Sayer (1989) argue that this sort of mass-produced choice is not due to market fragmentation by single manufacturers at all, but is rather a direct result of the penetration into the market of increasing numbers of overseas producers, something that Nixon (1996) hinted at above. This, and not an increase in the range of products being made by single firms, might therefore explain the increase of goods on the market. Major industries, including fashion, still mass produce; it is just that there are quite simply more firms putting such goods onto the market. Benetton can therefore be seen to be an atypical illustration of post-Fordism in an industry which remains largely dependent upon Fordist mass production. As Harvey (1989) points out, though 'there has certainly been a sea-change in the surface appearance of capitalism since 1973 . . . the underlying logic of capitalist accumulation and its crisis tendencies remain the same' (Harvey, 1989: 189).

Traditionally, as Leopold (1992) suggests, commentators have seen fashion as a product of consumer demand. Leopold sees this approach as problematic and suggests that more emphasis should be put on addressing the nature of the fashion system.

> Loosely defined as the interrelationship between highly fragmented forms of production and equally diverse and often volatile patterns of demand, the fashion system is a hybrid subject; it incorporates dual concepts of fashion: as a cultural phenomenon, and as an aspect of manufacturing with the accent on production technology. (Leopold, 1992: 101)

The essential problem with analyses of fashion as far as Leopold is concerned, then, is that they have tended to concentrate, somewhat disproportionately, on high fashion, while neglecting class relationships which underpin the development of mass markets in cheap, standard-ized fashionable clothing. The fashion industry was characterized, in the years following the Second World War, as an increasingly perishable industry which exploited a compliant body of small-scale contractors and concentrated, in turn, on producing short-term design runs. Most importantly, Leopold (1992) argues that what is being described here is not a straightforward trickle-down system. Mass-produced goods such as Levi 501s, for instance, have a powerful stranglehold on the market in an upwards, as well as downwards, direction. But the key question at this stage centres on the extent to which fashion might be said to dictate to consumers rather than vice versa and whether or not the limited technological and organizational innovations I described above actually serve to increase this tendency. For instance, in their book *Marketing Today's Fashion*, Mueller and Smiley (1995) argue that, far from dictating what customers should wear, the successful process of marketing a garment begins and ends with the consumer. In their next breath, however, they go on to discuss the value to fashion marketing of fashion consultants, fashion magazines, trade publications, advertising and store image, all of which actively construct a sense of what fashion *should* be in order to ensure that the consumer consumes it.

Some authors do not then accept that the clothing fashion industry actively prioritizes the needs of its consumers. In this respect, Colin

McDowell (1994) presents a particularly robust critique of fashion in arguing that, as an industry, it actively sets out to alter consumers' buying habits in order that they come to believe that luxuries are, in fact, necessities. Noting that fashion is no longer the preserve of the rich, McDowell acknowledges the apparently liberating nature of contemporary fashion but suggests that the fashion industry has intentionally moulded a culture where what defines a person depends upon what labels he or she is wearing.

> The designer scam sets out to convince us that a certain level of wealth, a certain style of living, a certain assessment of what is important in life raises us above criticism and accountability. To be fashionable, it suggests, is not merely to live on a level of privilege. It is also about being able to do so on the level of Caesar's wife. (McDowell, 1994: 4)

By prioritizing low cost at the expense of quality, the needs of the consumer, as far as McDowell is concerned, are increasingly being ignored. Thus, McDowell quotes the example of Giorgio Armani's range of A/X Exchange merchandise which he claims is little more than a slight variation on classic items of American sportswear embossed, as a token gesture, with a designer label. The industry therefore continues to exploit feelings of social uncertainty and insecurity by offering the illusion that fashion can answer, or at least lead us to forget, the problems of everyday life (see McDowell, 1994: 138). Ultimately, the fashion industry is an industry in crisis.

> Over the last decade, in my opinion, we have been abused and misled by a frequently ruthless and immoral industry determined to scam us in to believing that high fashion is a birthright, a proof of worth, an adjunct of character, even an indication of social desirability. That industry is now running scared at what it fears might prove a permanent shift in consumer aspirations and spending. It is terrified in case luxury ready-to-wear becomes profitable again. It stares bleakly at a future dominated by the likes of Benetton and the Gap. (McDowell, 1994: 225)

Regardless of the so-called democratization of fashion, there does, indeed, seem to be an argument for suggesting that to a large extent manufacturers set the fashion agenda. As a means of debating whether the fashion industry is in this sense authoritative I will now consider a series of key related issues.

The communicative role of fashion

It might be argued that fashion is a more complex phenomenon than the above approaches suggest. As such, Malcolm Barnard (1996) sees fashion as a two-sided coin. He argues that while, on the one hand, fashion is inherently seductive and exciting, on the other it might be perceived to be fraudulent, dangerous and trivial. Essentially, Barnard sees fashion as being ambivalent, 'at once positive and negative' (1996: 4). However, he suggests that fashion cannot be trivial as such, precisely because it appears to be an inevitable consequence of the social and economic organization of the world. In this context, Barnard goes on to consider fashion in the context of power and ideology, pointing out that fashion can serve not only to constitute and communicate a position in the social order, but might also challenge positions of relative power within it. As such, 'Fashion and clothing are used as weapons and defences in that they express the ideologies held by social groups which may be opposed to the ideologies of other groups in the social order' (Barnard, 1996: 39). In other words, fashion can act as a resource by which social groups can maintain either dominant or subservient positions within a social order. In this context, authors such as Barnard (1996) and Hebdige (1979) before him use punk as an example of how fashion can actively be used as a means of assaulting dominant values in the form of the unconventional use of safety pins, for instance, which in actual fact amounts to a mode of dress diametrically opposed to the dominant order. In effect,

> the curious cultural profile enjoyed by fashion and clothing may be under-stood as the result of a conflict between the desire for there to be a 'beyond' to ideology, for there to be a place where class divisions, for example, are absent, and the realisation that there can be no such beyond. (Barnard, 1996: 45)

This point is an important one in reinforcing the ambivalent nature of fashion and the way in which, like consumption itself, it appears to promise so much and yet can never ultimately out-pace the structural constraints of society as a whole. Arguably, fashion actively reinforces such constraints. In this context, Barnard goes on to present a useful discussion of Marxist interpretations of fashion in which he suggests that fashion might be used as a means of constituting class positions; as a means, in effect, of making class positions seem legitimate through servant uniforms, for instance. As far as Barnard is concerned, then, status is the underlying motivation for fashion in capitalist societies. And in this respect the work of Veblen (1899), which I discussed in some detail in Chapter 2, is particularly pertinent in that he argued that fashion can be used to communicate and reproduce positions of economic status, much like consumers use labels and logos nowadays in order to achieve the same effect (see Barnard, 1996: 110).

Fashion, argues Barnard, plays an especially important role in the context of gender constructions. This is said to be especially true when considering the argument that the creation or maintenance of a look or appearance is a defining feature of femininity, though it is apparently not so significant in constructions of masculinity (1996: 115). Thus, it could be argued that historically women have been encouraged to express themselves through the frivolities of fashion. 'The gender identity of women, then, may be said to be constructed, signalled and reproduced by means of fashion and clothing insofar as women wear the sorts of things that a society deems appropriate for them and insofar as they continue to be "obsessed" with their appearances' (Barnard, 1996: 115).

Intriguingly, Barnard (1996) goes on to use Derrida's (1978) notion of 'undecidability' to express the ambiguity inherent in the fashion experience; that is, the idea that meaning invested in a particular good may be evident, but that meaning may simultaneously be dissipated by those relations that constructed it. Taking a postmodern stance in this respect, Barnard argues that the meanings with which people endow fashion are not undecidable at all, but are, in fact, largely reliable and finite in that, as knowledgeable consumers, we make judgements about people's fashion sense one way or the other. The key point here is that as far as wider theoretical issues are concerned, fashion and clothing are mass produced and *do* incorporate a common cultural knowledge concerning the meanings constituted in them. Fashion can therefore be described as ambiguous. In effect, clothing and fashion 'represent something like a border or a margin between a public, exterior person and a private, interior identity' (Barnard, 1996: 173). Fashion is essentially mass produced and consumers arguably use mass produced garments to construct who they are. Despite thousands of copies of that garment having being made, as Barnard notes, we see it as being 'us' and, as such, 'identity shades into difference, and difference into identity' (1996: 174). The meaning of fashion is expressed by the tensions that exist as a result of its complex ambiguities. Any understanding of fashion is a product of the interrelationship of a variety of conceptual positions, and debates will continue because there is no means of resolving such positions. In effect, fashion is characterized by conflicting desires – desires which reflect the abstract uncertainties of a so-called postmodern world (see Miles, 1996).

In this respect, Wilson's (1992) insightful discussion of the relationship between postmodernism and the body can be used to build upon Barnard's (1996) conception of fashion and the role it plays in the experience of an increasingly fragmented world. She suggests that fashion can either be seen to glue together false identities on the surface or to provide a sense of playfulness – props, if you like, that can be adapted from one postmodern experience to another. In this sense, Wilson argues that fashion is far more than a mere language. True, it communicates, but it is also tactile and visual and thus, in effect, embodies culture (Wilson, 1992: 14.) Our value systems are actively embodied in our dress:

Perhaps what was wrong with the eighties was not a style obsession, but that styles, of dress at least, expressed all too well the enterprise-culture ethos of the eighties of the times. In a kind of reverse resistance, the riot-engendered style of the poor (Punk) was converted into the style of dominance and of a success whose boots were for walking, and were indeed going to walk all over you. (Wilson, 1992: 14–15)

The global impact of fashion

What do the above arguments mean for fashion as an industry? As a means of answering this question it may well be worth while considering Fred Davis's (1992) discussion of the fashion system. Davis considers the suggestion that the fashion industry has structured its very survival on the managed excess of change, pointing out that 'Typically, fashion is charged with furthering the superficial and spurious while undermining the substantial and genuine' (1992: 194). However, Davis argues that, on the contrary, the fashion system has allowed increasingly complex systems of taste. Distinguishing between the fashion cycle (the passing of time from the introduction of a fashion to its being supplanted by a new fashion) and the fashion process (the diverse influences and exchanges on an individual, organizational and institutional level that are transmitted to such a cycle), Davis argues that, rather than the traditional three- to five-year fashion cycle, what has emerged in its place in the late twentieth century is a plethora of 'microcycles' each of which is associated with a different identity segment of the apparel market (Davis, 1992: 157). In effect, fashion has become increasingly plural. In order to explain this development, Davis (1992) borrows some of the thoughts of Daniel Bell (1976) on the cultural contradictions of capitalism. He therefore suggests that, as a mass-based culture of consumption arises and as it becomes increasingly global and uniform in nature, there emerges an increasing thirst for individuality. In this context, Davis (1992) argues that the previous long-term incarnations of the fashion cycle came to be replaced by an increasingly identity-conscious reactivity resulting in more pluralistic micro-fashions which in turn created a framework for the communication of self.

Davis (1992) goes on to ask whether or not *everything* is subject to fashion and argues that this could indeed be the case, although certainly not in the extreme form that it occurs in the realm of clothing. But he does not see fashion as something that *necessarily* has a negative impact upon people's lives. Indeed, Davis argues that fashion has opened upon all sorts of taste strata that consumers are able to exploit, and that fashion potentially provides a frame for counteracting the standardized nature of a global consumer culture.

Ironically, fashion has furthered . . . expressive possibilities for many
individuals and groups notwithstanding the fact that many of the materials
employed in the quest are the very same ones produced and promoted by the
multinationals themselves. What is different, of course, is the symbolic uses to
which such materials are put and accordingly, the meanings they acquire in
more local and diversified cultural contexts. (Davis, 1992: 199)

Davis (1992) feels that fashion is characterized by the contradiction
that exists between the powerful, highly integrated corporate units in a
global marketplace of fashion and peculiarly localized expressions of
fashion. That is, advances in consumer capitalism have made possible
increasingly complex systems of taste which have seen a rapid growth in
the interdependence of people at a variety of levels such as the economic
and the environmental. At the same time, outcrops of regional and local
particularisms have also emerged, thereby undermining the very character of the nation state. As far as Davis is concerned, then, there seems
to have been some form of local action against the encroachment of a
global centre, while the flexibility of that centre continues to be
sustained by the diversity of the periphery. Contemporary fashion is a
product of a multi-global marketplace which has developed alongside a
localized sense of style and ethnicity. Either way, the influence of
fashion appears likely to reassert its stranglehold on the spending power
of the world's population. A question I will consider by the conclusion
of this chapter is how far localized expressions of fashion can be seen to
liberate the consumer from the conformity upon which it depends.

Does fashion shape social life or is it shaped by it?

The fashion industry, as Craik (1994) points out, appears to be constantly striving to be new in order to perpetuate a system of 'newness'
that depends on the desire to acquire fresh modes of fashion. Western
fashion is economically driven and as such could well be described as
'the trumpery of capitalist consumer culture' (Craik, 1994: 6). But a key
concern here is the balance that operates in the realm of consumption
between the application of meaning in the context of fashion and the
process of constant economic exchange and its ideological dimension.
Fashion is undoubtedly a product of capitalist enterprise and cultural
expressions of that enterprise. But the question that fascinates Craik
(1994) is why it is that, despite being aware of the stereotyping and
falsity characterized by the fashion industry and its advertising, women,
and increasingly men, are prepared to get involved with the wares and
the glamour that surround that industry as a whole.
     Craik argues that fashion has become a dominant system in the sense
that obsolescence has become a key feature of contemporary forms of

fashion. The variety that the fashion industry did come to offer came to satisfy market niches, but only through the development of cheap synthetic fibres, mass production providing the consumer with an illusion of exclusivity and quality (Craik, 1994: 212). What Craik describes is therefore a highly exploitative industry – an industry that exploits both the worker and the consumer, in terms of working conditions and the artificial differentiation between product lines. In this environment, the licensing of the name of designers has, in recent years, become a profitable business. Meanwhile, an equally profitable business in counterfeits has emerged which leaves the industry in a difficult position in so far as such developments advertise the designer's name, while arguably increasing sales of the original as a form of inverted advertising.

> Once again, counterfeit emphasises the distinction between the hand-finished and the mass-produced item, either elevating the status of the former or revealing little difference between the 'real' thing and the fake. Indeed, counterfeiting is merely an overt form of the practice of prestigious imitation on which the fashion industry is based – namely, the popularisation of a new style or idea by its modification and differentiation for different markets. (Craik, 1994: 213)

In this climate, fashion has emerged as the everyday norm. Indeed, Craik (1994: 225) argues that, at least to an extent, clothes create the parameters of a person's living environment: 'At a collective level fashion maps social conduct and, in turn, is shaped by it. Fashion statements appear to mark a moment, but the fashioned body is never secure or fixed. The body is constantly re-clothed and re-fashioned in accordance with changing arrangements of self.' The point here is that it is actively in the interests of consumer capitalism to ensure that such arrangements are never fixed. Fashion may shape social conduct, but it is consumerism that shapes fashion and the ideology of consumerism that permeates everyday life.

If we accept that fashion shapes social conduct, it is clearly necessary to consider an illustration of a form of consumption that operates in this context. To this end, Susan Willis's (1990) discussion of the fitness industry as a realm of fashion consumption, and its relationship to the construction of gender relations, is particularly useful. Willis argues that the consumption of exercise, which was particularly fashionable during the 1980s, represents a partial, not to say paradoxical, victory in women's struggle for equality with men. During the 1980s, exercise became a consumer-based experience within which the consumer purchased the latest Jane Fonda workout video and bought the most fashionable leggings or exercise step. Willis argues that this new wave of fitness fashion was liberating for women in the sense that it contrasted with earlier visions of macho male exercisers, while presenting images of women as successful, independent, enterprising and fulfilled individuals. But Willis also suggests that, while the fitness fashion allowed women to take control of their bodies, it also simultaneously obliged women to define themselves *through* their bodies. As a result, the fitness workout could be seen to substantiate male domination inasmuch as men, unlike women, do not feel the need to proclaim themselves as gendered objects.

> Most women who appear in public *à la* exercise choose not to cover up their luminescent body socks, with blouse, skirt or dungarees. In doing so, they unashamedly define themselves as workout women. In making a public body statement, a woman affirms herself as someone who has seized control over the making and shaping of her body . . . However, all these affirmative, apparently liberatory aspects of a woman's public-exercise statement are negated by the simple fact that men do not appear in public similarly clad. (S. Willis, 1990: 7)

Women, in effect, use the fashionable opportunities that fitness provides as a means of proclaiming their gender identities, because gender provides the only means by which they define their struggle for equality. Men's identities do not need to be constructed on similar grounds precisely because they are the dominant sex. In other words, the realm of fitness illustrates quite vividly the paradoxical role that fashion can play in constructing social relations 'in a society where only one gender needs definition' (S. Willis, 1990: 8). In considering Susan Willis's (1990) work, it could therefore be argued that, though the consumption of fashion offers women hope, it also reasserts their subordination. More importantly, perhaps, that subordination is in the interests of consumer capitalism as a whole which has served to make fitness more than something people do, but something people *consume*. The point here is that people are not merely consuming products or fashions, but they are also reproducing consumerism as a legitimate way of life. By consuming the fashions associated with fitness, the dominant role of consumer capitalism is assured, as are the social relations that prop it up.

Conclusion

The overriding issue with which the above concerns seem to be related (and one that runs throughout this book) appears to be the extent to which fashion, and in turn consumerism, can provide the individual with a realm in which he or she can freely express him or herself, or whether that realm is preconceived to such an extent that any degree of individual expression becomes negligible. In this context, Simmonds (1990) asks whether or not fashion has actually been democratized as a result of mass production. Concluding quite unreservedly that this is not the case, Simmonds suggests that fashion represents an especially powerful means of creating desire and thereby extending the lifetime of the economy precisely because it has an omnipresent media and advertising profile. Indeed, 'The mere existence of fashion as an industry and integral part of capitalism means it is, by definition, undemocratic; and so further underlies the impossibility and futility of the question' (Simmonds, 1990: 136). What is fashion? How best can the sociologist conceive of fashion while avoiding the temptation to see it as little more than a tool of consumer capitalism? In this context, Lang and Lang (1965: 323) ask 'whether public taste is first manufactured and then disseminated through organized channels and foisted upon the mass or whether changes in the moods and life conditions lead to irrational and widespread changes of taste without promotion'. Indeed, they go as far as to argue that 'The world of fashion is not so much available to people as imposed upon them. In one way or another it dictates to everyone. It is contagious. Any individual group may resist a particular fashion, but fashion, as such, cannot be resisted' (1965: 323).

In considering the above arguments, fashion can in some ways be regarded as an irresistible social force, even perhaps, in some form or another, a tool of consumer capitalism, but it also gives consumers something that they want and in this respect the fashion arena is an arena that gives *and* takes. In many ways, the beauty of consumerism as ideology, as I will argue throughout the remainder of this book, is dependent upon the self-gratification that it provides the individual. In this context, in my research into the relationship between youth consumption and the construction of identity, I found the consumption of 'retro' forms of sportswear to be especially fascinating (Miles, 1995, 1996). By buying into this particular fashion, young people feel part of something; they feel as if they belong to a mini subculture of consumption. Yet, on the other hand, they also feel that they can express their individuality by wearing a different colour of retro trainer compared with that of their peers. Young consumers appear, in general, to be fully aware of the structural pressures, notably in the form of the media and advertising, which are intended to influence their consumption patterns. But, ultimately, they are willing to trade a certain sense of individuality that is inevitably lost through consumption in order to secure a sense of stability in what is in many respects an unstable world. In a world where transitions into adulthood are extended and the job market is increasingly uncertain, consumption provides young people with some semblance of stability in what Beck (1992) describes as a 'risk society'. This is an issue to which I will return in Chapter 9. All I want to say at this stage is that fashion, perhaps more so than any other social arena, serves to reinforce ideologies of consumerism. But this is not purely in the interests of consumer capitalism alone. Fashion is not a trivial matter as far as the individual is concerned, but often plays an active and positive role in his or her life. The problem is that this creates a perpetual cyclical process within which consumerism fails to offer the luxuries and freedoms that it appears to promise and yet simultaneously offers *enough* to ensure that the consumer continues to crave for more.

The argument that fashion provides a framework of convention is, in this sense, an appealing one. There may well be evidence, as Davis (1992) suggests, of continued tensions between global and local expressions of fashion. But what is so interesting about fashion is that such localisms will always be incorporated into the fashion system as a means of fuelling the apparent diversity of such a system while retaining its bread and butter, namely the global realities of mass consumption. In this sense, fashion is indeed disciplining: 'It is a reflection of a common sensitivity and taste. Fashion then is the epiphenomenon of convention, the disciplining force of consumer choices in the face of an expanding market of alternative goods' (Minchinton, 1982: 222).

The convention that fashion offers is one that is based on a masquerade of individuality and to an extent it *can* offer the individual the sense of commonality that he or she craves. But, ultimately, it does so while portraying the illusion that consumerism can offer the consumer anything he or she wants. Fashion does not simplify choice for the consumer, but exaggerates it. Fashion 'provides for an orderly march from the immediate to the proximate future' (Minchinton, 1982: 222) inasmuch as it offers the individual well-channelled routes of consumption all of which seem to be uniquely individualistic. In fact, these routes are essentially pre-ordained by consumerism itself. The illusion is created that the answer to all an individual's problems can be found in the marketplace, when all that marketplace can do is offset those problems temporarily. There is no doubt, as Giddens (1991: 200) argues, that 'standardisation can often be turned into a mode of creating individual qualities . . . Mass produced clothing still allows individuals to decide selectively on styles of dress, however much the standardizing influence of fashion and other forces, affect those individual decisions', but, ultimately, such selective decision-making is expressed through the constraints enforced by a set menu. That menu was chosen by consumer capitalism (see Chapter 9). It is actually in the interests of consumer capitalism, as Craik (1994) implies, actively to *discourage* the extent of fashion choice available to the consumer. Too much diversity would only cripple a system that thrives on the *illusion* of choice when, in fact, the key to the successful reproduction of consumer capitalism is actually mass production. Consumers satisfy themselves that they can consume fashion as they please; in fact, they are consuming fashion as consumer capitalism pleases: along a well-trodden and easily reproduced path.

To conclude this chapter, there can be little doubt that, nearly a hundred years after the conception of his argument, Simmel's (1904: 301) contention that fashion illustrates both 'the need of union and the

need of isolation' remains highly pertinent to a discussion of consumerism as a way of life. This in itself is testament to the power of consumerism as an ideological framework. The problem is that Simmel's
arguments concerning the figurative role of money in the construction
of life have proved more prophetic than even he could have imagined.
Ultimately, the need to be an individual can only be contested within an
arena where consumerism is lauded not merely as *a* way of life but as
the way of life.

Recommended reading

Malcolm Barnard (1996) *Fashion as Communication*. London: Routledge.
   Discusses the way in which fashion communicates class, gender, sexuality
   and social identities.
Jennifer Craik (1994) *The Face of Fashion: Cultural Studies in Fashion*. London:
   Routledge. An interdisciplinary analysis of fashion as a cultural phenomenon
   which is particularly effective in discussing gendered aspects of consump-
   tion.
Fred Davis (1992) *Fashion, Culture and Identity*. London: University of Chicago
   Press. This book is especially useful in terms of developing an understanding
   of fashion as both cycle and process.
Grant McCracken (1990) *Culture and Consumption*. Bloomington, IN: Indiana
   University Press. Includes a useful discussion of theoretical aspects of the
   material properties of fashion.
Colin McDowell (1994) *The Designer Scam*. London: Hutchinson. An illuminating
   if rather populist account of goings on behind the catwalk in the fashion
   industry.
Sean Nixon (1996) *Hard Looks: Masculinities, Spectatorship and Contemporary
   Consumption*. London: UCL Press. An indepth analysis of the increasing
   significance of consumption in the construction of masculinities during the
   1980s.

7

CONSUMING POPULAR MUSIC

Is there anything more to the pop music industry than the maximization of profit and the commodification of sound? Today's music charts are dominated by image-conscious groups and 'artists', who appear, at least on the surface, to be more concerned with their 'street cred' than with the actual substance and creativity of their music. Decrying the current state of popular music is an age-old generational tradition. My parents did it; so probably did yours. But having said that, there might well be an argument for suggesting that popular music *has* reached new extremes of consumer-oriented imagery. Pop music is a commodity which can be bought and sold in the marketplace. The question is whether the consumer is being exploited as a result. In order to address this question, I will begin by briefly discussing *the music industry in context*, moving on to look at whether we should consider *popular music as protest or control*. In developing this argument, I will then consider two key questions. Can we, in fact, identify *a 'common universal pop aesthetic'*? And, to what extent do *consumers invest their own personal meanings in music*? I then look at two types of music that might be described as exceptions that prove the rule – *world music and dance music* – in a discussion of the 'authenticity' of contemporary pop music. On this basis, I come to an overall conclusion about the relationship between consumerism and popular music.

The debate here centres on how far music has become a focus for the construction of lifestyles at the expense of musical creativity and what this development, if it can be said to have occurred, says about consumerism as a way of life and about music as a realm of innovation and rebellion (Burnett, 1996). A key approach to this question, as Burnett (1996) notes, is therefore that of Marcuse (1964) who argues that an especially important characteristic of modern industrial societies is their ability to incorporate ideas within the dominant culture, such as those characteristic of rebellious aspects of popular music which could potentially serve actively to negate that culture. Regardless of the degree of rebellious content in contemporary pop music, one thing is for sure:

Pop music is now one of the most ubiquitous and evident commodities in popular culture, an accompaniment to other forms of cultural experience and stimulant to consumption. As a cultural form of great sensuousness and adaptability, pop music is a register for many of today's dominant tensions around identity, community and gender, and of their unconscious concomitants in patterns of need and phantasy. (Richards, 1994: 108)

The music industry in context

In order to contextualize the nature of pop music consumption, I will briefly consider the actual structure of the music industry. In particular, it is interesting to note that in 1994 more than 90 per cent of the gross sales of recorded music worldwide came from albums, singles and music videos owned by one of only six multinational corporations: Time Warner, Sony, Philips, Bertelsmann, Thorn-EMI and Matsushita (Burnett, 1996). The stranglehold that these companies, all of which are transnational subdivisions of powerful multinational electronics or communications conglomerates, have on the music industry is quite phenomenal. Indeed, it is fair to say that the music industry is becoming increasingly concentrated in the hands of the major players. Meanwhile, the production and sale of records, cassettes, mini and compact discs had an annual turnover in 1994 of £21 billion or $33 billion worldwide, arousing particular controversy over the apparently unnecessarily inflated price of compact discs.

The music industry is big business, the British music industry alone being worth around £2.5 billion, and will clearly do anything to maximize profits. This pandering to profit has meant that in recent years the industry has self-consciously avoided taking commercial and therefore creative risks, not least as a result of the declining popularity of the Top 40 singles charts in both Britain and the USA during the course of the 1980s. As such, Sanjek and Sanjek (1991) point out that during this period several adult-oriented radio stations employed programming consultants in order to investigate how best to maximize their audiences. Interestingly, they were advised to offer 'not what listeners actually like but what they find least offensive', and to 'play it safe, whatever you do' (1991: 249). Sanjek and Sanjek go on to note how the 1980s was a difficult decade for the music industry in general with the sale of pre-recorded cassettes dropping below $2 million or £1.3 million for the first time since 1977. In this context, the 1980s saw a series of take-overs occur which concentrated the industry into the hands of the six companies mentioned above who continue to negotiate 'non-competitive strategic alliances' as a way of avoiding the risk inherent in new ventures (Burnett, 1996: 23).

Music is a massive multimillion dollar industry not only in terms of the music produced but also in respect of the vast sums of money invested in musical hardware worldwide. In this context, Burnett (1996) describes the international music industry as a major player in processes of globalization. You have to wonder what the consequences are for the promotion of new talent, however, when record companies such as Warner Brothers are reportedly investing over $80 million in established performers such as REM, the worlds highest-paid band, over the course of a five-album contract. Is, in this sense, the diversity on offer to the consumer purely illusory? REM purport to be a radical band. Indeed, lead singer Michael Stipe ironically goes as far as to proclaim on the track 'King of Comedy' on the 1994 album 'Monster' that, 'I'm no commodity.' Despite this sentiment, critics might well argue that far from being innovative REM's respective albums merely tread a well-worn path which, in turn, amounts to a 'formula' that sells records in large quantities.

The problem here seems to be that the music industry is more concerned with protecting the assets it already has than providing the consumer with the diversity that he or she may or may not crave. Yes, independent labels control between 5 and 10 per cent of market sales, enabling 'the inquisitive consumer to sample forms of music the majors have avoided or denigrated' (Burnett, 1996: 259), but ultimately these labels do not have the power or the resources to compete on an equal basis.

Capital invested in REM is capital not invested elsewhere, and in this context you have to wonder if the industry is protecting the best interests of the consumers it serves. Far from extending the boundaries of musical diversity and creativity, at least on the surface the music industry appears to be an industry intent on risk limitation. In this context, it may well be argued that music is no longer a realm within which consumers can generally express their discomfort with dominant social orders.

Popular music as protest or control?

David Rowe (1995), in his book *Popular Cultures*, points out that the dual activities of formulating music and generating capital have produced continuing disputes over the nature and control of popular music. Such disputes arguably came to a head during the 1980s and, in this context, often focus upon the question of authenticity. As such, Rowe acknowledges a long tradition whereby rock history has been characterized as the continued subordination of singers, musicians and composers to the imperatives of capitalism. In this respect, punk rock, which started as an underground movement characterized by the early days of the Clash, provides a useful illustration, converging as it did into an influential musical movement and finally becoming a sanitized form of commercial pop, as heard in the sounds of such bands as the Buzzcocks.

One of the most important contributors to the above debate is undoubtedly Theodor Adorno in collaboration with Max Horkheimer. Horkheimer and Adorno (1973) discuss the 'mass deception' that they see as being perpetuated by the culture industry which ensures that consumers are compelled to buy and use its products despite the fact that, at least at a superficial level, they see through them. Their argument is that capitalist production in effect comes to control people's lives, so much so that they have no choice but to accept what the resultant social system has to offer. Stressing the commodified nature of popular music, Adorno (1990) argues that pop music has degenerated to the extent that it never actually creates new ideas, preferring instead to regurgitate old ones in a safe and predictable fashion. In this context, it is interesting to note that Oasis, one of the biggest selling bands in the world, are continually compared, often critically, to the sound of the Beatles.

During the mid-1990s and despite the death of John Lennon, the Beatles themselves underwent a tremendously lucrative revival with the re-mastered reproduction of several collections of their records as well as new recordings such as 'Free as a Bird' upon which, with a technological slight of hand, the voice of John Lennon was superimposed. Despite not existing as a band as such, in 1994 the Beatles earned £10 million from records and music publishing. This in the year *before* their big marketing push when several CDs were released alongside television documentaries and books as part of the re-emergence of a full-scale Beatles' industry. As Davidson (1995: 11–12) puts it, 'Now the Beatles are cashing in, exploiting ostensibly, the pent-up demand of their fans for new products.' Meanwhile, Davidson (1995) points out that the American television network ABC allegedly paid $20 million for the privilege of showing the six-hour documentary series, *Beatles Anthology*, while *Forbes* magazine estimates that the project as a whole, including television, CDs, videos and books will earn the Beatles more than $100 million in total (Davidson, 1995: 12).

Perhaps the remaining members of the Beatles were encouraged by the continued success of ageing rockers the Rolling Stones, who were touted during their 1995 tour as 'The greatest rock band in the world', despite Wroe's (1995: 12) dismissal of the band as 'glamorous car salesmen'. This comment was not meant to be a slight upon the quality of the Rolling Stones 'product' or the possibility that the band might be past its best, but rather a dig at the fact that, to coincide with their 1995 European tour, sponsors Volkswagen launched what they described as 'the fabulous new Volkswagen Golf Rolling Stones collection'. This limited edition car comes emblazoned with its own Rolling Stones logo and the band's name stitched into the seat fabric (see Wroe, 1995: 12). At the time Volkswagen estimated that they would sell 150,000 Rolling Stones cars at a mere £16,000 a time. Clearly, the intention on the part of Volkswagen was to tap a relatively young, loyal and generally affluent audience and at the cost of a mere £6 million which is how much the company invested in the tour. The band itself sold 6.5 million tickets at the cost of a cool £100 million, a figure that rocketed with the additional benefit of merchandise sales.

What is of interest here is the fact that the Rolling Stones can still command such massive sponsorship and that a big enough audience is still out there to justify Volkswagen's investment. The company is clearly banking on the long-term appeal of the Stones and the massive following they have collected over the years. But are these ageing rockers really producing the best sounds and performances currently available in the world of rock music or is it indeed formula, predictability and nostalgia that the consumer is buying into (see Burnett, 1996)? It is in this sort of context that Horkheimer and Adorno (1973: 134) argue that:

> [Capitalist] culture consists of repetition. That its characteristic innovations are never anything more than improvements in mass production is not external to the system. It is with good reason that the interest of the innumerable consumers is directed to technique, and not to the contents – which are stubbornly repeated, outworn, and by now half-discredited.

As far as Horkheimer and Adorno (1973) are concerned, as Longhurst (1995) notes, popular music is interchangeable. In particular, it depends on a process of 'pseudo-individualization' whereby the essential structure of popular music always remains the same with very slight changes in detail serving to appeal to the taste of the consumer, thereby convincing him or her of the individuality of his or her choice (Longhurst, 1995: 5). Thus, from this point of view, popular music becomes produced in a uniform fashion as a means of standardizing audience reaction while maximizing economic dividends. The standardization of music has a distinct ideological function in so far as it makes the consumer more pliant, a passive subject for the purpose of programmed consumption. Thus, Adorno (1990) speaks of the reification and fetishization of music in its commodity form. Music is reified in the sense that the process robs the consumer of any real pleasure, while offering a standardized and essentially inauthentic product.

One vivid example of this formulaic approach to pop music is the 'boy band' phenomenon which really took off in the United States during the late 1980s and early 1990s with groups like New Edition and New Kids on the Block and more recently with Take That who had considerable chart success, notably in Britain where they achieved eight number one hits. As a result of the latter's influence on the charts, there has been an explosion of 'boy bands'. Record executives recognized the economic potential of what up to then had been a largely untapped niche market occupied by young adolescent girls keen to watch attractive young men singing and dancing to catchy pop tunes. One of the more extreme examples of the manufactured nature of such bands is surely that of Upside Down, who had limited chart success in Britain during the mid-1990s after they were first brought to the British public's attention in a BBC television documentary *Inside Story* which portrayed how the band was put together. Perhaps a more appropriate word to use here is 'manufactured' in that the main criteria for membership of the band appeared to be the degree to which the overall package would appeal as a *product* to a female teenage audience who are apparently more concerned with the sexuality and image of the bands they consume than their musical talent.

Despite bands like Upside Down fitting in with Horkheimer and Adorno's (1973) conception of the formulated nature of modern music, their rather elitist approach has been criticized on several counts, these criticisms being most effectively summarized by Longhurst (1995). In particular, Longhurst (1995: 12) quotes Middleton's (1990) suggestion that music can never simply be a product reducible to exchange value as, to whatever degree, it always has at least some form of artistic value. This appears to be a reasonable suggestion albeit one that focuses on the production side of the equation. The question is: how far is the actual consumption of music, in itself, a creative artistic experience?

Middleton (1990) argues that the music industry is actually more complex than authors like Horkheimer and Adorno (1973) suggest and that, in turn, actual musical forms are more diverse than they might be prepared to admit. In particular, there is more choice available now than when Horkheimer and Adorno undertook their original work during the 1930s and 1940s, while the meanings with which consumers endow popular music are not as prescribed as they suggest. Indeed, the variety of pop music available in the marketplace and the choice that this engenders might be said to undermine the sorts of generalizations characteristic of Horkheimer and Adorno's work. For instance, it may well be that consumers who listen to Upside Down may have very different reasons to do so compared to those who prefer Iron Maiden. In this respect, Horkheimer and Adorno's approach is dangerous in so far as it underestimates the lived cultures of everyday social relations. How far the nature of this experience, regardless of the ways in which it is played out, continues to be determined by the ideological imperatives of consumer capitalism is very much open to debate.

Is there a 'common universal pop aesthetic'?

In discussing the above issues, Simon Frith (1988), one of the most cited commentators on the evolution of pop, talks about the industrialization of music and, in particular, the constant conflict that consumers feel between music-as-expression and music-as-commodity and how this effectively defines the twentieth-century pop experience. That is, however much consumers use its products, people retain a sense that the music industry is first and foremost an essentially bad thing and that they are inevitably being manipulated by the global sounds of Dire Straits, for example. In effect, consumers cannot help but think that music is alienating in the sense that it involves the taking of a creative act and the artificial transformation of that act into a commodity. 'What is bad about the music industry is the layer of deceit and hype and exploitation it places between us and our creativity' (Frith, 1988: 12).

But Frith (1988) makes an important point when he says that this common-sense approach forgets that the industrialization of music is not something that happens to music *per se*, but is actually a form of communication which determines what songs, singers and performers are and can be. In other words, performers cannot exist independently of the industrial process in that they are a product of that process and, in turn, cannot be assessed from any other perspective. Having said that, Frith bemoans the monopoly of prepackaged acts and argues that the most important development in this respect was the emergence of the pop video which passed more power in determining which records actually made the charts directly into the hands of the record companies. Music that makes 'good pop television', as Frith (1988) notes, is music that will sell. Indeed, he goes as far as to argue that 'the rise of the pop video has been dependent on and accelerated the decline of the ideology of youth-as-opposition' (Frith, 1988: 213). Frith (1989: 2–3) therefore argues that the holy grail of authentic pop music is beyond the reach of the consumer inasmuch as the world of pop music has become predetermined by a 'universal pop aesthetic'. The diverse sounds of music on the margins, such as 'world music', which I will discuss in more detail below, therefore come to have particular appeal precisely because they are an exception to a rule which has seen pop music in general become increasingly uniform. On the other hand, and more recently, Frith (1992: 74) has conceded the fact that:

> The industrialization of music hasn't stopped people from using it to express private joys or public griefs; it has given us new means to do so, new ways of having an impact, new ideas of what music can be. Street music is certainly an industrial noise now, but it's a human noise too so it is perhaps fitting to conclude that the most exciting and political music of the early 1990s should be the hip-hop sounds of young urban black bands like Public Enemy, groups that are heavily dependent on both the latest technology and street credibility.

A key issue here, then, is how far consumers can construct their own meanings in the context of the music produced for them by the music industry. Earlier in his career, Frith (1983) carried out some research on the make-up of young consumers of music, concluding that those individuals and groups that most stressed the degree of individual choice in the context of music also stressed the importance of shared

musical tastes (see also Longhurst, 1995). Such groups felt that they
personally transcended the mass tastes of the music scene in general
and yet depended upon their peers for confirmation of that fact. This is
a key point and one that was equally relevant to my discussion of
fashion in Chapter 6. Such a process is symptomatic of the ideological
influences of consumerism as a way of life. In effect, consumption offers
consumers a framework within which they can construct a sense of
identity; that sense of identity ultimately being subject to wider structural forces such as the impact of the media or advertising – forces that
tend to be reproduced through the more immediate concern for acceptance in a group setting. In order to become accepted, young consumers
have to consume what is perceived to be acceptable taste and must
often buy peer-acceptable music, which in this sense is barely individualistic at all. In this light, as Longhurst (1995) points out, Frith
(1990) criticizes his own work for underestimating the role of consumption in the creation of musical meaning. Ultimately, however, as
Frith's (1983) work so clearly illustrates, such meaning can only be
partially agentic. Indeed, the influence of the major players in the music
industry is such that a creative consumer is the very last thing that the
industry wants to encourage. In effect, the music industry, much like
the fashion industry, self-consciously 'fears . . . an active audience,
whose tastes can't be predicted, whose use of music can't be completely
controlled' (Frith, 1983: 270).

In his book, *Producing Pop*, Keith Negus (1992) focuses on the discovery and development of recording artists, looking in particular at the
personnel within the music industry and how they actively contribute
to or construct the 'sounds and images of pop' (1992: vi). Pointing out
that pop music arises from a constant dialogue between production and
consumption, Negus argues that the pop music industry is, in turn,
characterized by a constant *negotiation* between commerce and
creativity. In this context, he does not believe that commerce is bad
for art, but that the industry itself is a very risky environment for all
those concerned – commercial failure resulting in potentially severe
human costs. Negus does recognize, however, that marketing staff
within the industry must actively construct consumers as identifiable
markets and therefore quotes Middleton (1990: 249) who argues in turn
that:

> We do not choose our musical tastes freely; nor do they reflect our
> 'experience' in any simple way. The involvement in subjects in particular
> musical pleasures has to be constructed . . . subjects themselves . . . have a
> role to play (of recognition, assent, refusal, comparison, modification); but it is
> an articulatory, not a simplistically creative or responsive role.

In this respect, the visual image of a performer is paramount and, as
such, record companies are obliged to have some degree of control over

the image of their artists, the video playing a particularly important role as a vehicle for presenting image above substance. As Negus (1992) points out, the dominance of imagery in modern pop music is illustrated by the way in which different genres of music have become associated with different modes of dress (for example, the heavy metal rocker with long hair and leather; the rap artist with training shoes and baseball cap); visual images that appear to confirm to the individual wearer that an artist or genre actually represents or reflects his or her personality in some way. In this sense, images rather than musical content are the most powerful means of reinforcing an artist's musical identity. Having said that, Negus (1992: 70) suggests that debates over the authenticity of an artist are also paramount 'for the very practical reason that an artist has to live with their image and carry it convincingly in a range of settings . . . Not only does the artist have to be comfortable with and committed to their image in some way, but the audience has to believe it.'

In some ways Negus's analysis of the music industry is inherently paradoxical. For instance, when discussing the 'branding' of artists, far from suggesting an equal two-way relationship, he actually tends to imply that the music industry holds far more cards than the actual consumer. Negus (1992: 71–2) quotes a senior executive in the music industry:

> You try and brand the artist, in the way that U2 are branded. The most brilliant corporate branding I have ever seen, without anyone ever thinking that they were being corporately got. Brilliant. You never saw a picture of U2 if it wasn't in front of the joshua tree. Bono was out there [clenches fist]. He was an okay kind of guy because he was saying the right things. I say this as a huge U2 fan. Brilliant piece of marketing.

An equally important part of the production of pop music is the targeting of a market, notably by age range. Between the 1950s and the 1970s, pop music was specifically targeted at an age range between 15 and 24. As a result of demographic change, however, this age group has declined as a total percentage of the population, as has the nature of the pop music consuming public. What has emerged is an expanding market of middle-aged music buyers and the industry has had to adapt as a result. Hence, the continued success of the Rolling Stones. Negus argues that this reflects a general trend towards the segmentation of consumer markets elsewhere. While, on the one hand, the music industry appears to divide its audience into market segments in order to construct identifiable markets, on the other Negus insists that this basically amounts to a process of negotiation:

> Music is not simply received as sound, but through its association with a series of images, identities and associated values, beliefs and affective desires.

> Marketing staff are acutely aware of this and strategically attempt to create these links – between the music and the image, and between the artist and the consumer. (Negus, 1992: 79)

Negus therefore concludes that greater attention needs to be paid to interactions between the music industry and its consumers inasmuch as pop music is the product of tensions between corporate strategists, artists and audiences.

Do consumers invest their own meanings in music?

Despite the above arguments, an individual can invest a wide variety of meanings in a piece of popular music. He or she may see it as an investment, a source of relaxation, a source of happiness or perhaps as a means of reinforcing his or her identity by, for instance, signposting that individual as a heavy metal fan (Longhurst, 1995: 243).

Longhurst (1995) goes on to debate how far pop fans can actually be productive. To this end, he discusses the work of John Fiske (1992) who notes that consumers can be semiotically productive through the sense of identity that they construct around music and how they communicate that to others. Fans may also be textually productive by circulating literature within the fan community itself. For example, a fan might draw or write about pop musicians placing them in unfamiliar contexts as they do so, thereby providing a basis for discussion with other fans. In this context, Paul Willis (1990) sees young people as being very adept at the symbolic work of developing their own styles and of reading off and decoding musical orientations in the construction of an overall lifestyle. If a particular type of music does not fit that lifestyle then it will be rejected; hence the demise of Upside Down whose sales may well have suffered as a result of their potential fan-base perceiving them to be overly manufactured. From this point of view, music can be seen to be creatively consumed in five major ways: first, listening and buying; secondly, home taping; thirdly, interpreting sounds; fourthly, dance; and finally, interpreting songs and symbols. In this context, the personal stereo plays a key role in the construction of personal 'soundscapes' (P. Willis, 1990: 64).

Bearing in mind Willis's contribution to this debate, Longhurst (1995) discusses the productivity and creativity of young people's music consumption, emphasizing as he does so the complex interrelationships that exist between musical production and consumption. It is very important from this point of view actively to set about contextualizing music in its social context. As Longhurst (1995) argues, the consumption of Madonna and her music is a case in point. Some consumers may see Madonna as little more than a pornographic pin-up for male consumption; others may argue that she is an empowering role model for young women. Such decisions are actively made by consumers themselves and, as such,

> even what seem to be the most commodified products of the culture industry need to be examined in their social contexts of production and consumption before any judgements of value can even begin to be made. I am suspicious of accounts which 'write off' whole forms of music because they do not seem to conform to traditional standards of high art or because they have mass appeal. (Longhurst, 1995: 251)

In effect, Longhurst acknowledges that the consumption of pop music is a complex and essentially *interactive* process. In discussing Warde's (1992) contribution to debates over consumption, Longhurst (1995) points out that music is consumed through a diversity of social relations and that, in this context, consumers of popular music are, at the very least, *potentially* powerful.

> [I]t is possible to trace a process by which someone who begins as a relatively passive consumer of pop music becomes a communal producer. As music affects them they become more interested in particular types of music. They may define themselves (or be defined by others) as a fan, and begin to use arguments about authenticity to defend their tastes in arguments concerning music with other people. They may be enthusiastic enough to form their own band with other like-minded people. This band might rehearse in facilities which are part-sponsored by the local state as part of an attempt to use cultural production to stimulate the local economy. This might lead to the production of new records which are then sold locally or on the international market, moving into the commercial sector . . . general theories which suggest simple relations between the dimensions of production, textual structure and consumption are likely to prove increasingly unhelpful in a future of increased cultural complexity and fragmentation. (Longhurst, 1995: 247)

There is, indeed, an argument for suggesting that the extent to which the music industry actively sets about controlling its consumers is exaggerated. As David Rowe (1995: 18) points out in his discussion of rock music, 'Even attempts to define rock as a particular musical style are undermined by the diverse musics which claim the rock label or have had it affixed to them, so that today rock increasingly appears to be more of an expedient market niche than a deep-rooted, significant cultural form.' Despite these sentiments, Rowe warns against over-deterministic analyses of the relationship between rock or popular music and capitalist production which he sees as tending to under-estimate the instabilities characteristic of contemporary forms of capitalism. He goes on to suggest that it is quite simply misguided to describe the social relations entailed in the production of pop music as a straightforward product of the logic of commodification and uses the prominence of independent labels to illustrate this point. Rowe argues that during the late 1970s and early 1980s the music industry experienced a period of considerable flux which resulted in a 'crisis' in rock economics, culture and politics. In particular, Rowe notes that many commentators see the increase in independent rock activity as reflecting a sea-change whereby consumers have become increasingly dissatisfied with what the major labels can offer them. In effect, independent labels were prepared to take more risks. In reality, the independents exploited a period during the early 1980s when the majors were financially vulnerable due to overcapacity, falling sales, rising costs, high overheads and rigid organizational practices (Rowe, 1995: 40). What is therefore seen to emerge in this context is not only a shift in the economic balance of forces, but also a significant cultural and ideological transformation of the consumption of pop music.

Rowe (1995) therefore points out that it is possible to conceive of a consumer symbolically escaping through music while remaining subject to the structures of transnational economies. As such, a shift in the production practices employed by the music industry has apparently seen the emergence of an increasingly post-Fordist regime of niche marketing and sub-contracting which has made the major record companies increasingly flexible. Meanwhile, music retailers have become increasingly responsive to consumers' needs (see du Gay and Negus, 1994). Though Rowe's (1995) analysis of the implications of these developments is somewhat limited, his work clearly shows that it is probably too much of a simplification to suggest that the music industry simply exploits consumers. The complicated balance of power that exists between producers and consumers is well illustrated by the recent history of the independent labels, many of whom have been bought up by the majors. In recent years, labels, much like bands, appear to have become branded, so much so that, having bought an independent label, a major label will often retain the name of the independent in order to ensure the brand loyalty of consumers. Meanwhile, major labels also create their own subdivisions or pseudo-independent labels in order to attract a particular segment of the market; a good example is Oasis's relationship with Creation records, a subsidy of Sony, which none the less retains the street-cred of its original name. For the consumers of many 'indie' bands, the idiosyncratic identity of the label is important in their relationship with the music concerned. 'Indie-kids' may take a lot of pride in the fact that their favourite band can be perceived to be more autonomous and creative than the majority of the 'pop fodder' available on the market. Yet, ironically, such independence is often a façade which amounts to little more than a sophisticated marketing ploy on the part of the majors.

In this context, the extent to which pop music can express any resistance to dominant orders must be limited. Significantly, more often than not political rock (for example, Manic Street Preachers 'Generation

Tourists') is perceived, notably by critics in the music press, as being little more than clichéd. In the end, political protest has a limited role to play in contemporary expressions of pop music. This point is reinforced by one of the musicians interviewed by Rowe (1995: 75):

> But there's always that danger of pushing yourself into too much of a dilemma and making yourself look a real hypocrite because you're in the marketplace just as anyone else, you know. Your job, not your job, but your preoccupation, is to sell records, you know, and by doing that you're involved in like capitalist processes as much as anyone else. It's the degree of autonomy you can do whilst achieving that end that's important, really retaining your integrity.

Although in the end the music industry *is* characterized by more dynamism than a deterministic analysis of relations to the mode of production can account for, inevitably it is the music industry itself that lays down and restricts the guidelines within which consumers can exercise their own degrees of creativity and dynamism.

World music and dance music

In the interests of extending this debate, which appears to focus on the question of the authenticity of popular music, I want briefly to consider two types of music which might be said not to conform to a rigid conception of the ideological role of popular music: world music and dance music.

J. Barnett (1996) discusses the emergence in recent years of 'world music', an umbrella term which was invented in 1987 to represent an eclectic and diverse style of marginal forms of music with some form of mainstream appeal. The emergence of such a category is seen by J. Barnett (1996) to represent a general trend towards diversification in an oversaturated pop market. Indeed,

> aspects of the production of World Music tend to be overstated to collude with the fantasy that the recordings represent unmediated cultural experiences. The star system – an essential factor in the pop domain – scarcely applies to World Music artists, because they are pressured to be spontaneously 'being themselves' rather than taking on performative roles, and because their lifestyles are not considered parallel to the aspirations of the music audience. (J. Barnett, 1996: 240)

In this respect, it might be suggested that world music performers have more of a proactive role in the recording process than their mainstream counterparts. They apparently have an inherent left-wing dissatisfaction with modernism and a desire to address the alienation of Western society (J. Barnett, 1996). Kershaw (1991: 63) goes as far as to suggest that 'World Music is constituted as the ideological antithesis of "mass produced corporate pop"'. The marginal status of world music might therefore be seen to appeal to a more critical and creative audience than that described by Horkheimer and Adorno (1973).

Another type of music that might be discussed in a similar vein is 'dance' which can itself be divided into various subcategories such as 'jungle', 'techno' or 'swingbeat'. Interestingly, Thornton (1995) considers dance music in the context of musical authenticity. Noting that authenticity has historically been associated with live performance, Thornton points out that, as recorded music has become increasingly influential, records come to command their own form of authenticity, so much so that under these conditions it would seem that the mass-produced cultural commodity is not necessarily imitative or artificial, but plausibly archetypal and authentic (Thornton, 1995: 26–27).

Dance music is thus seen to be authentic inasmuch as it is integral to a particular subculture. In this sense, new technologies act as a catalyst to innovations in authenticity. More specifically, the buzz created in British dance clubs through the interrelationships between records, DJs and dancers create 'subcultural authenticities', which are symbolized by the excitement generated in and around a rave (Thornton, 1995: 30). Thornton describes dance music as characteristically experimental. Dance records are sought after for their rarity. Foreign imports are particularly prestigious, while 'the ideological vagaries of music genres like their communication of bodily "soul" or their revelation of technology play a main role in whether [dance] records come across as genuine' (Thornton, 1995: 66). The DJ plays a formative role in dance music as a mixer and innovator of sound. In this context, Thornton (1995) argues that 'house' records are not recordings of performances, but are actively performed by the DJ him or herself, allowing spontaneity, surprise and creativity.

The spontaneity of the event and the spontaneity of sound (and its relationship to drug culture) are the key to any experience of dance, in that it is more than a mere type of music, but represents a subcultural experience. What is perhaps most important about rave culture, for instance, is that it is selfconsciously non-political. Dance music in general purposefully avoids a political critique in favour of a search for pure escape. Dance music is political only in the sense that it is selfconsciously non-political (see Rietveld, 1993). Dance is therefore seen to be remarkable in so far as it incorporates a complex interaction between the body, nature and technology, a world where consumption arguably becomes a personal experience rather than an afterthought of capitalist production. Such arguments again serve as a critique of some of Adorno's theories. Dance is seen to be an escape from everyday reality. It is not the commodification of sound that is going on here apparently, but the appropriation of sound as a means of escape from the everyday world which consumerism inhabits.

My suggestion is that world music and dance music are, in the above respects, exceptions that prove the rule. Both world music and dance are, in some respects, anti-commercial. The notoriety of a DJ, for instance, is often based on his reputation rather than any image that may have been constructed around him, while people who listen to world music are often consumers of artists with very little chart success and high standards of musicianship. The same cannot be said, however, of the vast majority of popular music available to consumers in the marketplace.

Conclusion

Having discussed the work of some of the major contributors to debates over the authenticity of popular music, and having briefly looked at examples of music that might claim to be free from the ideological imperatives of consumerism, what might we conclude about the role that pop music plays in our experience of consumerism as a way of life? The first point I would like to make, in this context, is that although it might be accepted that some types of music are less prone to commercialization than others, in the final analysis the product that artists produce will inevitably be tempered by the demands of consumer capitalism. Dance music may well be characterized by an innovative localized culture backed up by technological developments, but ultimately any mixes that a DJ creates are judged according to their *commercial* potential. If a DJ produces mixes that do not appeal to consumers in general, then he or she will not attract the work that he or she wants. Creativity is inevitably tempered by the demands of the marketplace. Indeed, it could be argued that in many ways dance, which was once a subversive underground movement, has actually been commandeered by the mainstream music industry. Having noticed that the dance scene was rapidly gaining a following, the major labels have tried to exploit the commercial potential of dance by making dance remixes of songs over which they already have control, while simultaneously poaching talent from the underground scene. What appears to be occurring here is a process whereby a genuinely creative and subversive movement is subsumed into the industry, so much so that most mainstream pop songs incorporate some form of a dance drumbeat.

As far as world music is concerned, it might well be argued that the designation of such a label merely represents a means of giving diverse types of music a quasi-common identity, in order that they are saleable in the marketplace. This provides world music with a market niche precisely because it brings with it an air of authenticity that other types of music cannot achieve. It commands such a niche because other types of music are in some respects inauthentic, but need to comply with the sorts of labels associated with this inauthenticity if they are to survive in the same commercial arena. It is in this sense that world music is an exception that proves the rule of inauthenticity.

Some of Lash and Urry's (1994) arguments, which among other things consider the role pop music plays in patterns of late capitalism, are of particular interest here (see Rowe, 1995: 47). They argue that in recent years pop music has become more and more about the selling of a brand, which is personified in the artist who has already been established in the marketplace. This process therefore takes the focus off the creative object itself and puts it onto the artist, creating an environment in which the image of the artist becomes far more important than the songs that he or she produces. Michael Jackson is a good example of how a performer's image or the cult of his or her personality becomes commodified. The same might be said of Madonna whose forays into the worlds of art and cinema have tended to upstage her music, while providing a springboard from which her music attracts increasing media and consumer attention. The prioritization of image in pop music is further illustrated by the increasing influence of MTV (music television) on the industry as a whole. Indeed, as Wollen (1986) points out, many commentators go as far as to credit MTV, the ultimate promoter of music videos, with responsibility for the resurgence of the music industry in the USA. The key point here is that MTV prioritizes image over sound and thereby encourages the promotion of brand awareness over and above the quality of music. The way bands are packaged and the money invested in special effects in a video format have almost become more important than the songs themselves. Sanjek and Sanjek (1991) note that new acts debuting on MTV enjoy an increase in sales of between 10 and 15 per cent. Companies are therefore prepared to spend large sums of money in signing exclusivity contracts with MTV in order to ensure that their artists have the best chance of being in 'heavy rotation' and that they are therefore seen by the biggest audiences available.

Many commentators see MTV as having a negative impact, both in the way it promotes consumerism in such an unadulterated fashion and in the extent to which it constructs false images of physical perfection in the form of a mass-mediated spectacle. It has also been criticized for restricting musical diversity (Goodwin, 1992). Goodwin does go on to argue that the role of 'good looks' in promoting a band's video career is generally exaggerated, but by the same token he also acknowledges the suggestion that music video works ideologically against non-market solutions to social problems and, as such, serves to sustain dominant power relations.

The overall implication here is that the pop music industry is producing products that appeal to a mass market; products that conform to a standardized, rationalized formula and that, as such, pop music is irredeemably commercial. There is no doubt that this is part of a long-term historical process, as Goodwin (1992) notes. However, the evidence seems to suggest that the commodification of pop music has been taken to extremes in recent years. Note the popularity of tribute bands such as the Australian Doors, No Way Sis, the Bootleg Beatles and Bjorn Again. The pop music market is surely going a step too far when, Hysteria, who have discovered a niche as a tribute band to Def Leppard, which in itself might seem somewhat strange, advertise for a one-armed drummer in order to ensure absolute authenticity (Inverdale, 1997)! Tribute bands are safe because they do not require much imagination on the part of the consumer. What is worrying is not only that such predictability sells concert tickets, but that in turn the music industry is not prepared to take the risks to challenge the imagination of consumers. A cyclical process therefore develops within which the dominant order is reproduced and where the big six record companies retain what is virtually monopolistic control.

Consumers are not dupes of the capitalist system, but they can only consume creatively within the parameters laid down by the music industry. Such parameters are often unsavoury in nature. For instance, Goodwin (1992) discusses the particularly unfortunate nature of many music videos which in order to gain the attention of the male audience have denied the subjectivity of women by repeatedly depicting them as helpers, assistants, groupies and, most often, as sexual objects. These sorts of images sell records in a male-dominated industry. Meanwhile, the extent to which Madonna challenges the traditional role of gender in the realm of musical production and consumption remains open to question. The same can also be said of the Spice Girls who emerged towards the end of the 1990s as a major marketing phenomenon and as a living example of the power of image in the pop industry. Carefully put together as an amalgam of five distinct images, the Spice Girls were 'manufactured' by the major record label, Virgin, with the intention of attracting as wide an audience as possible. Masquerading under the banner of a distinctive brand of pseudo-feminist ideology known as 'girl power', the band's overt sexuality is equally appealing to the male consumer. Catchy pop tunes and relentless marketing saw the Spice Girls catapult themselves into the public consciousness over a very short period of time. The Spice Girls are a brand dependent not on public performance but on a slick marketing campaign intent on capturing the moment and maximizing its commercial potential before that moment passes. The debate as to whether girl power is a genuine political stance is questionable inasmuch as ultimately all girl power actually appears to achieve is a justification for the commodification of female sexuality and the prioritization of image over substance.

At this juncture there appears to be no real likelihood of the emergence of a new musical movement to take up the mantle of punk which, although it challenged the dominant values of rock music and presented a dissenting 'structure of feeling', ultimately entered the mainstream, lost its potency and increasingly submitted to the consumer culture that emerged during the 1980s (see Rowe, 1995: 41). Similarly, the emergence of 'Britpop' in the mid-1990s illustrates the power which the music industry can deploy in actively determining what is fashionable. Bands that previously had little in common, such as Pulp, Blur, Elastica and Oasis, were hyped through Britpop as the saviours of British guitar-playing music. The industry actively marketed a new musical movement that may in reality have only existed in the minds of music journalists and marketers, the end result being a prefabricated and more than likely short-lived renaissance of the British music scene.

In conclusion, though we can accept that the consumption of pop music is more complicated than a straightforward discussion of the immanent logic of commodification allows; pop music offers the consumer all sorts of symbolic escapes; and, at least to an extent, consumers are able to extract their own meanings from the pop music they listen to – if these factors are accepted uncritically then we run the risk of underestimating the ideological power of consumerism. To accept as a commonplace that the music industry provides the consumer with massive choice without recognizing that this choice is highly constructed and that ultimately one boy band is very much like another would be dangerous. It is precisely because consumerism allows the individual to construct his or her own meanings, while constructing consumerism as the only legitimate way of life, that we need to look into the complex interrelationships involved in the music industry in detail. New scenes such as punk and dance do, every now and then, emerge and to some degree consumers do have an active role to play in guiding the direction of musical consumption. The problem is that all too often these scenes are quickly subsumed into mainstream chart music where the values originally invested in the music become diluted in order that the 'product' can be closely controlled by the industry. In the final analysis, you cannot help but wonder how much the meanings consumers endow pop music with are liable to be eroded in a consumer culture where the image incorporated in the records you buy is considered to be more important than the reason why you bought them.

Recommended reading

Theodore Adorno (1990) 'On popular music', in Simon Frith and Andrew Goodwin (eds), *On Record: Rock, Pop and the Written Word.* pp. 301–14, London: Routledge. A classic though much criticized treatment of the popular consumption of standardized popular music in a 'mass' society.

Robert Burnett (1996) *The Global Jukebox: The International Music Industry.* London: Routledge. An illuminating analysis of the international music industry. The chapter on the consumption of popular music is especially worth reading.

Simon Frith (1988) *Music for Pleasure*. Cambridge: Polity Press. A key contribution by one of the most important commentators on the sociology of pop music.

Brian Longhurst (1995) *Popular Music and Society*. Cambridge: Polity Press. An excellent overview of the sociology of popular music which is particularly effective on the culturally productive potential of fans.

Richard Middleton (1990) *Studying Popular Music*. Milton Keynes: Open University Press. A comprehensive analysis of various theoretical and practical aspects of popular music.

Keith Negus (1992) *Producing Pop: Culture and Conflict in the Popular Music Industry*. London: Edward Arnold. Perhaps the most effective and comprehensive discussion of complex workings of the music industry.

David Rowe (1995) *Popular Cultures: Rock Music, Sport and the Politics of Pleasure*. London: Sage. Looks at rock music and sport as realms of social life that serve to express tensions between the commercial nature of popular cultural forms and their potential for resistive independence.

Sarah Thornton (1995) *Club Cultures: Music, Media and Subcultural Capital*. Cambridge: Polity Press. Makes a case for the consumption of dance music as musical creativity and subcultural expression.

Paul Willis (1990) *Common Culture*. Milton Keynes: Open University Press. An important work that looks at the situated nature of young people's cultural life, including a chapter on music and symbolic creativity.

8

CONSUMING SPORT

Sport is perhaps the single area of contemporary social life to have been most profoundly altered in recent years by the everyday impact of consumerism as a way of life. What is perhaps more interesting, as I will go on to argue during the course of this chapter, is that the processes associated with the commercialization of sport appear to be actively increasing the profile of sport as a legitimate diversion from the actualities and tensions of everyday life. The debate here centres on whether or not such developments have ideological implications for the broader impact of consumerism upon modern or (post)modern life. In this chapter, I will suggest that consumerism not only infiltrates all aspects of social life including sport, but does so in such a way as to alter the *overall* construction of that social life as well as its constituent parts.

The very essence of the sporting endeavour seems to have undergone considerable change over the past two or three decades. This reflects the continuation of a long-term trend which has seen sport as a participatory experience become superseded by sport as a spectator event. During the nineteenth century, sport increasingly took on the mantle of a team pursuit structured by team rules; while during the late nineteenth and early twentieth centuries, sports became mass-attended spectator events. In this respect, whereas sport had previously been all about actual participation in athletic competition, such participation was gradually eroded in favour of locally based spectators paying to view events. Nowadays, people's experience of sport is increasingly about participating *third* hand, through the media in general and television in particular.

During the course of the twentieth century, sport has emerged as big business to the extent, as Schlossberg (1996) notes, that in 1993 it accounted for $2.5 billion of US marketing expenditure. Sport clearly offers an attractive option to marketers and advertisers alike inasmuch as the emotional investment fans have for particular sporting teams make it a 'natural' arena for the promotion of products. As Coakley (1994) notes, companies actively seek to graft their product onto a team's image in the hope that product loyalty will emerge out of team loyalty. These sorts of commercial imperatives appeared to have gone somewhat far when, in the summer of 1997, two sponsors, Nike and Adidas, put together a two-man run-off, ostensibly to crown the fastest man in the world. What took place was a race-off between Donnovan Bailey, Olympic 100 metres champion and Michael Johnson, 200 metres gold medallist, over 150 metres. However, such an event could equally be derided as a sporting circus staged by two multinational sportswear companies desperate to gain the upper hand over their nearest competitors. Meanwhile, also during the summer of 1997, the world's most expensive soccer player, Ronaldo, speculated that he might leave one club, Barcelona, to join another, Internazionale of Milan. Ronaldo's sponsor, Nike, made a public statement to the effect that they did not approve, primarily because Nike already sponsored the world champions Brazil and were hoping to strike a similar deal with Barcelona. Eventually, the player moved regardless, but not before the fragile economic foundations of top-class sport were laid bare.

Sport clearly has a crucial role to play as a means of maintaining the health and vitality of major related industries such as the media and advertising (Rowe, 1995). The problem here, however, is that sport itself has arguably become a product to the extent that the essential character of the sporting enterprise has been lost to market imperatives. Rottenberg (1956: 249), in his discussion of baseball, neatly illustrates this point:

> Two teams opposed to each other in play are like two firms producing a single product. The product is the game, weighted from the revenues derived from its play . . . In one sense the teams compete; in another they combine in a single firm in which the success of each branch requires that it be not 'too much' more efficient than the other. If it is, output falls.

Such observations illustrate how the actual nature of sporting endeavours may actually be transformed by market interests. Not only are companies with large marketing budgets able to ride on the back of sporting success, but sport itself can be seen to have emerged quite simply as a commodity to be bought and sold in the marketplace. In this respect, Schwartz (1994) argues that sport has been allowed to develop into little more than a business intent on competing with other businesses for the leisure dollar, while the athletes themselves mercilessly pursue money at every opportunity. Such developments have clearly not occurred overnight and, as Rowe (1995) notes, many sports, notably Rugby Union, have been forced to professionalize for fear of being left on the fringes of the sporting marketplace. In this context, Coakley's (1994) suggestion that athletic performance is actively being corrupted by the need to mould sport into a product, rather than being something worth while for its own sake, has meant that sport is in danger of degenerating into nothing more than a commodified spectacle. As such, Coakley goes on to discuss the move away from an emphasis in sport on ability and the mastery of technical skills, namely an 'aesthetic orientation', to an emphasis on 'style' and the mastery of dramatic expression, namely a 'heroic orientation'. Coakley believes that what has emerged historically is a situation where there is an increasing need on the part of sports people to please naïve audiences while undermining the essence of their own sport. A particularly good example of this scenario is the move within ice skating, in recent years, towards the prioritization of crowd-pleasing, though potentially dangerous, jumps and away from the simple aesthetics of artistic impression.

If you marry the actual physical transformations sport has undergone in recent history, and the way in which marketers have exploited such changes to their own ends, then Lipsyte and Lewis's comments are worth consideration:

> As a mirror of our culture, sport now shows us spoiled fools as role models, cities and colleges held hostage and games that exist only to hawk products. And the truth and beauty of sport itself – a pleasure of the flesh to the participant, an ennobling inspiration to the spectator – seem to have been wiped off the looking glass. (quoted in Mitchell, 1995a: 10)

The key issue here centres on whether Lipsyte's vision of sport is a misguided, romantic one or whether sport has actually changed for the worse as a direct result of commercialization and commodification. In short, has a consumer ethic engulfed the sporting experience and, if so, why should we necessarily assume that this is a bad thing? After first considering the *Marxist* angle on the commodification of sport, I will go on to focus on this issue more directly in the context of the following four major areas of investigation. What is the relationship between *the Olympic Games and the consumer ethic*? In what ways does *American sport illustrate the power of consumerism*? How has *English soccer been affected by the consumer ethic*? And what *role does television play in the commodification of sport*?

Marxism and the commodification of sport

Throughout this book I have tried to outline some of the most important ways in which contemporary society has in recent years become increasingly dependent upon its relationship with the consumer ethic. It might well be said in this context that sport provides the most graphic expression of some of the ways in which this ethic appears not always to operate in the best interests of the consumer. Having said that, any approach that bemoans the current state of professional sport could be said to do nothing more than romanticize exactly what that sporting experience is all about. In this light, consider Davies's (1995: 2) thoughts on the current state of English football:

> Football should not be run like a supermarket, or Alton Towers, a Take That concert or a raincoat factory. Football is not about profit and loss. It is about glory and excitement, about loyalty and legends, about local identity and family history, about skills and talents, none of which can be computed on balance sheets. Football doesn't have a product. Every year United fans have their ashes scattered on the turf at Old Trafford. How often do you see that happening at Tescos?

Many commentators are arguably overly critical of sport as nothing more than another example of a new dimension of capitalist alienation (see Bocock, 1993). From this Marxist perspective, sport alienates not only the athlete who is exploited by the modern money-making machinery which is out of his or her control, but also the spectator, inasmuch as modern consumers are generally more and more physically *passive*. They watch sport, often from the comfort of their own living rooms, but rarely actively participate in it. They are, in effect, mentally active, yet physically *passive*. Though sports and leisure clubs are apparently increasing in popularity, the general trend appears to be away from sporting participation and towards media-based spectating. The consumption of sport therefore becomes an experience primarily located in the head. The consumption of sport is largely pre-packaged and apparently encourages the existence of a culture where lethargy is lauded as a positive attribute. As a result, the ideological dimensions of the consuming experience, as I will discuss in detail in Chapter 9, are conveniently overlooked. In this sense, it could be argued that sport plays an active role in camouflaging the excesses of consumer culture by providing a form of escape from the everyday tensions of capitalist exploitation while reinforcing the very excesses that this exploitation propagates. In other words, consumer capitalism promotes accumulation and in the process simultaneously legitimizes itself.

There is, indeed, a long Marxist tradition which sees sport as playing an important role in terms of capitalist class relations. Particularly vocal in this regard is Jean-Marie Brohm (1978) who argues that sport is essentially a class practice which is intricately geared into the mechanisms of the capitalist system. Sport must, according to Brohm, be smashed like capitalism itself. 'As the biggest mass spectacle, sport operates as an apparatus for transforming aggressive drives. Instead of expressing themselves in the class struggle, these drives are absorbed, diverted and neutralised in the sporting spectacle' (Brohm, 1978: 180). Similarly, Gruneau (1984) suggests that capitalist class interests have come to dominate sport as a business interest. By moving into the realms of sport, capitalism has served its own interests by producing new wants and discovering and creating new use-values. Some commentators, Whannel (1992) included, see this approach as inherently one-dimensional. As such, Brohm (1978) is seen to portray sport as a one-way street – a dominant ideology that remains uncontested – when, in fact, sport is a product of a complex set of interrelationships between structures of social control and the actual experiences and expressions of sporting culture. By considering the relationship between the Olympic Games and the consumer ethic, I hope to begin to shed light upon this debate.

The Olympic Games and the consumer ethic

The Olympic Games have always been synonymous with the amateur ideal. Yet, some commentators have argued, on the contrary, that in the late twentieth century the Olympics have become synonymous with a consumerist ethic. Gruneau (1984) goes as far as to contend that the commercialization of the Olympics is symbolic of a broader reduction of sport into a cross between the entertainment and light consumer-goods industries. Gruneau notes how, by associating themselves with the Olympic ideals of youthfulness, physical prowess and achievement, companies are assured of massive profits, whether through the Games' official snack bar, soft drink or beer. It is estimated, for example, that the top ten sponsors of the Atlanta Olympics alone invested $1.5 billion (Rodgers, 1996). The Olympic Games have come a considerably long way since 1912 when the American athlete Jim Thorpe was stripped of his two gold medals after officials learnt that he had once played semi-professional baseball.

Early moves towards the professionalization of the Olympics during the second half of the twentieth century were not, however, uniformly successful. For instance, over 20 years after the Games of 1976 the dire financial implications of the Montreal Olympiad are still being felt throughout the local Canadian economy. Similarly, the 1980 Olympic Games in Moscow cost somewhere between $2 billion and $9 billion, ironically putting the Olympic Organizing Committee into a situation where it simply *had* to sell itself as a commodity in order to remain financially viable (Gruneau, 1984). By 1984, the marketing potential of the five rings, and the sense of quality with which those rings were imbued, were well and truly on track as companies pursued the priceless image that the Olympics could transfer to their own products. The marketing frenzy which has come to characterize the Olympic Games is captured nicely by Rodgers's (1996) vision of the Olympic Village in Atlanta where no fewer than six McDonald's restaurants served 7,500 free meals a day, while a Burger King hot-air balloon simultaneously dominated the sky above.

It is not so much the way in which sponsors desire the attributes of the Olympic ideal to rub off on their own products that is so startling, but the way in which consumerism appears to be undermining the very fabric of the sports themselves and, in particular, the sportsmen and women who participate in them. The 'Dream Team', the US basketball team which entered the 1992 Olympics in Barcelona, provide a clear illustration of how commercial imperatives have come to dominate the Olympic experience. Detractors claim that the Dream Team, comprised of the major professional stars of the most commercially successful basketball league in the world, was merely an elaborate marketing exercise engineered in order to maximize commercial advantage for both the players and the sport alike (see Schlossberg, 1996). Ironically, in achieving the status of gold medal winners, two Dream Team players, Michael Jordan and Charles Barkley, both of whom were endorsed by Nike, refused to wear the US team's tracksuit because it was emblazoned with the logo of one of Nike's major competitor's, Reebok. Barkley, famously commented that, 'Us Nike guys are loyal because they pay us a lot of money . . . I have 2 million reasons not to wear Reebok' (Perspectives, 1992). A compromise was finally reached when the US Olympic Committee allowed the two basketball players to unzip their jackets in order to conceal the Reebok logo. This incident reflects wider concerns about the commercialization of the Games in general and the worrying trend that professional sports such as basketball, tennis and even athletics, once lauded as bastions of amateurism, are being invaded by a consumerist ideal. The following quotation from the *Chicago Tribune* (18 September 1991), which considers the commercial impact of the Dream Team, says a lot about how far the Olympics have come since the Jim Thorpe incident in 1912.

> It's the first time NBA players will compete in the Olympics, and perhaps the principal area of expansion on the NBA agenda is international. The NBA wants to sell its game and its merchandise overseas. So why not bring its biggest stars? It's a walking billboard for the NBA. And are they going to lose? . . . The talent is overwhelming and the opposition dubious. And the corporate sponsors who hire these people will be wearing the widest grins. (quoted in Schlossberg, 1996: 59)

The Olympic Games cast off any last vestiges of amateurism in 1981 when the President of the International Olympic Committee, Juan Antonio Samaranch, officially dissolved the 'pure amateur code' which many felt by this time had become unenforceable despite Samaranch's claim in the same year that 'The commercialisation of the Olympic Games will never be tolerated. They will remain the only sports event in the world where there is no advertising in the stadia or on the athletes' vests' (quoted in Whannel, 1992: 1). It is true to say that Olympic advertising is restricted inasmuch as Olympians do not partake in direct advertising during the Games themselves and advertising within the stadia is not permitted. However, to suggest that the Games have not been commercialized is to invite ridicule. The Olympic movement readily courts sponsors in the form of TV companies who invest millions of pounds and dollars in order to transmit the Games world-wide. For instance, as Lucas (1992) admits, the American television network ABC agreed to pay the International Olympic Committee a staggering $326 million in order to secure the American rights for the Winter Olympic Games in Calgary in 1988. Meanwhile, the Coca-Cola company spent $22 million in order to guarantee that no other soft drinks company could display the Olympic rings or sell their product at Olympic stadia. The athletes themselves *are* sponsored, in a way that surreptitiously subverts the International Olympic Committee's (IOC) guidelines while superficially maintaining Olympic principles of amateurism (Coakley, 1994). For instance, athletes may be seen wearing Ray-Ban sunglasses or drinking bottled Evian water in front of the cameras. In many respects, then, the Olympics appear to be an adver-tising platform first and a sporting endeavour second.

Those defending the apparent move towards the commercialization of the Olympics argue that there is no real reason why the Olympic movement should not benefit from the huge funds that multinational companies are clearly prepared to invest. Lucas (1992) argues that what is of more concern is that the Olympic movement does not merely transmute into a giant money-making machine. In this sense, Lucas (1992: 80) argues that the Olympic spirit should and indeed *is* being defended at all costs.

> The Olympic Movement, especially the IOC, is bedazzled by its new found avenues of financial opportunity and will continue exploring them for some years to come. By the millennial year 2000, the IOC will have accumulated in properties, investments, credits, and cash sufficient billions of dollars so that it can 'ease off.' It will pull back appreciably from this financial focus and be able at last to devote nearly all of its vast power, influence, and new wealth to educational and altruistic efforts at an even higher level and through a more universal presence than are now possible.

Sadly, any vision of an altruistic Olympic movement investing its vast funds in the future of sport at the grass roots is tempered by the image of privileged members of the IOC jet-setting around the world in order to be fêted by potential host cities determined to gain their support by whatever means necessary. There appears to be little motivation for the Olympic movement to put the brakes on the commercialization of what is evidently one of the most potentially profitable investments in the world.

If the ultimate symbol of amateurism, the Olympic Games, become so forcibly directed by the consumer ethic, then that is as evocative a sign as you are likely to get that consumerism is indeed a way of life or that our way of life is being subjected, first and foremost, to a consumer ethic. Gruneau (1984) is right when he suggests that the commercialization of the Olympics is a long-term process with significant social implications. The Games have evidently become too bound up in economically motivated vested interests for sport to be anything more than another focus for the accumulation of capital. The key concern here is that the very nature of sport is being diluted by commercial imperatives and that the consumers of sport, the fans, are being exploited as a result. I will begin to look at the implications of this process further after considering aspects of the relationship between consumerism and sport in both the USA and Britain, at which point I will consider the commercialization of 'soccer' in particular.

American sport and the power of consumerism

The USA leads the world in promoting the instillation of the consumer ethic into sporting ideals. Whether this is a direction in which the world wants to be led is open to question. In this context, some of the issues raised by Coakley (1994) are especially pertinent in that he describes how American sport has increasingly become a target for the 'entrepreneurial spirit'; in turn creating a model which the rest of the world, including Britain, has relentlessly followed. The irony inherent in such a model is that:

> Investments in sport are often risky, but they have paid off very nicely for owners and sponsors who have been able to use monopolistic business practices to keep costs down and revenues up. Profits have also been enhanced by public support and subsidies. It is ironic that North American professional sports are often used as models of competition when, in fact, they have been built through a system of autocratic control and monopolistic organization. (Coakley, 1994: 328)

What the above more than hints at is the fact that the commercialization of sport is not necessarily of mutual benefit. That is, the interests of the sport itself, the TV companies selling that sport and the individual sports fan do not necessarily match. A TV company, for instance, might want to schedule a sporting fixture in a peak viewing slot. This may concern that particular sport's governing body which might prefer the fixture to be played at another time in order to ensure equity across the fixture list between clubs. Meanwhile, the individual fan who is only able to attend matches on a Saturday is left disappointed. Ultimately, the unusual scheduling of that game results in disappointment all round. There may well be a reduced attendance, which not only results in reduced revenue for the sport, but also detracts from the on-screen spectacle. It seems likely that, ultimately, the fan is bound to lose out in a world where sports are becoming less and less dependent on income provided by gate receipts and more and more determined to maximize other aspects of their business profile.

American sports stars command vast amounts of money, much of it through endorsements, while at the bottom of the ladder less well-known or less successful sportsmen and women are often left to live life on the bread line. For instance, in the summer of 1997, Barry Sanders of the Detroit Lions became the highest paid footballer in National Football League (NFL) history when he signed a five-year deal worth a basic $34 million, alongside a further $12.75 million in projected bonuses. The living embodiment of the riches that sport can bring, however, is Michael Jordan, who after briefly flirting with baseball in 1994 returned to play basketball with the Chicago Bulls in order to recommence a breath-takingly successful and lucrative sporting career. Companies pay Jordan $30 million a year to hype their products (Putnam, 1995: 15). Jordan, one of the world's most famous sportsmen, spent 18 months 'in exile' and returned as an even more marketable commodity. In this context, Putnam (1995: 15) quotes Brandon Steiner of Steiner's Sports Marketing in New York, who argues that Jordan is worth 'a few hundred millions' in terms of total sales to the NBA as a whole. Meanwhile, Gatorade have a 10-year contract with Jordan worth $18 million and Nike sell more than $200 million worth of Air Jordan footwear and Jordan clothing. Jordan earned a mere $20 million from such an endorsement. As for Jordan's return to his favoured sport, he himself says that 'It was never a financial decision . . . I came back because I missed the game' (Jordan in Putnam, 1995: 15). Regardless of Jordan's underlying motives, he is the world's highest earning sportsman. He allegedly collects more than £34 million a year, a figure which *excludes* his salary.

An important issue here is the extent to which the money-making potential of sports and their most saleable commodities, the athletes, transcends the actual nature of the sport concerned. It seems likely that as a sport basketball is *having* to transcend itself. Basketball is a par-ticularly interesting example of this process in so far as it has become imbued with notions of 'street style' and 'street cred' that have arguably become more important to many fans or consumers than the sport itself. This is especially true as far as the worldwide marketing of the NBA is concerned. Certainly, in Britain, the image associated with NBA basket-ball, which has become increasingly popular through TV exposure, is less of a technically proficient and exciting sport and more of an enterprise associated with style and 'hipness'. This reflects a general trend whereby sports are increasingly more synonymous with the con-sumption of leisure than they are with undiluted sporting participation and observation. In this context, Schlossberg (1996: 176) discusses the emergence of American sports stadia as merchandizing and promotion arenas, today's ballparks have ATM machines, virtual shopping malls, and restaurants and hotels. Is it any wonder that corporate sponsors and advertisers are flocking to [these] splendid palaces, even to the point of paying for the privilege of putting their names on them, while fans are paying more and more for the privilege of being exposed to these marketing communications messages? Yes, people pay for the privilege of being advertised to.

The extent to which the power brokers of sport are prepared to go to ensure the economic viability of the sporting enterprise is perhaps best illustrated by the rather questionable practice of actually relocating a team or club in order to maximize revenue. There are several examples, as Coakley (1994) notes, of owners of team franchises abandoning or at least threatening to abandon their fan-base in order to seek new and more lucrative venues and their associated catchment areas; clubs desert the loyal fan-base they may have cultivated over many years in favour of the financial potential that resides elsewhere. Situations therefore arise where clubs 'sportmail' (as opposed to blackmail) the city in which a franchise is resident with the intention of getting more money invested by the city. In one example, the St Louis Cardinals moved to Phoenix, while the Minneapolis North Stars moved to Dallas and the Minneapolis Moose to Winnipeg, Canada, much to the disgust of the much-maligned local supporters whose interests apparently amounted to a minor consideration in what was, first and foremost, a business decision.

What is certain is that the professional ethos of sport pervades American society as a whole with sport, in turn, playing a key role in the maintenance of the American Dream. The priority given to sporting ideals is well illustrated by the vast amounts of money invested in school- and university-level sports notably in the form of sports scholarships. Sports teams in American universities operate at a semi-professional level with stadia often larger than their professional counterparts in Europe. Young sportsmen and women are given considerable financial support, often more so than their academic colleagues, largely because university authorities recognize the economic spin-offs inherent in having a high-profile university sports team. The spin-off in terms of attracting new students through a university's sporting reputation and in terms of attracting large crowds, in the tens of thousands for big games, is more than worth the initial outlay. Whether a sports person *should* receive the advantages of a university education purely because of his or her sporting prowess and ahead of other students with superior academic credentials is undoubtedly questionable, as is the extent to which the consuming ethos can ever hope to benefit all consumers all the time. This is a point I will reconsider shortly in terms of the commercialization of English 'soccer'.

The American relationship with 'soccer', the world's favourite sport, is further illustration of how consumerism affects the essential nature of sport. The mere fact that I refer to 'soccer' here, as opposed to football, illustrates the extent to which commercial values have infiltrated the world's most popular sport in recent years. Perhaps a watershed in this respect, an inevitably American one at that, was the 1994 World Cup. The World Cup competes with the Olympic Games as the world's most popular sporting event. In an effort to popularize 'soccer' in the world's biggest sporting market, the Federation of International Football Associations (FIFA), football's governing body, decided to stage the tournament in the USA. The competition was, in fact, a considerable success, despite rumours circulating prior to the tournament that the rules were to be changed in order to appeal to the domestic American audience who are generally uncomfortable with low-scoring sports. In this context, Schlossberg's (1996: 150) comments about American attitudes to 'soccer' are deeply ironic: 'The American audience, despite the World Cup and the $4 billion that was expected to trickle down to American merchants because of it is still barely knowledgeable about the sport. Soccer's inability to adjust to American tastes – as other sports have done – is the reason for this. . . .'

The long-term effect of 'soccer' on America's sporting psyche has been limited. At present, a professional 'soccer' league, something that has always failed in the past, is struggling to gain a foothold. If anything, the major impact of the 1994 World Cup on the American audience, at least, was the innovative use of advertising. Because 'soccer' entails two uninterrupted halves of 45 minutes each, advertising opportunities are inherently limited. As such, during the 1994 World Cup, American television audiences were treated to sponsors displaying their icons *during* the game. Meanwhile, as Schlossberg (1996) notes, companies such as Canon, Coca-Cola, Fuji, MasterCard, McDonald's, Snickers and Gillette paid up to $20 million each for the privilege of associating their name with the world's biggest single sport event.

English 'soccer' and the consumer ethic

What then of the commercialization of English 'soccer'? It would certainly be true to say that English football is currently undergoing a consumer revolution which is fundamentally altering its essential character. Advertisers, marketers and the media have suddenly realized the potential of football as a vehicle for profit. The 1994 World Cup certainly had some role to play in this process inasmuch as it gave the game a significant boost, much as its predecessor had done in Italy in 1990. However, since the 1994 World Cup in the USA, there appears to have emerged a collective awareness of the long-term financial under-achievement of football, an awareness that culminated in the establishment of the Carling Premiership in 1992. A key element in this process has been the relationship between sport and television which I will go

on to discuss in more detail shortly. The emergence of satellite television in Britain has played a major role in providing the initial capital
which has underlain a boom in the football 'industry'. Football is indeed
a business. Reports about major football clubs such as Manchester
United, Liverpool and Newcastle United are almost as likely to appear
on the business section of national newspapers as they are on the sports
pages.

Such developments can be best illustrated through a brief discussion
of Manchester United. One of the richest football clubs in the world,
Manchester United has somewhat ironically, though accurately, been
described as 'a multi-division entertainment and leisure conglomerate
that is expanding its business and seeking new profit opportunities
based on a successful core business' (*Independent on Sunday*, 1996). As
such, Fox (1996) puts United's stock-exchange value at £280 million and
their financial turnover during 1995 at £60.6 million. During 1995 they
earned approximately £19.7 million (rising to approximately £24.7m)
through gate receipts; £41 million through commercial enterprises; £6.7
million through sponsorship and advertising (rising to approximately
£10 million in 1996); £20 million through the sale of merchandise; £3.4
million through catering and conference facilities and £350,000 through
the rights to videos and fan magazines. Meanwhile, the club can earn
£15 million through a successful run in the Champions League, the
competition to find Europe's best football club (Fox, 1996: 24). Maurice
Watkins, a Manchester United director, says that all this has been made
possible in the aftermath of a period when the sport in general was
largely associated with hooliganism, allowing football finally to become
'politically acceptable' to the extent that nowadays the country's major
political leaders go out of their way to strap their allegiances to particular clubs. Indeed, during the 1990s English 'soccer' is increasingly
dependent on its growing popularity among the middle classes. Meanwhile, as Maurice Watkins recognizes, Manchester United are 'a world
brand name', a brand name which for too long was underexploited
(Fox, 1996: 24). The implication here, as David Blatt of the English
Football Supporters Association notes in his discussion with Steve
Boggan (1996) is that, although:

> Clubs have never treated fans well . . . they are now taking advantage.
> Among football fans, there is a brand-loyalty that Coca-Cola would kill for.
> Your team can lose, you can be given lousy seating, blocked views, poor
> toilets and dreadful catering facilities but you will still go back because it is
> your team . . . They exploit fans' loyalty and they'll carry on exploiting it
> because they know they can. They know it goes way beyond rational
> behaviour. It's true love. (Boggan, 1996: 19)

The word 'exploitation' is an emotive one but is on occasion used by
Manchester United's fiercest critics. Manchester United have been the

subject of considerable public and political criticism most particularly for their merchandizing policy. It is interesting to note that, during a recent survey of the readership of the club magazine *United*, which doubles as a ready sales tool for the club, 83 per cent of those questioned said that they only visited the ground once a season (Wilson, 1995: 14). Clearly, Manchester United's commercial influence reaches far beyond the immediate confines of their stadium. As such, United has been the recipient of particular criticism for a somewhat over-enthusiastic replica shirt policy. Replica shirts represent a massive market to big clubs (the Brazilian national team alone is sponsored to the tune of $400 million), and Manchester United have not been slow in pursuing this market. At any one time, United generally have a home kit (their traditional red), an away kit, a third, and on occasion, a fourth kit. Each of these kits is changed at least biennially, often with the tiniest alteration in detail. Indeed, the conflict of interests inherent in the commercialization of sport, and in this case between kit suppliers, sales and team performance, was neatly illustrated when the Manchester United team refused to wear a grey version of their kit because they claimed that it contributed to them losing a match particularly heavily as they were unable to identify one another on the pitch! The kit was subsequently withdrawn, leaving thousands of frustrated children, parents and supporters with redundant merchandise and the club with a further opportunity to release yet another replica kit onto an unsuspecting marketplace.

What is significant here is that football clubs are trading not only on the market-value of their team, but also on the value of football *per se* which itself has become something of a media and fashion darling. Yet, as Anthony (1996) notes, the shirts themselves are of a poor quality and reflect a commercial imperative rather than a desire to provide the life-blood of the club – the supporter – with value for money. Commercial imperatives appear to be all, so that,

> a generation of kids now know various teams by the corporation that rents the chest space: JVC, Carlsberg, Sharp. But even these names move on eventually. In the non-stop bidding of football, it's possible for a new player to be wearing a new number on a new kit designed by a new manufacturer, featuring a new sponsor. Only the fans remain the same. (Anthony, 1996: 1)

Anthony (1996) estimates that in Britain replica kits are worth £100 million a year in business. Manchester United's contract with kit manufacturers Umbro alone is said to be worth somewhere between £40 million and £60 million. Meanwhile, when Alan Shearer, one of the most expensive 'soccer' players in the world, was signed by Newcastle United from Blackburn Rovers for £15 million, Newcastle made a massive £250,000 on sales of Shearer's number nine shirt in a single day (Anthony, 1996: 4). Nobody is forcing supporters to purchase the merchandise which clubs produce. Or are they? Critics might say that, if you create a situation where young children pester their parents to purchase the latest Manchester United kit for fear of losing face among their peers, and regardless of the quality of the garment concerned, you are being exploitative. The key point here, as noted by Connett and Tomas (1996: 10) who quote Alex Flynn, is that 'There is a difference between a fan and a customer. A fan cannot take his business elsewhere.'

British football has woken up to the economic benefits of sporting passion. In recent seasons English football clubs, in particular, as well as, to an extent, Celtic and Rangers in Scotland, have been able to attract some of the best footballers in the world with massive financial incentives. Such a trend has been exacerbated by the 'Bosman case'. This case, brought by a Belgian footballer to the European courts, means that footballers from European Union countries are designated free agents at the end of their contracts as a result of which they are now able to pick and choose the most lucrative deal for their futures wherever that deal might be offered in the world. A by-product of this ruling is that English supporters are being entertained by some of the most skilful players in the world. But the question that has to be asked is: how long can this last?

Many football clubs have attempted to cash in on the increasingly high public profile of English football and continue to do so, notably through the holy grail of the stock market, in which many clubs are seeking a quotation. Football supporters believe passionately in their teams, but the money markets are passionate about profits and this appears to create a tension that may well alter the very character of the game. As teams face the threat of relegation, their economic destiny could prove to be far more serious than their sporting one. In addition, the big question here, as John Williams, as quoted by Moyes et al., notes, is:

> are the interests of shareholders always synonymous with those of the fans? The answer to that is obviously no. As soon as a company floats, its ultimate and complete loyalty is to the shareholders . . . The big clubs don't care where their supporters come from or if they never come as long as they buy a hat or shirt. (Moyes et al. 1997: 17)

In this respect, as Howard Wilkinson, the English Football Association's current technical director, points out, 'Money is pouring into the game more quickly than it can be dealt with. Given these rewards, the fear of failure intensifies to an illogical point. We should all remember every time somebody wins, someone else must lose' (Tooher, 1997: 21). Much could apparently be learnt from the American example where many American football and baseball clubs, having gone public, have been forced later to revert to private ownership as a direct consequence of the volatile nature of the marketplace, notably in light of the massive wage demands made by star players. In this light, will, indeed, the financial attractions of the English game persist or will it all come shuddering to an abrupt halt? Perhaps the answer to this question lies in a consideration of the impact of television on the sporting 'enterprise'.

Television and the commodification of sport

Television is probably *the* single most influential driving force under-lying the commodification of sport. Television companies invest millions of pounds in sport in the full knowledge that this is a sure-fire way of attracting viewers and thereby justifying high advertising rates. Advertisers are attracted, in turn, by the hope that supporters who are deeply committed to their club will invest the same com-mitment in the products they advertise. In effect, advertising exploits emotion. The fact that, in Britain at least, sports such as football are attracting an increasingly middle class following in a post-hooligan age gives advertisers an increasingly attractive target audience. Indeed, the satellite TV company BSkyB was so impressed by the make-up of this audience that in 1995 it agreed to pay £674 million or just over $1 billion for the right to cover Premiership football matches in England over a period of five years. What is of interest is that the Office of Fair Trading has challenged the BSkyB deal and as such has described the Premier-ship as a cartel which charges artificially high prices for television rights (Garrett, 1997).

In this financial climate sport can be seen to have transcended its role as a pastime and to have well and truly entered the realm of the business world. However, there is a further issue here: the financial benefits of the commercialization of sport often appear to go only as far as the elite clubs or personalities. The £674 million BSkyB deal only includes the English Premiership. It excludes the rest of the league which negotiates its own comparatively limited sponsorship deals. But what of the lesser clubs? How can they ever compete in the same ballgame? Does the commercialization of sport merely represent a widening of the gap between those clubs with massive resources and those that are forced to exist on the verge of bankruptcy?

In reality, television companies are most concerned with the financial windfalls inherent in top-class sport. There is no immediate pay-back as far as they are concerned in developing the grass roots. What is important is money, and money, largely through advertising, is only generated through those performers setting the highest standards.

In this context, it is briefly worth considering the sporting invest-ments of the global media baron, Rupert Murdoch. As S. Barnett (1996) notes, Britain has been a testing ground for Murdoch's policy of paying whatever it takes to prise exclusive rights out of sporting bodies. Every sport will have its price and any price is worth paying if the subsequent dividends far outweigh the initial investment, as devoted supporters are apparently always willing to pay for the opportunity to watch their chosen team. But worryingly, in this context, S. Barnett (1996: 10) quotes the feelings of one BSkyB executive who commented that 'Sport owes nothing to the armchair viewer.' Meanwhile, the TV rights to the 2002 World Cup have gone to a private satellite operator with whom Rupert Murdoch has recently announced a financial alliance. In this context, S. Barnett's (1996) account of the power of Rupert Murdoch's televisual sporting empire is thought-provoking to say the least. In the USA, Murdoch's company Fox TV paid £1 billion for four years' coverage of the NFL National Conference and also holds the rights to the World Baseball Series at a cost of an estimated £370 million. In turn, A. Barnett (1997) reports that Murdoch is spending $350 million in order to buy the LA Dodgers, the USA's most glamorous baseball team, whilst he has also entered a venture deal to buy 40 per cent of the company that owns Madison Square Garden, the New York Knicks basketball team and the New York Rangers ice hockey team. He has also invested around $150 million in the National Hockey League. Among other deals Murdoch has struck, the company Star TV, 63 per cent of which belongs to Murdoch, is paying £11 million for ten years of Asian badminton, while Channel Seven, of which Murdoch owns 15 per cent, has paid £32 million for rights to Australian rules football and £7 million for five years of 'Super 12', a Rugby Union tournament (S. Barnett, 1996). As such, Mitchell (1995b) expresses concern that it is the media power-brokers including men like Murdoch, Mark McCormack (who 'owns' and markets many of the world's leading sports stars through his company International Management Group, and who simultaneously organizes some of the major sporting events, including golf's World Matchplay – critics might suggest that this creates a fundamental conflict of interests) and Don King (who has dominated the promotion of top-class American boxing for many years) who really hold the reins in world sport, and the chances are that these people put their own interests before those of the sporting public or, indeed, sport itself.

The current major development in TV sports coverage is 'pay-per-view' where viewers pay for the privilege of watching single sporting events. This is a development that up to now has largely been associated with boxing, particularly in the USA, but which is bound to have far more universal effects in the next few years with the emergence of digital technology. Indeed, there is currently much talk of the entire English Premiership football programme *only* being available through pay-per-view; individuals paying between £5 and £10 for the privilege of watching their team play from the comfort of their own homes, a move that would earn Premiership clubs millions of pounds a year. In this respect, Rick Parry, the Premiership's first chief executive, argues that 'pay-per-view is the ultimate in consumer choice. Consumers will want plenty of it. The potential revenue is huge' (Murray, 1997: 6).

Meanwhile, sports fans in France are already able to watch any first division football match at home as and when it takes place. In this context, Williams (1996: 3) quotes Greg Dyke, head of Channel 5 in Britain, who argues, in turn, that 'Football will have to learn to look at television in a completely different way. Once you can deliver a couple of thousand channels, TV will become an extension of the turnstile. So you'll have 30,000 in the ground and thousands more paying at home.'

Clearly, such developments have far-reaching implications for the future of sport. Sports are increasingly at the beck and call of television companies, the influence of BSkyB in Britain being such that football matches are now played virtually every night of the week when in the past equity was reflected in a fixture list within which all teams played at the same time. The perennial danger here is that big clubs will continue to benefit at the expense of smaller ones and, in turn, at the expense of the individual supporter who will inevitably struggle to keep up with the inflated cost of his or her continued support.

Conclusion

In a world in which the nine members of the International Cricket Council have agreed to take part in a series of one-day tournaments in Disney World, Florida, and where Mike Tyson biting Evander Holyfield's ears in a world championship fight gets talked about as a marketing opportunity, aspects of global sport may appear at first glance to reinforce a Marxist interpretation of sport within which capitalist enterprise is all. My suggestion, however, is that, broadly speaking, the Marxist approach actually underestimates the complexity of contemporary expressions of sport. In this regard, a discussion of Christopher Lasch's (1985) work on sport might well be worth considering in some detail. Lasch argues that as capitalism has developed modern industry has become increasingly characterized by routinized jobs, this having served to give sport a new function in that workers seek out some of the benefits, both physical and intellectual, in sport, that they would have previously found in their work.

> The rise of spectator sports to their present importance coincides historically with the rise of mass production, which intensifies the need sport satisfies while at the same time creating the technical capacity to promote and market athletic contests to a vast audience. But according to a common criticism of modern sport, these same developments have destroyed the value of athletics. Commercialized play has turned into work, subordinated the athlete's pleasure to the spectator's, and reduced the spectator himself to a state of passivity – the very antithesis of the health and vigour sport ideally promotes. (Lasch, 1985: 51)

Going on to argue that sports have been diluted by the requirements of mass production, Lasch is not impressed with the 'exploding scoreboards' and 'recorded cavalry charges' that characterize the development towards a larger but less well-informed sporting audience intent on sensation-seeking (as illustrated by the ice-skating example above). In effect, Lasch argues that it is not the professionalization of sport itself that corrupts athletic performance, but the way in which such developments foster ignorant audiences. Lasch therefore regards sport as being beset by ulterior motives such as profit-making, which are essentially degrading in the sense that the techniques associated with the game itself becomes incidental. But Lasch's approach to sport is not a left-wing analysis. He describes approaches which see sport as perpetuating the 'false consciousness' of the masses as offensive, in so far as the theorists concerned imply that they understand the needs and interests of the masses more than the masses themselves. Lasch argues that sport is more than a mere mirror of society which indoctrinates the masses with dominant values. 'Sport does play a part in socialization, but the lessons it teaches are not necessarily the ones that coaches and teachers of physical education like to impart. The mirror theory of sport, like all reductionist interpretations of culture, makes no allowance for the autonomy of cultural traditions' (Lasch, 1985: 60).

What is most interesting, in this context, is Lasch's argument that, in fact, the 'reactionary values' perpetuated by sport no longer even reflect the dominant needs of American capitalism. I agree with Lasch's point here and would point out in addition that the needs of American, and indeed world, capitalism have undoubtedly changed in recent years. Lasch points out that the professionalization of sport has led athletes to adopt thoroughly professional and individuated attitudes which, in turn, have served to undermine the old ideals of team spirit. The athlete is no longer representative of his or her class or race, but represents only him or herself. This comment appears to be particularly pertinent in light of the recent media frenzy surrounding the emergence of Tiger Woods, the black American golfer, who, though lauded as a great black hope in a white, middle-class game, is perhaps best thought of, in this day and age, as a boundless focus for commercial and advertising investment – as exemplified by the Nike advertisement, 'I'm Tiger Woods' – and as part of a process within which his race arguably becomes little more than a global economic convenience where next to nothing appears to be free from the process of commodification.

In this context, sport, argues Lasch, is indeed no more than an object of mass consumption. In this sense Lasch agrees with Novak (1976) in that 'The invasion of sport by the "entertainment ethic" . . . breaks down the boundaries between the ritual world of play and the sordid reality from which it is designed to provide escape' (Lasch, 1985: 64). Thus, in a world dominated by the production and consumption of images, sport is bound to be dominated by spectacle and Lasch feels that this reflects an attempt to set up a separate sphere of leisure uncontaminated by the world of work and politics.

Lasch's analysis of sport is useful in that he sees it in terms of the extension of commodity production. Above all, sports teams must win because they are in a business where success is all and this has implications for the nature of the spectacle that the spectator is watching. 'Prudence and calculation, so prominent in everyday life but so inimical to the spirit of games, come to shape sports as they shape everything else' (Lasch, 1985: 65). In essence, sport has been degraded much as work was before it, the degradation of work creating the need for commercialized recreation. People turn to sport to find diversion and as a result sport becomes a 'thing of no consequence' (Lasch, 1985: 66). This attempt to create a realm of pure play is, as far as Lasch is concerned, counterproductive inasmuch as all it achieves is the creation of yet another business subject to the same pressures and tensions as all the rest. The end result is that 'What began as an attempt not only to invest sport with religious significance but to make it into a surrogate religion in its own right ends with the demystification of sport, the assimilation of sport to show business' (Lasch, 1985: 66).

So how does all this fit in with the apparently increasing commodification of sport which I discussed above? First of all, I agree with Lasch (1985), but also with Whannel's (1992) suggestion that sport is not in fact one-dimensional. I would argue that contemporary sports continue to serve the interests of the dominant orders but do so while simultaneously serving the interests of those who get involved in the sporting spectacle. This is the attraction of sport. It is too much of a simplification to describe this process as 'false consciousness'. Nor is it fair to describe sport as entirely passive. What I want to suggest is that, at least to an extent, consumers are in fact aware of the ideological parameters within which they partake of sporting experience and hence of consumption. They are fully aware, for instance, that the sports they watch are dominated by the interests of multinational media barons. People are, however, prepared to put up with the nature of such parameters in so far as they provide the positive benefit of giving structure to life in a world which offers very little, as I will argue in Chapter 9, in the way of a sense of stability. In many ways, as I have highlighted throughout this chapter, sport is a unique consumer product. A supporter or consumer may intensely dislike aspects of what he or she is purchasing, a club's management or a particular player or even the style of play, but is still passionate enough about that club to pay more money to see his or her team perform. What exists is a dogged conviction on the part of the fan that his or her particular team will one day come good and that conviction will perennially provide him or her with an escape from everyday woes, despite the fact that such a conviction will rarely, if ever, be fulfilled.

In this respect, though it could equally be argued that sports have created false markets for themselves, they have done so with the acquiescence of consumers whose passion is ready and waiting to be explored to its commercial limit. As far as consumers of sport are concerned, the commercial model is the *only* model:

> unaware of alternative models, they simply continue to express a desire for what they get, and their desires are based on limited information manipulated by commercial and corporate interests. Therefore changes will occur only when people connected with sports are able to develop visions for what sports could and should look like if they were not so overwhelmingly shaped by economic factors. (Coakley, 1994: 328)

What is so striking about a discussion of the commercialization and commodification of sport is that it so vividly expresses the tensions that exist in a society where consumerism is a *way of life*. It could well be argued that the commercialization of sport has gone out of control and that the character of sports have had to submit to broader social processes as a result of which consumerism has emerged all powerful. This reflects Crook et al.'s (1992) contention that contemporary culture is undergoing processes of (hyper)commodification. That is to say, there is an argument for suggesting that the commodity has spread into all spheres of modern life, thereby negating the distinction between commodified and non-commodified realms. It is in this sense that the needs of consumer capitalism must be extended into new realms. In order to change and expand, consumer capitalism must create new needs and, as such, the imagery and day-dreams that are generally associated with the consuming experience no longer need to be oriented to a non-commodified region of meaning. Commodities, in effect, become self-referential (Featherstone, 1991). In this context, as Rowe (1995: 121) notes:

> Irrespective of particular summations of the state of the sports industry, the significance of the proliferation and circulation of images as integral to the increasing alignment of culture and economics in cultural production cannot be ignored (Hall, 1989). This trend does not presuppose the evacuation of politics from popular cultural forms like sport, but marks their insinuation into an expanding range of sites in which the material and the symbolic intertwine in increasingly complex and contradictory configurations. For this reason, a reflexive analysis is required of sport's ideologies and their associated modes of politics.

I will end this chapter where it began, by acknowledging the possibility that the consumption of sport helps to reinforce broader ideologies of consumerism. To some extent it would indeed be fair to say that sport provides an escape from the tensions of everyday life, but if that escape encapsulates the very ideologies that pervade everyday life then it is no more than illusory. Consumerism offers consumers a sporting product which they gratefully consume, an arena within which the stresses and strains of modern life can be put to one side. By its very existence, professional sport legitimizes consumer capitalism. Consumerism cannot provide the escape that it so vociferously offers. All it can do is provide an *illusion* premised on the emotional and personal commitment that people invest in sporting teams and personalities. In Chapter 9, I will consider these sorts of issues in a more concerted fashion as part of a concluding discussion which will consider, in particular, the ideological dimensions of consumerism as a way of life.

Recommended reading

Jean-Marie Brohm (1978) *Sport: A Prison of Measures Time.* London: Inks Links. An important, though somewhat extreme, Marxist interpretation of sport.

Jay Coakley (1994) *Sport in Society: Issues and Controversies.* London: Masby. A wide ranging account of the sociological aspects of sport; American sport is particularly well covered.

Richard Gruneau (1984) 'Commercialism and the modern Olympics', in Alan Tomlinson and Gary Whannel (eds), *Five Ring Circus: Money, Power and Politics at the Olympic Games.* pp. 1–15, London: Pluto. The Olympics provide a powerful illustration of the relationship between consumerism and sport. This article identifies the ideological implications of such a relationship.

Howard Schlossberg (1996) *Sports Marketing.* Oxford: Blackwell. This book is intriguing in the sense that it looks at the relationship between sport and consumption from a commercial perspective.

Gary Whannel (1992) *Fields in Vision: Television Sport and Cultural Transformation.* London: Routledge. An excellent discussion of the impact of television upon contemporary sports.

9

THE CONSUMING PARADOX

During the course of this book I have used a series of case studies to highlight the ways in which consumerism is manifested as a way of life. There seems to be considerable evidence to suggest that consumerism *does* have an influential role to play in constructing our everyday experience in an array of social realms. Those realms of life I discussed above are merely symptomatic of the nature of social change that I am attempting to describe. My discussion might equally have considered countless other areas of social life all of which have in recent years been transformed by a consumer ethic, such as education, health care, tourism and transport. Those areas of social life I have discussed are therefore intended not as definitive summations of the impact of consumerism, but as contextualized illustrations of the impact of consumerism as a way of life. Had an attempt been made to identify a prime mover in the construction of life experience 30 or 40 years ago, that prime mover might well have been work, our everyday experience of work and the social relationships that were engendered in work. In the late twentieth century, I contend that our experience of work is *potentially* less important than the impact of consumerism which provides the primary arena within which 'citizens' of contemporary Western society conduct their everyday lives.

In Chapter 1, I identified what I described as the 'consuming paradox': the idea that while, on the one hand, consumerism appears to offer us as individuals all sorts of opportunities and experiences, on the other hand, as consumers we appear to be directed down certain predetermined routes of consumption which ensure that consumerism is ultimately as constraining as it is enabling. In order to discuss the complex implications of the 'consuming paradox', I want to consider two crucial questions, both of which are fundamental to any social scientific understanding of consumerism as a way of life. First, what is *the relationship between consumerism and inequality?* And, secondly, what are *the ideological implications of consumerism as a way of life?* I will then conclude by considering how social scientists might best begin to *understand the impact of consumerism in a risk society.*

Consumerism and inequality

A fundamental concern of this book centres on the debate as to whether consumerism can actually provide the sorts of freedom of choice that it appears to offer on the surface. The problem here is that discourses associated with consumerism, and notably those conducted by right-wing politicians, tend to underestimate or even ignore the fact that a considerable percentage of people are effectively disenfranchised from consumer culture. The point here is that, though consumerism is attractive inasmuch as it appears on the surface to offer the individual all sorts of freedoms, the extent to which those freedoms are freely available is highly debatable. This issue is discussed by Mica Nava (1991) who looks at the relationship between consumerism and power. She argues that consumerism is essentially liberating and that the sorts of political ideals that are expressed through consumer discourses encourage a situation in which individuals have a stronger say in determining what social life can offer them. In other words, as a political arena consumerism has the *potential* for bringing about a kind of utopian collectivism in which the rights of the consumer become a key concern of political and social debate. Nava also argues that there is a tendency to underestimate the extent to which consumers use the opportunities provided for them by consumerism. In this context she suggests that,

> twentieth-century Western consumerism . . . has already generated new grass-roots constituencies – constituencies of the market-place – and has enfranchized modern citizens in new ways, making possible a new and quite different economic, political and personal and creative participation in society. The full scale of its power is yet to be imagined. (Nava, 1991: 173)

This, some would say middle-class, vision of an empowering culture is all well and good, but what I want to suggest is that in many ways the consumer society we live in is more remarkable for the way in which it divides than for the ways in which it provides. In this respect, Gabriel and Lang (1995) point out that much of the rhetoric surrounding the empowering nature of consumerism is superficial and that the opportunities consumerism provides are exaggerated. Their argument is that historically the range of choice available to the consumer has actually been reduced. In this context, Gabriel and Lang point out that British shoppers in the 1960s actually spent *less* of their income on shopping than British shoppers in the 1860s because they had more fixed costs and that, regardless of the opportunities available in the marketplace, people often do not get the opportunity to take advantage of them. The suggestion here is that consumerism is often more about rhetoric than it is about substance. An increase in the range of choice available to consumers does not always bring with it the resources or the opportunity to explore such choices at will. The consumer is assumed to be a citizen of a consumer culture, but that citizenship often involves a prohibitive membership fee.

> The key barrier to consumer choice is money. The message? If you want choice, and who doesn't, you have to get out there and get going. Money gives choice. Choice gives freedom. Whatever the area of consumption, from crime protection to clothes, from health to education, from cultural industries to cars, money is the final arbiter. (Gabriel and Lang, 1995: 32)

Consumerism is not, in effect, an unqualified right. It often has more power to force home to us what we do not have as consumers, than it does to give us what we want. As Gabriel and Lang (1995) point out, the idealized vision of consumerism, drawn upon by many politicians, does not necessarily equate with the everyday experience of consumers. Thus, a supporter of a football club may have been supporting his or her team for 30 or 40 years, but as sport has become increasingly commercialized such a person may have found it impossible to justify the increasing costs that this entails. The commercialization and commodification of sport, which I discussed in Chapter 8, may make sport more of an attractive source of entertainment, but while doing so it might also serve to alienate particular sectors of its support. As far as English 'soccer' is concerned, for example, though the renovation of sports stadia may have made the game more attractive, many spectators have been driven away unable to keep up with the economic costs that these changes incur. In this respect, consumerism is a double-edged sword.

In Chapter 5, I discussed the sorts of opportunities that technological innovation appeared to offer the individual. This serves as a useful illustration of the paradoxical nature of consumerism. The opportunities so often touted by the media as beneficial to the consumer, such as the Internet, CD ROMs and the latest innovations in musical reproduction, are clearly beyond the means of the majority of people. In particular, the Internet is largely the preserve of a privileged few who access it through business or education. To give a similar example of a realm of life in the late twentieth century that has not been discussed in any detail in this book, namely education, there certainly seem to be more opportunities to allow parents to pick and choose the most favourable school for their child. This is particularly true in the British case where legislation has been introduced actively to encourage such choice. But, ultimately, these sorts of choices are limited by the financial burdens involved. Certain schools will always be beyond the financial means of the majority of people. Consumerism is a way of life in the sense that the rhetoric employed suggests that such schools are available to all, when of course they are not.

The inequalities that have become associated with consumption are even more evident when you consider the global impact of consumerism as I noted in Chapter 3. For those who can freely enjoy the benefits of consumerism as a way of life, globalization apparently brings with it an endless appetite for fragmented diversity. Consumerism seemingly provides consumers with a global village within which they can be who they please. However, the same cannot be said for those people and, indeed, countries, that do not have the necessary resources. One of the more interesting approaches to this question is that of Serge Latouche in his book, *In the Wake of the Affluent Society* (1993). Latouche argues that the drive on the part of individuals to improve materially has become a driving force behind Western society, and that this force is exalted by the media and by politicians alike to the extent that it has actively invaded the social world. A myth has therefore been perpetuated which centres on the belief that everyone can be a winner in a consumer society; that by extracting prodigious quantities of wealth from nature everybody can be given what they need; and everyone can co-operate against humanity's fundamental foe which appears to be nature itself. This represents a social contract within which people believe that it is entirely possible for everybody to share in a general prosperity. But, as Latouche (1993) goes on to suggest, the idea that everyone can win in a consumer society is quite simply naïve. Everybody can gain from consumerism in one sense or another. Subscription to cable and satellite television are often greatest in some of the poorest urban areas, for instance. The benefits of consumerism in this sense appear to be filtering down. However, such a filter is only partial and merely serves to promote the idea that any form of consumption is inherently liberating when clearly it is not.

The biggest loser in the world of consumerism, as far as Latouche (1993) is concerned, is the Third World. The fact that in the West wealth and personal advancement have been lauded as the way forward has worked against the population of the Third World inasmuch as what the Western world gains in surplus the Third World loses in wage income. In this sense Latouche's argument reflects some of the debates associated with world systems theory, evident in the work of Immanuel Wallerstein (1979), but more specifically the idea that Western capitalism and consumption is perpetuating inequalities through national debts that constantly need to be paid off. Thus, Third World countries find themselves in situations where they are forced to develop markets that will do little to help their long-term economic cause but, rather, merely serve to prop up the major economies of the world while increasing dependence upon them. In effect, the developed world ensures that the Third World is underdeveloped in a situation where it is constantly paying off its debts and as a result is unable to produce for itself.

As far as the Western world itself is concerned, Latouche (1993) argues that the rise in per capita standards of living has been obtained at the cost of a deeper malaise in a spiritually empty and immoral society where money is all and where the soul is degraded in a constant cycle of selfishness and manipulation. In this context, Latouche argues that modernity encourages the emergence of an essentially inhuman society which pursues the principle of 'maximine': maximum results and enjoyment through minimum cost and effort. The problem with such a social system lies in the fact that,

> The happiness of persons, if this is taken as an objective of a society, cannot be a simple addition of states of pleasure of all its members separately obtained, each to the detriment of others. Even if happiness is no more than the mere symbolic enjoyment felt by the subjects as a consequence of that of a ruler, it still possesses an irreducible personal aspect. A society cannot be said to be perfectly happy if one of its members is in misery. (Latouche, 1993: 241)

Returning to the impact of consumerism upon the West, Zygmunt Bauman (1988) suggests that choice, and especially consumer choice, represents the foundation of a new concept of freedom in contemporary society, and that the freedom of the individual is constituted in his or her role as a consumer. Modern consumption, argues Bauman, has opened the possibility of choice to increasing numbers of people. However, the system that constructs the 'free' individual also generates massive oppression inasmuch as those who are excluded from making such choices become disfranchised and oppressed. Bauman therefore distinguishes between the 'seduced' and the 'repressed'. The 'seduced' are those members of society for whom consumption becomes a major arena of liberation; the 'repressed' are those who simply do not have access to the necessary resources to become involved in what such a society has to offer. This section of the population therefore becomes dependent upon the support services and institutions provided for them by the state. In effect, there is clearly a price to pay for the sorts of benefits that consumerism provides. Consumerism cannot be all things to all men and women. Rather, it protects those with resources from those without.

Clearly, there are all sorts of pressures to consume in certain ways in contemporary consumer society as my discussion of 'McDonaldization' in Chapter 4 illustrated. But the irony is that perhaps those pressures are greatest on the very people who do not have the resources to take advantage of the opportunities consumerism provides. In this respect, some of Campbell's (1987) comments about the daydreaming qualities of consumption, and the fact that thinking *about* consumption is often more important than the act of consumption itself, are highly pertinent. The nature of consumerism is such that as soon as somebody consumes something they immediately transfer their wish to consume onto something else as part of a constant cycle of desire. The concern here is that many people who are subject to consumerism as a way of life experience consumption as nothing but an imaginary sphere. Perhaps the less access you have to the wares that consumerism can offer, the more it becomes fundamental to your self-conception. A world has been created where consumerism is all. This is a particularly dangerous state of affairs for those people who can do no more than dream about what consumerism might have to offer them.

The ideological role of consumerism

Jameson (1984) points out that culture is no longer ideological. It no longer provides a means of disguising the economic activities of capitalism, but is itself an economic activity, perhaps the most important economic activity of all. Such activity is most vibrantly expressed within the context of consumerism which has itself emerged in the late twentieth century as the dominant mode of cultural reproduction to develop in the West over the course of modernity (Slater, 1997). As Slater (1997) suggests, consumption is not merely a consequence of industrial modernization, but is actually part and parcel of the very making of the modern world. Far more than a mere product of modernity, chameleon-like, consumption plays a fundamental role in its actual constitution. However, consumerism *is* an ideological beast. The ideological dimensions of consumerism are, in effect, shielded from consumers by their ability to consume.

The above argument appears to be somewhat deterministic. It might indeed be argued that some of the thoughts I have presented are rather reminiscent of the Frankfurt School's contribution to debates concerning the cultural manifestations of capitalism. At least in some respects, the following quotation encapsulates what I am attempting to say about the ideological influence of consumerism:

> The culture industry perpetually cheats its consumers of what it perpetually promises. The promissory note which, with its plots and staging, it draws on pleasure is endlessly prolonged; the promise, which is actually all the spectacle consists of, is illusory: all it actually confirms is that the real point will never be reached, that the diner must be satisfied with the menu. (Horkheimer and Adorno, 1973: 139)

Although I would agree with many critics that members of the Frankfurt School, who are often criticized for the elitist nature of much of their work, take an extreme position on this debate, they do provide a useful starting point. I do not agree, however, with the implication here that consumer culture is necessarily a culture of the lowest common denominator. On the contrary, consumer culture has made available all sorts of cultural experiences that were previously the preserve of the middle and upper classes. What I would say, however, is that consumerism as a way of life is dependent upon the fact that consumers are never satisfied by what they consume and that they continue to consume in pursuit of the false promises offered to them by consumer capitalism. Consumers are partially fulfilled through consumption – more than the Frankfurt School were prepared to admit – in the sense that consumption provides a framework within which people can actively negotiate their position in the world. Consumers do have certain freedoms, but such freedoms are only partial in the sense that they can only extend as far as they serve the intentions of the status quo. Wilson's (1992) reference to Frederic Jameson's conversation with Stuart Hall about postmodernism is particularly enlightening in this respect.

> Postmodernism has this odd double standard where you're convinced that capitalism has triumphed: there's the market on the one hand and everybody's better off and everybody plays their different music, but on the other hand we're also equally convinced that there's incredible misery in these societies, they're getting worse rather than better . . . And we know that both things are true and also that they are incompatible. (Wilson, 1992: 4)

Regardless of whether or not we accept the contention that capitalist societies are going through some form of an epochal shift, and whether or not we accept that this shift has been adequately catered for in discussions of postmodernism, in this statement Jameson pinpoints the fact that consumerism is essentially characterized by contradictions and by the inequalities that accompany those contradictions. Wilson (1992: 4) also sums this point up very nicely when she says: 'Postmodernism expresses at one level a horror at the destructive excess of Western consumerist society, yet, in aestheticising this horror, we somehow convert it into a pleasurable object of consumption.'

The power and subsequent longevity of consumerism as a way of life is therefore rooted in the fact that the pleasures which consumers find through consumption outweigh any comparable concern as to its ideological underpinnings. For example, consumers want reality to be distorted when they visit Disney despite any recognition on their part that Disney is quite clearly controlling their patterns of consumption. Consumerism is ideologically powerful because, despite being at least partially aware of its influence and power, consumers are prepared at least to explore the extent to which they can use consumerism as a framework for the construction of their identities. A person might not construct an identity directly through what he or she consumes, but they may well construct who they are as a result of *why* they consume that particular item. Young people, for example, do not construct their identities through what they consume, but rather through peer group relationships in which the consumption of what are deemed to be appropriate consumer goods plays a key role (see Miles, 1995, 1996). As such, the ways in which consumers ascribe meaning to consumer goods is very important, the irony being that, however expressively and creatively people consume, the arena within which they do so is ultimately prescribed for them by consumer capitalism.

Before concluding, and in order to consider how far consumerism actually manipulates consumers in this regard, I want briefly to consider the work of Conrad Lodziak (1995). Lodziak notes that the infatuation with debates over modernity and postmodernity have led to a concomitant neglect of the ways in which capitalist societies are reproduced. In this respect, the work of Jameson (1984) can be described as the exception that proves the rule. Lodziak points out that the preoccupation with social change that characterizes recent social theory has led theorists to neglect the ways in which the capitalist system is monitoring such change 'while at the same time securing its own stability' (1995: 21). The key point here is that social change does not occur in isolation but is beneficial to and indeed generates the capitalist system as a whole. The capitalist system grants the consumer autonomy while 'At the same time, and consistent with this, it has been busy in commodifying experiences and human relations, and in formally regulating spheres of life that were once open to informal or democratic control, or left to individuals to sort out for themselves' (Lodziak, 1995: 22).

Where I diverge from Lodziak is the point at which he argues that consumers are therefore automatically steered towards an increasingly trivial and meaningless existence as a result of their inability to express themselves in more meaningful and oppositional areas of life. Much like many of the arguments associated with the Frankfurt School, it would be fair to say that this is taking the argument somewhat far. Though there are strong reasons for suggesting that the commodification of culture has had an increasing role to play in people's lives, that role is not necessarily a trivializing one. Consumerism has indeed tended to divert and actively dissuade people from opposition to dominant social orders, but it is not therefore in itself necessarily insubstantial or 'inauthentic'. People can invest their own personal meanings in what they consume, and consumption can be a significant source of creativity. For example, regardless of the impact of consumerism on sport, a supporter of a football club can still get considerable satisfaction from seeing his or her team succeed. Regardless of how manufactured a particular piece of music may be, there is always the possibility that an individual will find in that song particular lyrics that resonate with important aspects of his or her own individual life experience.

One issue that Lodziak (1995) does raise and which is worth considering in this context is the extent to which consumerism might be described as a 'dominant ideology'. That is, there could be an argument for suggesting that the basis of capitalistic economic structure is hidden from the consciousness of agents of production and that consumerism serves this very purpose. It is, however, surely an exaggeration to imply that consumers are somehow controlled by a 'false consciousness' within which they are unaware of the real motivations of powerful elites. In this context, Hebdige (1979) argues that human beings actually reproduce themselves through a process of 'naturalization'. They accept particular ways of organizing the world and of organizing social life as being 'natural' and as a result ideology becomes an essential element of social life. Ideologies are therefore lived, not merely thought, and become projected as values of humanity as a whole (Eagleton, 1994). It is in this respect that we can argue that consumerism has come to be accepted as a way of life and has therefore been able to stratify every aspect of that life. Consumerism is perceived to be a 'natural' way to live, when it in fact encourages inequalities, the irony being that these inequalities are apparently necessary if those higher up the social scale are to enjoy the benefits that consumerism so vocally offers. From this point of view, then, consumerism has an essentially *unnatural* influence on the construction of our everyday lives.

Consumerist ideology works at the level of the practical unconscious and this is made possible by the potential for personal freedom that consumerism appears to offer to the individual. Consumerism offers consumer sovereignty which, as authors such as Keat (1994) argue, actually acts as an ideological disguise for other more pressing projects, such as the restoration of the fortunes of capital accumulation and the increased power of the state. Consumerism is essentially seductive and as such, as I noted in Chapter 2, it plays a crucial role in linking 'together the lifeworlds of the individual agents and the purposeful rationality of the system' (Bauman, 1988: 807). In other words, consumerism is more concerned with the sorts of structures it imposes in the form of a social system than the specific freedoms it provides for the individual consumer who is seduced by the latter and therefore, at least partially, unaware of the former. The interesting point here, as Lee (1993) notes, is that consumer goods live a double life in that at one and the same time they are agents of social control and yet actively construct consumer cultures. Consumerism should not be considered to be a purely manipulative weapon of dominant social orders. To take this position would be to underestimate the subtleties of consumerism as a way of life. Consumption, in effect, both constrains *and* enables. It is in this sense that consumerism reflects the underlying tensions characteristic of the relationship between structure and agency in contemporary societies.

You could argue, as Fiske (1989: 14) does, that, 'we "live" capitalism through its commodities, and by living it, we validate and invigorate it'. However, though the economic system is ideologically reproduced through commodities and in this respect 'a commodity is an ideology made material' (Fiske, 1989: 14), the producers and distributors of commodities are not necessarily deliberate propagandists. In fact, Fiske argues that consumption is at least partially and potentially liberating inasmuch as it provides a basis from which people can act *against* the ideological imperatives of capitalism. For instance, ripped jeans might signify a resistance to the idea that consumer goods automatically become obsolete and should therefore be replaced (see discussion in Chapter 3). The key point here is that resistance is activated in the cultural sphere rather than the economic sphere. Economically, such a gesture will have little, if any, impact, but a display of poverty is a visual affront to consumerism as a way of life: 'It is a refusal of com-modification and an assertion of one's right to make one's own culture out of the resources provided by the commodity system' (Fiske, 1989: 15). As far as Fiske is concerned, then, consumerism is empowering in the sense that people can interpret the wares that consumerism offers in their own ways. This argument is, however, limited as Lee (1993) notes, by Fiske's (1989) tendency to equate the active role consumers may have in the realm of consumption with power. Just because consumption is active, it does not necessarily follow that it is liberating. Consumer goods should be seen as objects of social struggle rather than as arbiters of power (Lee, 1993). Consumerism trades off the degree of agency that consumers invest in consumer culture as a means of ensuring the long-term dominance of consumer capitalism. Consumer capitalism is able to assert itself as a way of life precisely because the act of consumption is active and is therefore automatically equated with power. The real power relationship between the consumer and the producer is inevit-ably camouflaged by the superficial appeals of apparently liberating and creative consumer lifestyles.

Consumer capitalism is not about false consciousness as such because many consumers are fully aware and critical of the sorts of inequalities and injustices that are associated with consumerism. Nor is consumer-ism about false needs. Consumerism is so all powerful precisely because it requires a certain degree of individuality on the part of consumers in order to ensure the maintenance of segmented markets. If consumers were simply 'dupes' of the capitalist system that system could not extend its boundaries. Consumer capitalism actively wants consumers to experience what might be described as 'pseudo-sovereignty'. The individual's experience of consumerism is therefore clearly a balancing act between structure and agency. The structures intent on ensuring the longevity of consumerism as a way of life actively provide room within which consumers can apply their own meanings. The consumer is offered a veneer of sovereignty and maximizes his or her personal freedom within the veneer provided, despite a tacit acceptance that consumerism is a more powerful beast than any one individual at any one time. At a routine everyday level, people simply do not feel the need to question the validity of consumerism as a way of life. The dreams that people engender in consumerism give meaning to people's lives. It is in this respect that Bocock (1993) argues that in the contemporary world alienation has been extended into the realm of consumption. This has been made possible through the perpetuation of consumerism as a mental activity, rather than a purely physical activity that can only fulfil biological needs.

Understanding consumerism in a risk society

If we accept that consumerism has an influential role to play in our lives precisely because it is in the interests of consumer capitalism to provide some degree of agency within which consumers can explore the possibilities provided for them by the marketplace, then this raises some issues about how social science might best come to terms with consumerism as a way of life. The 'consuming paradox' is an intriguing issue for contemporary social theorists in the sense that it reflects the essential stresses and strains that are characteristic of contemporary life experience.

The first point to make is that consumerism is necessarily an arena of conflict in the sense that the individual is perpetually trying to come to terms with the sorts of stresses, strains and tensions that characterize the multi-dimensional nature of the consuming experience. The consuming experience is multi-dimensional in so far as it plays on the structure and agency question. It could indeed be argued that consumerism is the foremost arena within which structure and agency is contested. At one and the same time, consumers feel constrained and controlled, yet liberated and sovereign. This paradox represents an underlying influence upon how people conduct their everyday lives because it appears to provide a sense of stability in what is essentially an unstable world. In this respect, Beck's (1992) conceptualization of the 'risk society' is especially pertinent. Beck (1992) describes a process whereby individuals 'become the agents of their own livelihood mediated by the market' (Beck, 1992: 130). In this context, the individual's life experience is an increasingly precarious one. The support mechanisms that are traditionally associated with modernity, such as social class, family and community, have apparently been replaced by secondary ties such as fashion, economic cycles and markets which in turn undermine the individual's degree of control and leave him or her open to the ups and downs of an increasingly insecure life experience (Beck, 1992). In this context, predictability and certainty become a thing of the past, as a new set of risks is brought into existence at both a macro- and micro-level. Beck (1992) therefore identifies a new mode of socialization, a 'metamorphosis' or 'categorical shift' in the make-up of the relationship between the individual and society. He suggests that in advanced modernity the individual becomes removed from traditional support mechanisms and support relationships and that consequently the constraints of everyday life as experienced by the worker and the consumer take on new significance.

In a risk society, consumerism has an increasingly important role to play as a framework within which people conduct their lives. The irony here is that, though people live in an increasingly individualized culture, the individual experiences a less autonomous private existence in the sense that he or she is subject to public criteria of individuality. In other words, individuality is increasingly subject to external forces and arguably standardization, thereby creating a situation within which the individual is increasingly susceptible to personal crises (Beck, 1992). The focus of an individual's life, bereft of stable sources of support, therefore becomes focused on the maintenance of an individual biography. While consumerism offers the individual an arena within which he or she can seek out an individual biography, that biography is inevitably tempered by the fact that the individual can never be entirely unique within this realm. What is therefore constructed is an environment within which the individual is dependent upon both the standardizing *and* the diversifying tendencies of consumer capitalism. Such dependency ensures the constant reproduction of consumer capitalism. The cost we, as consumers, have to pay for consumerism as a way of life is perpetual insecurity because consumerism cannot provide us with the stability that we so fervently desire. As Beck (1992) argues, what emerges is an ego-centred world-view. The individual is opened up to an increased risk of uncertainty in the sense that any failure is perceived on his or her part as implicating the inadequacies of the individual. The individual receives all sorts of conflicting messages when he or she consumes. Not only is the individual never quite satisfied by what he or she consumes – not only does the individual always want that bit more – but when he or she gets whatever he or she may want, it only serves to intensify the precarious nature of that person's everyday existence.

If the key to an understanding of consumerism lies in its expression at a micro-level inasmuch as the micro-level represents the arena within which tensions over structure and agency are expressed, then the everyday nature of consumerism *as a way of life* needs to be a more fundamental sociological concern than it has been in the recent past. As Miller (1987) notes, both theory and research need to consider in tandem, not only the transformative nature of consumption, but also the inherent limitations of such transformations. The ways in which consumers adapt to consumerism as a way of life need to be incorporated into a critical understanding of how that way of life came about. Assumptions about the power of consumerism, negative or positive, should therefore not be made. The time has come to leave the sort of office-bound theorizing that has characterized the emergence of consumption as a key focus of social scientific debate behind in order to welcome a more concerted and contextualized social scientific conceptualization of consumerism as a way of life.

To conclude, it should be reiterated at this stage that the intention of this book has not been to portray consumers as objects of false consciousness. On the contrary, my argument is that, as Thomas and Thomas (1928: 572) argue, 'If men [sic] define situations as real, they are real in their consequences.' Consumerism clearly constructs rules about how consumers should behave and promotes consumer goods as a resource which individual consumers can use as a means of constructing their social life. Despite and indeed because of the structural nature of this relationship, what matters is what the consumer perceives to be *real*. Regardless of whether the individual underestimates the ideological impact of consumerism, what is important is that this is a *subjective* conception of reality. Consumerism is a way of life in the sense that regardless of the power relationships it engenders it also actively constitutes a subjective reality. What I am therefore suggesting is that a critical approach to the sociology of consumerism should use as its starting point the construction of consumer meanings. In this respect, the focus here should not be on the extent to which consumerism is an inauthentic focus for people's everyday lives. If consumers experience consumerism as a way of life then that life is necessarily authentic. It is up to the sociologist to discover why and how consumers live within the ideological parameters that consumerism lays down for them. Such a task should begin by reflecting on the fact that consumerism makes us feel we belong in a world where we perhaps very rarely feel that we belong otherwise. It is in the interests of consumer capitalism to massage our individualistic desire to express ourselves to others through what we consume and why we consume it. In decades and centuries to come people might well think about implementing new ways of constructing social life that do not prioritize consumerism as a way of life. Given the ideological power of consumerism, however, the likelihood is that they will do so through a pair of designer-tinted spectacles which ultimately taunt them into focusing on nothing more than the countless new ways in which they can achieve pseudo-sovereignty through the goods provided for them in the marketplace.

Recommended reading

Zygmunt Bauman (1988) *Freedom*. Milton Keynes: Open University Press. One of Bauman's most important books in which he discusses the contradictory freedoms that are created through consumption.

Ulrich Beck (1992) *Risk Society: Towards a New Modernity*. London: Sage. The foremost contribution to the debate as to what constitutes a risk society.

Yiannis Gabriel and Tim Lang (1995) *The Unmanageable Consumer*. London: Sage. Looks at the nature of consumerism from an impressive array of angles.

Frederic Jameson (1984) 'Postmodernism, or the cultural logic of late capitalism', *New Left Review*, 146: 53–93. A highly influential and well-contextualized essay on the nature of postmodernism.

Serge Latouche (1993) *In the Wake of the Affluent Society*. London: Zed Books. Considers the global implications of consumerism.

Conrad Lodziak (1995) *Manipulating Needs: Capitalism and Culture*. London: Pluto Press. Looks at the ideological dimensions of capitalism and could be said, at times, to overestimate them.

Mica Nava (1991) 'Consumerism reconsidered: buying and power', *Cultural Studies*, 5: 157–73. A useful article on the apparently liberating nature of consumerism.

Don Slater (1997) *Consumer Culture and Modernity*. Cambridge: Polity Press. A theoretically minded book which considers the relationship of consumer culture to modernity.

REFERENCES

Aaronovitch, D. (1996) 'Strange new world', *The Independent on Sunday*, The Sunday Review, 29 September: 7.

Abercrombie, N. (1994) 'Authority and consumer society', in R. Keat, N. Whiteley and N. Abercrombie (eds), *The Authority of the Consumer*. London: Routledge. pp. 43–57.

Adorno, T. (1990) 'On popular music', in S. Frith and A. Goodwin (eds), *On Record: Rock, Pop and the Written Word*. London: Routledge. pp. 301–14.

Ang, I. (1992) *Living Room Wars: New Technologies, Audience Measurement and the Tactics of Television Consumption*. London: Routledge.

Anthony, A. (1996) 'Fashion item in polyester as worn by Stuart Pearce: Yours for £40', *The Observer*, Review 11 August: 1–4.

Appadurai, A. (1986) 'Commodities and the politics of value', in A. Appadurai (ed.), *The Social Life of Things: Commodities in Cultural Perspective*. Cambridge: Cambridge University Press. pp. 1–63.

Archer, M. (1995) *Realist Social Theory: The Morphogenetic Approach*. Cambridge: Cambridge University Press.

Barnard, M. (1996) *Fashion as Communication*. London: Routledge.

Barnett, A. (1997) 'Hopes high as takeover season takes off', *The Observer*, Business, 27 July: 9.

Barnett, J. (1996) 'World music, nation and post-colonialism', *Cultural Studies*, 10 (2): 237–47.

Barnett, S. (1996) 'Turn on, pay up', *The Guardian*, Sport, 26 July: 10.

Barthel, D. (1989) 'Modernism and marketing: the chocolate box revisited', *Theory, Culture & Society*, 6: 429–38.

Baudrillard, J. (1980) 'The implosion of meaning in the media and the implosion of the social in the masses', in K. Woodward (ed.), *The Myths of Information: Technology and Post-industrial Culture*. London: Routledge & Kegan Paul. pp. 137–48.

Baudrillard, J. (1988) *Selected Writings*. ed. M. Poster. Cambridge: Polity Press.

Baudrillard, J. (1993) *Symbolic Exchange and Death*. London: Sage.

Bauman, Z. (1988) *Freedom*. Milton Keynes: Open University Press.

Bauman, Z. (1992) *Intimations of Postmodernity*. London: Routledge.

Beauregard, R. (1986) 'The complexity of gentrification', in N. Smith and P. Williams (eds), *Gentrification of the City*. London: Allen & Unwin. pp. 35–56.

Beck, U. (1992) *Risk Society: Towards a New Modernity*. London: Sage.

Bedell Smith, S. (1985) 'Who's watching TV? It's getting hard to tell', *New York Times*, 6 January: 21.

Bell, D. (1973) *The Coming of Post-industrial Society*. New York: Basic Books.

Bell, D. (1976) *The Cultural Contradictions of Capitalism*. London: Heinemann.

Benjamin, W. (1973) *Charles Baudelaire: A Lyric Poet in the Age of High Capitalism*. London: New Left Books.

Benson, J. (1994) *The Rise of Consumer Society in Britain, 1880–1980*. London: Longman.

Bocock, R. (1993) *Consumption*. London: Routledge.

Boggan, S. (1996) 'A game of two halves: the rich and the poor', *The Independent*, 12 October: 19.

Booth, P. and Boyle, R. (1993) 'See Glasgow, see culture', in F. Bianchini and M. Parkinson (eds), *Cultural Policy and Urban Regeneration: The West European Experience*. Manchester: Manchester University Press. pp. 21–47.

Bourdieu, P. (1984) *Distinction: A Social Critique of the Judgement of Taste*. London: Routledge & Kegan Paul.

Braudel, H. (1974) *Capitalism and Material Life, 1400–1800*. New York: Harper & Row.

Braun, E. (1995) *Futile Progress*. London: Earthscan Publications.

Breakwell, G. (1983) *Threatened Identities*. Chichester: Wiley.

Brohm, J.-M. (1978) *Sport: A Prison of Measured Time*. London: Inks Links.

Brubaker, R. (1984) *The Limits of Rationality*. London: Allen & Unwin.

Bryman, A. (1995) *Disney and His Worlds*. London: Routledge.

Buffoni, L. (1997) 'Rethinking poverty in globalized conditions', in J. Eade (ed.), *Living the Global City: Globalization as Local Process*. London: Routledge. pp. 110–26.

Bulos, M.A. (1995) 'CCTV surveillance: safety or control?', unpublished paper, BSA Annual Conference, University of Leicester, 10–13 April.

Burnett, R. (1996) *The Global Jukebox: The International Music Industry*. London: Routledge.

Butler, R. (1991) 'West Edmonton Mall as a tourist attraction', *Canadian Geographer*, 35: 287–95.

Callinicos, A. (1989) *Against Postmodernism: A Marxist Critique*. Cambridge: Polity Press.

Campbell, C. (1987) *The Romantic Ethic and the Spirit of Modern Consumerism*. Oxford: Blackwell.

Campbell, C. (1995) 'The sociology of consumption', in D. Miller (ed.), *Acknowledging Consumption: A Review of New Studies*. London: Routledge. pp. 96–126.

Chancellor, A. (1997) 'Pride and prejudice: Apple's unoriginal sin', *The Guardian*. Weekend, 8 February: 5.

Chaney, D. (1990) 'Subtopia in Gateshead: the Metro Centre as cultural form', *Theory, Culture & Society*, 7 (4): 49–86.

Chaney, D. (1996) *Lifestyles*. London: Routledge.

Clarke, C. (1991) 'Towards a geography of the consumer society', working paper 91/3, School of Geography, University of Leeds.

Coakley, J. (1994) *Sport in Society: Issues and Controversies*. London: Masby.

Cockburn, C. (1985) *Machinery of Dominance: Women, Men and Technical Know-How*. London: Pluto.

Combe, V. (1996) 'Church plc adopts logo "to solve identity crisis"', *Electronic Telegraph*, 524, 29 October.

Connett, D. and Tomas, J. (1996) 'A golden goal', *The Observer*, 27 October: 10.

Conran, T. (1996) *Terence Conran on Design*. London: Conran Octopus.

Corrigan, S. (1994) 'It is a town square for the next millennium: America's largest mall, where climate is controlled, you can get married . . . and where operators really care', *The Observer*, Life Magazine, 27 November: 38–44.

Craik, J. (1994) *The Face of Fashion: Cultural Studies in Fashion*. London: Routledge.

Crook, S., Pakulski, J. and Waters, M. (1992) *Postmodernization: Change in Advanced Society*. London: Sage.

Cross, G. (1993) *Time and Money: The Making of Consumer Culture*. London: Routledge.

Davidson, A. (1995) 'Money that's what I want', *Independent Magazine*, 28 October: 11–12.

Davies, H. (1995) 'Merchandise United', *The Guardian*, 4 April: 1–3.

Davis, F. (1992) *Fashion, Culture and Identity*. London: University of Chicago Press.

Davis, J. (1990) *Youth and the Condition of Britain*. London: Athlone Press.

de Certeau, M. (1984) *The Practice of Everyday Life*. Berkeley, CA: University of California Press.

Derrida, J. (1978) *Spurs/Eperons*. Chicago: University of Chicago Press.

Dittmar, H. (1992) *The Social Psychology of Material Possessions: To Have is to Be*. Hemel Hempstead: Harvester Wheatsheaf.

Dorfles, G. (1979) 'Sociological and semiological aspects of design', in Design Council, *Design History: Past, Process, Product*. London: Design Council. pp. 11–13.

Douglas, M. and Isherwood, B. (1996) *The World of Goods: Towards an Anthropology of Consumption*, 2nd edn. London: Allen Lane.

Druckery, T. (1995) 'Introduction', in G. Bender and T. Druckery (eds), *Culture on the Brink: Ideologies of Technology*. Seattle: Bay Press. pp. 1–14.

du Gay, P. and Negus, K. (1994) 'The changing sites of sound music retailing and the composition of consumers', *Media, Culture & Society*, 16: 395–413.

du Gay, P., Hall, S., Jones, L. Mackay, H. and Negus, K. (1997) *Doing Cultural Studies: The Story of the Sony Walkman*. London: Sage.

Dunkerley, M. (1996) *The Jobless Economy? Computer Technology in the World of Work*. Cambridge: Polity Press.

Dupuy, J.-P. (1980) 'Myths of the informational society', in K. Woodward (ed.), *The Myths of Information: Technology and Post-industrial Culture*. London: Routledge & Kegan Paul. pp. 3–18.

Eagleton, T. (1994) *Ideology: An Introduction*. Harlow: Longmans.

Earl, H.J. (1959) 'Design review – cars 59', *Industrial Design*, 2: 79.

Eco, U. (1986) *Travels in Hyperreality*. London: Pluto.

Ewen, S. (1976) *Captains of Consciousness: Advertising and the Social Roots of the Consumer Culture*. New York: McGraw-Hill.

Ewen, S. and Ewen, E. (1982) *Channels of Desire*. New York: McGraw-Hill.

Featherstone, M. (1991) *Consumer Culture and Postmodernism*. London: Sage.

Fine, B. and Leopold, E. (1993) *The World of Consumption*. London: Routledge.

Fiske, J. (1989) *Understanding Popular Culture*. London: Unwin Hyman.

Fiske, J. (1992) 'The cultural economy of fandom', in L. Lewis (ed.), *The Adoring Audience: Fan Culture and Popular Media*. London: Routledge. pp. 30–49.

Forty, A. (1986) *Objects of Desire*. London: Thames and Hudson.

Fox, N. (1996) 'League of the millions', *The Independent on Sunday*, 8 September: 24.

Friedberg, A. (1993) *Window Shopping: Cinema and the Postmodern*. Berkeley, CA: California University Press.

Friedman, M. and Friedman, R.D. (1980) *Free to Choose*. London: Secker and Warburg.

Frisby, D. (1985) 'Georg Simmel: first sociologist of modernity', *Theory, Culture & Society*, 2 (3): 49–67.

Frith, S. (1983) *Sound Effects: Youth, Leisure, and the Politics of Rock*. London: Constable.

Frith, S. (1988) *Music for Pleasure*. Cambridge: Polity Press.

Frith, S. (ed.) (1989) *World Music, Politics and Social Change*. Manchester: Manchester University Press.

Frith, S. (1990) 'Afterthoughts', in S. Frith and A. Goodwin (eds), *On Record: Rock, Pop, and the Written Word*. London: Routledge. pp. 419–24.

Frith, S. (1992) 'The industrialization of popular music', in J. Lull (ed.), *Popular Music and Communication*. London: Sage. pp. 47–92.

Gabriel, Y. and Lang, T. (1995) *The Unmanageable Consumer*. London: Sage.

Gardner, C. and Sheppard, J. (1989) *Consuming Passions*. London: Unwin Hyman.

Garrett, A. (1997) 'Premiership squares up for the big match over broadcasting bonanza', *The Observer*, Business, 27 July: 9.

George, F. (1977) *Machine Takeover: The Growing Threat to Human Freedom in a Computer-controlled Society*. Oxford: Pergamon Press.

Giddens, A. (1991) *Modernity and Self-identity: Self and Society in the Late Modern Age*. Cambridge: Polity Press.

Giedion, S. (1948) *Mechanization Takes Command*. New York: Oxford University Press.

Goodwin, A. (1992) *Dancing in the Distraction Factory: Music, Television and Popular Culture*. Minneapolis, MN: Minnesota University Press.

Gorz, A. (1982) *Farewell to the Working Class: An Essay on Post-industrial Socialism*. London: Pluto Press.

Gottdiener, M. (1995) *Postmodern Semiotics*. Oxford: Blackwell.

Gruneau, R. (1984) 'Commercialism and the modern Olympics', in A. Tomlinson and G. Whannel (eds), *Five Ring Circus: Money, Power and Politics at the Olympic Games*. London: Pluto. pp. 1–15.

Guy, C. (1994) *The Retail Development Process: Location, Property and Planning*. London: Routledge.

Hall, S. (1988) *The Hard Road to Renewal: Thatcherism and the Crisis of the Left*. London: Verso.

Hall, S. (1989) 'The meaning of new times', in S. Hall and M. Jacques (eds), *New Times: The Changing Face of Politics in the 1990s*. London: Lawrence & Wishart. pp. 116–34.

Hall, S. and Jacques, M. (eds) (1989) *New Times: The Changing Face of Politics in the 1990s*. London: Lawrence & Wishart.

Hammersley, M. and Atkinson, P. (1983) *Ethnography: Principles in Practice*. London: Tavistock.

Harvey, D. (1988) 'Foreword', in S. Zukin (ed.), *Loft Living: Culture and Capital in Urban Change*. London: Radius. pp. ix–xii.

Harvey, D. (1989) *The Condition of Postmodernity: An Inquiry into the Origins of Social Change*. Oxford: Basil Blackwell.

Harvey, D. (1995) *The Urbanisation of Capital*. Oxford: Blackwell.

Hebdige, D. (1979) *Subculture: The Meaning of Style*. London: Routledge.

Hinde, S. (1994) 'Death of the high street as big stores leave town', *The Sunday Times*. 12 June: 7.

Hinde, S. (1995) 'High streets boom as top shops return', *The Sunday Times*, 16 April: 7.

Horkheimer, M. and Adorno, T. (1973) *Dialectic of Enlightenment*. London: Allen Lane.

Independent on Sunday (1996) 'The one-minute expert', Business, 6 October: 1.

Inglehart, R. (1990) *Culture Shift in Advanced Urban Societies*. Princeton, NJ: Princeton University Press.

Inverdale, J. (1997) Nationwide with John Inverdale, *Radio 5 Live*, 15 January.

Jackson, P. and Thrift, N. (1995) 'Geographies of consumption', in D. Miller (ed.), *Acknowledging Consumption: A Review of New Studies*. London: Routledge. pp. 204–37.

Jaeger, M. (1986) 'Class definition and the aesthetics of gentrification: Victoriana in Melbourne', in N. Smith and P. Williams (eds), *Gentrification of the City*. London: Allen & Unwin. pp. 78–92.

Jameson, F. (1984) 'Postmodernism, or the cultural logic of late capitalism', *New Left Review*, 146: 53–93.

Keat, R. (1994) 'Scepticism, authority and the market', in R. Keat, N. Whiteley and N. Abercrombie (eds), *The Authority of the Consumer*. London: Routledge. pp. 23–42.

Keat, R., Whiteley, N. and Abercrombie, N. (eds) (1994) *The Authority of the Consumer*. London: Routledge.

Kershaw, A. (1991) 'World music', in P. Sweeny (ed.), *Directory of World Music: A Guide to Performers and their Music*. London: Virgin. p. 63.

Kingdom, J. (1992) *No Such Thing as Society? Individualism and Community*. Buckingham: Open University Press.

Knox, P. (1991) 'The restless urban landscape: economic and socio-cultural change and the transformation of metropolitan Washington, DC', *Annals: Association of American Geographers*, 81: 181–209.

Kumar, K. (1978) *Prophecy and Progress: The Sociology of Industrial and Post-industrial Society*. Harmondsworth: Penguin.

Lang, K. and Lang, G. (1965) 'Fashion: identification and differentiation in the mass society', in M. Roach and J. Eicher (eds), *Dress, Adornment, and the Social Order*. London: Wiley. pp. 322–46.

Langman, L. (1992) 'Neon cages: shopping for subjectivity', in R. Shields (ed.), *Lifestyle Shopping: The Subject of Consumption*. London: Routledge. pp. 40–82.

Lansley, S. (1994) *After the Gold Rush, the Trouble with Affluence: 'Consumer Capitalism' and the Way Forward*. London: Century.

Lasch, C. (1984) *The Minimal Self: Psychic Survival in Troubled Times*. London: Pan Books.

Lasch, C. (1985) 'The corruption of sports', in W. Uumphlett (ed.), *American Sport Culture: Humanistic Dimensions*. Lewisburg: Bucknell University Press. pp. 50–75.

Lash, S. (1990) *Sociology of Postmodernism*. London: Routledge.

Lash, S. and Urry, J. (1994) *Economies of Signs and Space*. London: Sage.

Latouche, S. (1993) *In the Wake of the Affluent Society*. London: Zed Books.

Layder, D. (1994) *Understanding Social Theory*. London: Sage.

Lee, M. (1993) *Consumer Culture Reborn: The Cultural Politics of Consumption*. London: Routledge.

Leopold, E. (1992) 'The manufacture of the fashion system', in J. Ash and E. Wilson (eds), *Chic Thrills: A Fashion Reader*. London: Pandora Press. pp. 101–17.

Levy, A. and Rayment, T. (1995) 'The internet? It's all in the mind', *The Sunday Times*, 16 April: 15.

Lloyd, C. (1995) 'Store wars', *The Sunday Times*, Style Magazine, 1 January: 8–9.

Lodziak, C. (1995) *Manipulating Needs: Capitalism and Culture*. London: Pluto Press.

Longhurst, B. (1995) *Popular Music and Society*. Cambridge: Polity Press.

Lucas, J.A. (1992) *Future of the Olympic Games*. Champaign, IL: Human Kinetics Books.

Lunt, P.K. and Livingstone, S.M. (1992) *Mass Consumption and Personal Identity*. Buckingham: Open University Press.

Lury, C. (1996) *Consumer Culture*. Cambridge: Polity Press.

Lyon, D. (1988) *The Information Society*. Cambridge: Polity Press.

Lyon, D. (1994) *Postmodernity*. Buckingham: Open University Press.

Lyotard, J.-F. (1984) *The Postmodern Condition: A Report on Knowledge*. Manchester: Manchester University Press.

McCracken, G. (1990) *Culture and Consumption*. Bloomington, IN: Indiana University Press.

McDowell, C. (1994) *The Designer Scam*. London: Hutchinson.

McKendrick, N., Brewer, J. and Plumb, J. (1982) *The Birth of a Consumer Society*. London: Europa.

MacKenzie, D. and Wajcman, J. (1985) *The Social Shaping of Technology*. Milton Keynes: Open University Press.

Marcuse, H. (1964) *One-Dimensional Man*. London: Routledge & Kegan Paul.

Marling, S. (1993) *American Affair: The Americanisation of Britain*. London: Boxtree.

Marx, K. (1867) *Capital: A Critique of Political Economy*, Vol. 1. Harmondsworth: Penguin, 1990, 2nd edn, trans Ben Fowkes.

Masauda, Y. (1990) *Managing the Information Society*. Oxford: Blackwell.

Middleton, R. (1990) *Studying Popular Music*. Milton Keynes: Open University Press.

Miles, S. (1995) 'Towards an understanding of the relationship between youth identities and consumer culture', *Youth and Policy*, 51: 35–45.

Miles, S. (1996) 'The cultural capital of consumption: understanding "postmodern" identities in a cultural context', *Culture & Psychology*, 2 (2): 139–58.

Milgram, S. (1992) *The Individual in a Social World: Essays and Experiments*. New York: McGraw-Hill.

Miller, D. (1987) *Material Culture and Mass Consumption*. Oxford: Basil Blackwell.

Miller, D. (1995) 'Consumption as the vanguard of history: a polemic by way of introduction', in D. Miller (ed.), *Acknowledging Consumption: A Review of New Studies*. London: Routledge. pp. 1–57.

Minchinton, W. (1982) 'Convention, fashion and consumption: aspects of British experience since 1750', in H. Baudet and H. Van der Meulen (eds), *Consumer Behaviour and Economic Growth in the Modern Economy*. London: Croom Helm. pp. 209–31.

Mitchell, K. (1995a) 'Hijackers of our dreams', *The Observer*, Sport, 9 April: 10.

Mitchell, K. (1995b) 'Moguls or monsters', *The Observer*, Sport, 10 September: 6.

Morley, D. and Silverstone, R. (1990) 'Domestic communication: technologies and meanings', *Media, Culture & Society*, 12: 31–55 .

Mosco, V. (1989) *The Pay-Per Society – Computers and Communications in the Information Age: Essays in Critical Theory and Public Policy*. Toronto: Garamond Press.

Moyes, J., Farrelly, P. and Culley, J. (1997) 'A funny old game', *The Independent on Sunday*, 12 January: 176.

Mueller, C. and Smiley, E. (1995) *Marketing Today's Fashion*. Englewood Cliffs, NJ: Prentice-Hall.

Murdock, G., Hartmann, P. and Gray, P. (1992) 'Contextualizing home computing: resources and practices', in R. Silverstone and E. Hirsch (eds), *Consuming Technologies: Media and Information in Domestic Spaces*. London: Routledge. pp. 146–60.

Murray, C. (1997) 'Premiership risks an own-goal over pay-per-view TV cash, says Parry', *The Observer*, Business, 30 March: 6.

Murray, R. (1989) 'Fordism and post-Fordism', in S. Hall and M. Jacques (eds), *New Times: The Changing Face of Politics in the 1990s*. London: Lawrence & Wishart. pp. 38–53.

Nava, M. (1991) 'Consumerism reconsidered: buying and power', *Cultural Studies*, 5: 157–73.

Negus, K. (1992) *Producing Pop: Culture and Conflict in the Popular Music Industry*. London: Edward Arnold.

Newby, P. (1993) 'Shopping as leisure', in D.F. Bromley and C.J. Thomas (eds), *Retail Change: Contemporary Issues*. London: UCL Press. pp. 208–28.

Nixon, S. (1996) *Hard Looks: Masculinities, Spectatorship and Contemporary Consumption*. London: UCL Press.

Noble, D. (1984) *Forces of Production*. New York: Alfred A. Knopf.

Novak, M. (1976) *The Joy of Sports*. New York: Basic Books.

O'Brien, L. and Harris, F. (1991) *Retailing: Shopping, Society, Space*. London: Fulton.

O'Connor, J. and Wynne, D. (1993) 'From the margins to the centre: cultural production and consumption in the post-industrial city', unpublished paper presented at the Fourth International Symposium on the Sociology of Consumption, Helsinki, 14–19 June.

Otnes, P. (ed.) (1988) *The Sociology of Consumption: An Anthology*. Oslo: Solum Forlag A/S.

Papanek, V. (1995) *The Green Imperative: Ecology and Ethics in Design and Architecture*. London: Thames and Hudson.

Parkhurst Ferguson, P. (1994) 'The *flâneur* on and off the streets of Paris', in K. Tester (ed.), *The Flâneur*. London: Routledge.

Pepperell, R. (1995) *The Post-human Condition*. Oxford: Intellect.

Perspectives (1992) *Newsweek*, 10 August.

Piore, M. and Sabel, C. (1984) *The Second Industrial Divide*. New York: Basic Books.

Putnam, P. (1995) 'Rivers of dollars flow with Jordan', *The Observer*, Sport, 9 April: 15.

Richards, B. (1994) *Disciplines of Delight*. London: Free Association.

Rietveld, H. (1993) 'Living the dream', in S. Redhead (ed.), *Rave Off: Politics and Deviance in Contemporary Youth Culture*. Aldershot: Avebury. pp. 41–78.

Ritzer, G. (1993) *The McDonaldization of Society*. Newbury Park, CA: Pine Forge.

Ritzer, G. (1995) *Expressing America: A Critique of the Global Credit Card Society*. Newbury Park, CA: Pine Forge.

Ritzer, G. and Liska, A. (1997) '"McDisneyization" and "post-tourism": complementary perspectives on contemporary tourism', in C. Rojek, and J. Urry (eds), *Touring Cultures: Transformations of Travel and Theory*. London: Routledge. pp. 96–109.

Rodgers, P. (1996) 'Winner takes all', *The Independent on Sunday*. Business, 4 August: 1.

Rottenberg, S. (1956) 'The baseball player's labour market', *Journal of Political Economy*, 64 (June): 242–58.

Rowe, D. (1995) *Popular Cultures: Rock Music, Sport and the Politics of Pleasure*. London: Sage.

Rubinstein, R. (1995) *Dress Codes: Meanings and Messages in American Culture*. Oxford: Westview Press.

Russell, D. (1983) *The Religion of the Machine Age*. London: Routledge & Kegan Paul.

Sack, R.D. (1992) *Place, Modernity, and the Consumer's World*. London: Johns Hopkins University Press.

Sampson, P. (1994) 'Postmodernity', in P. Sampson, V. Samuel and C. Sugden (eds), *Faith and Modernity*. Oxford: Regnum. pp. 29–57.

Sanjek, R. and Sanjek, D. (1991) *American Popular Music Business in the 20th Century*. Oxford: Oxford University Press.

Saunders, P. (1981) *Social Theory and the Urban Question*. London: Hutchinson.

Saunders, P. (1984) 'Beyond housing classes: the sociological significance of private property rights in means of consumption', *International Journal of Urban and Regional Research*, 8: 202–25.

Sayer, A. (1989) 'Postfordism in question', *International Journal of Urban and Regional Research*, 13 (4): 666–95.

Schiller, H. (1981) *Who Knows: Information in the Age of the Fortune 500*. Norwood, NJ: Ablex.

Schlossberg, H. (1996) *Sports Marketing*. Oxford: Blackwell.

Schwartz, B. (1994) *The Costs of Living*. London: W.W. Norton.

Silverstone, R. and Hirsch, E. (1992) *Consuming Technologies: Media and Information in Domestic Spaces*. London: Routledge.

Simmel, Georg (1957) 'Fashion', *American Journal of Sociology*, 62: 541–8. Originally published 1904.

Simmel, G. (1907) *The Philosophy of Money*. London: Routledge, 1990.

Simmonds, D. (1990) 'What next? Fashion, foodies and the illusion of freedom', in A. Tomlinson (ed.), *Consumption, Identity and Style*. London: Routledge. pp. 121–38.

Simmons, J. (1992) 'The changing pattern of retail location', University of Chicago, Department of Geography, unpublished research paper.

Slater, D. (1997) *Consumer Culture and Modernity*. Cambridge: Polity Press.

Sparke, P. (1986) *An Introduction to Design and Culture in the Twentieth Century*. London: Allen & Unwin.

Sudjic, D. (1993) *The 100 Mile City*. London: Flamingo.

Swingewood, A. (1977) *The Myth of Mass Culture*. Basingstoke: Macmillan.

Swingewood, A. (1991) *A Short History of Sociological Thought*. London: Macmillan.

Thomas, C.J. and Bromley, D.F. (1993) 'The impact of out-of-centre retailing', in D.F. Bromley and C.J. Thomas (eds), *Retail Change: Contemporary Issues*. London: UCL Press. pp. 126–52.

Thomas, W.I. and Thomas, D.S. (1928) *The Child in America: Behavior Problems and Programs*. New York: Knopf.

Thornton, S. (1995) *Club Cultures: Music, Media and Subcultural Capital*. Cambridge: Polity Press.

Toffler, A. (1981) *The Third Wave*. New York: Bantam Books.

Tomlinson, J. (1991) *Cultural Imperialism*. London: Pinter Publishers.

Tooher, P. (1997) 'The city warms up for its match of the day', *The Independent on Sunday*. Your Money, 12 January: 21.

Urry, J. (1990) *The Tourist Gaze*. London: Sage.

Veblen, T. (1899) *The Theory of the Leisure Class*. London: Constable, 1994.

Wajcman, J. (1991) *Feminism Confronts Technology*. Cambridge: Polity Press.

Wallerstein, I. (1979) *The Capitalist World Economy: Essays*. Cambridge: Cambridge University Press.

Warde, A. (1990a) 'Production, consumption and social change: reservations regarding Peter Saunders' sociology of consumption', *International Journal of Urban and Regional Research*, 14 (2): 228–48.

Warde, A. (1990b) 'Introduction to the sociology of consumption', *Sociology*, 24 (1): 1–4.

Warde, A. (1992) 'Notes on the relationship between production and consumption', in R. Burrows and C. Marsh (eds), *Consumption and Class: Divisions and Change*. Basingstoke: Macmillan. pp. 15–31.

Wark, McK. (1991) 'Fashioning the future: fashion, clothing and the manufacturing of post-Fordist culture', *Cultural Studies*, 5 (1): 61–76.

Waters, M. (1994) *Modern Sociological Theory*. London: Sage.

Weber, M. (1920) *The Protestant Ethic and the Spirit of Capitalism*. London: Allen & Unwin, 1971.

Weber, M. (1978) *Selections in Translation*. Cambridge: Cambridge University Press.

Webster, F. (1995) *Theories of the Information Society*. London: Routledge.

Whannel, G. (1992) *Fields in Vision: Television Sport and Cultural Transformation*. London: Routledge.

Whiteley, N. (1993) *Design for Society*. London: Reaktion Books.

Williams, R. (1982) *Dream Worlds*. Berkeley, CA: University of California Press.

Williams, R. (1996) 'Pitch fever', *The Guardian*, 29 April: 2–3.

Willis, P. (1990) *Common Culture*. Milton Keynes: Open University Press.

Willis, S. (1990) 'Work(ing) out', *Cultural Studies*, 4 (1): 1–18.

Willis, S. (1991) *A Primer for Daily Life*. London: Routledge.

Willis, S. (1993) 'Disney World: public use/private state', *South Atlantic Quarterly*, 92: 119–37.

Wilson, E. (1992) 'Fashion and the postmodern body', in J. Ash and E. Wilson (eds), *Chic Thrills: A Fashion Reader*. London: Pandora. pp. 3–17.

Wilson, P. (1995) 'Mr Greedy's healthy diet', *The Observer*, Sport, 22 January: 14.

Winner, L. (1995) 'Three paradoxes of the information age', in G. Bender and T. Druckery (eds), *Culture on the Brink: Ideologies of Technology*. Seattle: Bay Press. pp. 191–7.

Wollen, P. (1986) 'Ways of thinking about music video (and postmodernism)', *Critical Quarterly*, 28 (1–2): 16–37.

Wroe, M. (1995) 'Tarnished idols of rock roll to riches in a VW', *The Observer*, 9 July: 12.

Yoshimoto, M. (1994) 'Images of empire: Tokyo Disneyland and Japanese cultural imperialism', in E. Smoodin (ed.), *Disney Discourse*. London: Routledge. pp. 181–99.

Zeitlin, J. (1988) 'The clothing industry in transition', *Textile History*, 19 (2): 211–38.

Zukin, S. (1988) *Loft Living: Culture and Capital in Urban Change*. London: Radius.

Zukin, S. (1995) *The Culture of Cities*. Oxford: Blackwell.

INDEX